The Strategy of Social Protest

Second Edition

WILLIAM A. GAMSON

Boston College

Wadsworth Publishing Company
Belmont, California
A Division of Wadsworth, Inc.

In memory of PAUL COWAN,
writer and political activist,
whose warmth and wisdom
are sorely missed

SOCIOLOGY EDITOR: Serina Beauparlant
PRODUCTION EDITOR: Hal Lockwood, Bookman Productions
PRINT BUYER: Randy Hurst
COPY EDITOR: Candace Demeduc
TECHNICAL ILLUSTRATOR: Judy Levinson
COMPOSITOR: Weimer Typesetting Co.
COVER: Sandy Drooker

Printed in the United States of America

1 2 3 4 5 6 7 8 9 10—94 93 92 91 90

LIBRARY OF CONGRESS CATALOGING-IN-PUBLICATION DATA

Gamson, William A.
    The strategy of Social protest / William A. Gamson.—2nd ed.
        p.   cm.
    Bibliography: p.
    Includes index.
    ISBN 0-534-12078-4
    1. Social movements—United States.   2. Pressure groups—United
States.   3. Pluralism (Social sciences)—United States.   4. Elite
(Social sciences)—United States.   I. Title.
HN64.G23   1990   89-34947
303.48′4—dc20   CIP

Preface to
the Second Edition

Second editions are second chances. The first edition of *Strategy* allowed me to have a say on a number of issues concerning groups that try to mobilize people to change American society. Since 1974 I've continued to think about these issues, aided by many insightful discussions by American and European students of social movements. The question of how well the results described in *Strategy* apply to challenging groups after 1945 has come up often since the first edition was published, and the answer has never seemed obvious to me.

I've chosen to use my second chance to have a go at the same set of issues addressed in *Strategy*—this time focusing on the experiences of modern challengers. I have not, of course, tried to carry out the same kind of systematic research on these as I did with the earlier challengers. Instead, I present a theoretical argument, drawing supporting examples from major, well-studied movements (especially the unruly ones) of the last 25 years.

I have left unchanged what I had to say on these issues in 1974. Except for minor corrections of citations and the like, Chapters One through Nine here are identical to the first edition. "Challenging Groups since 1945"—a new chapter for this edition—analyzes how well the substantive arguments in *Strategy* help us to understand the careers of these challengers.

In carrying out this exercise, I frequently am critical of the way issues were handled in the first edition. My own subsequent research and reading of others' work has led me to emphasize many parts of the mobilization process that are treated lightly in the earlier version. And, of course, there are major societal changes since 1945—the rise of the national security state and of television, for example—that have major implications for the strategies of challengers and authorities. On almost all the issues discussed in *Strategy*, quite a bit more needs to be said.

Like the first edition, this one includes the original data set. A number of other researchers made use of this material for additional analysis, using a variety of multivariate techniques. One even substantially recoded central outcome variables. This edition includes some of these published analyses and a lengthy exchange between Jack Goldstone and myself which appeared in the *American Journal of Sociology*.

Finally, I would like to thank David Snow, University of Arizona; Robert Benford, University of Nebraska; Stan Kaplowitz, Michigan State University; Charles M. Bonjean, University of Texas, Austin; Maurice Zeitlin, University of California, Los Angeles; Roger Barnes, Incarnate Word College; and Mark Kassop, Bergen Community College, for reviewing the manuscript of this new edition.

WILLIAM A. GAMSON

Preface to the First Edition

This book examines the experiences of a representative collection of American voluntary groups that, between 1800 and 1945, have challenged some aspect of the status quo. It explores the strategies they used and the organizational characteristics that influenced the success of their challenges. The results raise some serious questions about the pluralist interpretation of the operation of power in American society.

I suppose it is relatively common to experience, even when engaged in research that one enjoys doing and finds enlightening, a certain frustration. In any effort in which I've been involved, I have found myself preoccupied at certain stages with the limitations of what I am doing. These feelings are troubling when they occur but I have learned to value them. From the seeds of this dissatisfaction, a future research effort may grow.

Thus it was with the work described in this book. By the summer of 1966, I found myself moving toward completion of a study of the Cold War that Andre Modigliani and I had been working on since 1962. Any sense of optimism about the impact of peace research had been snuffed out by the brutal American presence in Vietnam and the surrounding rhetoric which justified this military adventure. Understanding the dynamics of the Cold War conflict still seemed important to me, but I had no illusions that those who waged and justified war in Vietnam would be receptive to any insights or arguments that we might develop.

Another question seemed prior and paramount — what are the levers of change in American society? Two friends of mine at Michigan, Marc Pilisuk and Tom Hayden, had published a stimulating essay addressing many of the issues on my mind. "Is There a Military Industrial Complex Which Prevents Peace?" they asked (Pilisuk and Hayden, 1965). Although I was not completely satisfied by their answer, I was fully persuaded of the value of the quest. Understanding the operation of power in American society seemed necessary for the agenda of peace research.

During the academic year, 1966–67, I began meeting in an informal weekly seminar with two graduate students at Michigan, Samuel Friedman and James McEvoy, to discuss issues of power in American society and how one might fruitfully do research on them. By the end of that year, through some process of alchemy, we found ourselves digging through back issues of the *Missouri Farmer* for 1919 — apparently a far cry from the military-industrial complex. Actually, in our minds it was not a very far cry because we had come to see the permeability of the American political system as the primary issue that we wished to explore and a study of the careers of relatively powerless groups that attempt to make changes as a focus of investigation. The exigencies of doing research have moved us a few steps further from our starting point but I believe that this book still speaks to the original, motivating questions.

Eventually, the ideas we discussed led to a research proposal and the National Science Foundation supported the work with two essential research grants which enabled us to complete it. A large number of people participated at different stages and I find it more natural to use the word "we" in describing this work — not the editorial "we" but a literal one. John Evans joined the project and contributed an important effort in defining the unit of analysis as well as in doing a number of pilot studies on challenging groups. Arnold Lewis made a major contribution to the definition of the outcome of a challenge and helped to design the questionnaire.

Robin Lepore Thomas played a crucial role at two stages. First, as an Antioch co-op student, she and fellow Antiochian Locke Holmes did the major work on compiling the sampling frame. Later, after graduating, she returned to work full time on the study as supervisor of compiling the protocols on the groups in the sample and of the coding operation. It was largely due to her skillful and energetic efforts that we were able to get both high quality data and reasonable comparability on protocols for 53 groups compiled by 17 different people!

Most of the actual compiling of protocols was done by undergraduates — either Antiochians on co-op jobs or Michigan students. They included Jane Palmer, Mary Lawson, Carl Greenberg, Peter Hunt, Alden Mudge, Steve Gortmaker, Meredith Reid, Grant McCracken, Rick Bent, Paul Karsten, and John Alberti. Nancy Foster came on the project near the end to work full time and did an excellent job on the eight protocols she compiled. Rick Bent also made major contributions to the coding operation.

A number of graduate students also participated during various stages. Dee Wernette made major contributions both in adding to the theoretical clarity of the work and in developing the complicated codes for the outcome of challenges. John Angle, Stanley Presser, and Patricia Pastor worked for shorter periods as part of their NIMH traineeships. Steve Rytina helped in the data analysis phase and Bruce Taylor with the tedious but important job of checking references.

Several people read over an earlier draft of the manuscript and made helpful suggestions: Dee Wernette, Stan Presser, Robin Williams, Zelda Gamson, Stan Kaplowitz, Rudolf Vleeming. My colleague, Chuck Tilly, and his associates have used a draft of this book in a seminar on mobilization for collective action, and I have found their ideas and their own work immensely helpful at a number of points. I have been fortunate at both the Center for Research on Conflict Resolution where the project was originally located, and more recently at the Center for Research on Social Organization, in having colleagues whose work was closely related and who offered the kind of intellectual support and stimulation that is so helpful in a project of this sort.

In the end, of course, many of the answers we sought eluded us and I have begun new work in an attempt to remedy the shortcomings of this effort. That is a story for a future preface.

William A. Gamson
December 1974

Contents

chapter one

The Permeability of the Political Arena

In May, 1937, shortly before Memorial Day, 78,000 steelworkers began a strike against the "Little Steel" companies of Bethlehem Steel, Republic Steel, Inland Steel, and Youngstown Sheet and Tube. The CIO-backed Steel Workers Organizing Committee (SWOC) was less than a year old at the time but had already enjoyed some notable success. A few months earlier, it had signed collective bargaining agreements with the five largest U.S. Steel subsidiaries, and, by early May, SWOC had signed contracts with 110 firms.

The Little Steel companies, however, were prepared to resist. Under the leadership of Tom M. Girdler, president of Republic Steel, they refused to sign an agreement which they felt, in Girdler's words, "was a bad thing for our companies, for our employees; indeed for the United States of America" (Galenson, 1960, p. 96).

The decision to resist was made more ominous by the common practice of large employers of the time to stock arsenals of weapons and tear gas in anticipation of labor disputes. Much of our information comes from the report of the LaFollette Committee of

1

the United States Senate,[1] which investigated the events surrounding the Little Steel strike. The committee report noted, for example, that during the years 1933 to 1937, over a million dollars' worth of tear gas and sickening gas was purchased by employers and law-enforcement agencies but that "all of the largest individual purchasers are corporations and that their totals far surpass those of large law-enforcement purchasers" (quoted in Sweeney, 1956, p. 20). The largest purchaser of gas equipment in the country was none other than the Republic Steel Corporation, which "bought four times as much as the largest law-enforcement purchaser." The Republic Steel arsenal included 552 revolvers, 61 rifles with 1325 rounds of ammunition, and 245 shotguns in addition to gas grenades (Sweeney, p. 33).

The Little Steel strike began on May 26, 1937, and for a few days prior to May 30, picketing and arrests occurred near Republic Steel's mill in south Chicago. On Memorial Day, after a mass meeting at strike headquarters, the strikers decided to march to the plant to establish a mass picket line. A crowd of about 1,000 persons, "headed by two bearers of American Flags, . . . started across the prairie toward the street which fronts on the mill. There was a holiday spirit over the crowd" (Sweeney, p. 33).

Chicago police were there in force and the paraders were commanded to disperse. Within a few minutes, seven strikers were dead, three lay fatally wounded, scores of others were seriously wounded, and 35 policemen were injured. The LaFollette Committee concluded on the basis of testimony from many eye-witnesses and photographs that "the first shots came from the police; that these were unprovoked, except perhaps by a tree branch thrown by the strikers, and that the second volley of police shots was simultaneous with the missiles thrown by the strikers." The strikers fled after the first volley but were pursued by the police. Of the ten marchers who were fatally shot, ". . . seven received the fatal wound in the back, three in the side, none in front. . . . The medical testimony of the nature of the marchers' wounds indicates that they were shot in flight. . . . The police were free with their use of clubs as well as guns. . . . Suffice it to say that the evidence, photographic and oral, is replete with instances of the use of clubs upon marchers doing their utmost to retreat, as well as upon those

---

[1] Hearings before a Subcommittee of the Committee on Education and Labor, United States Senate, 75th Congress, (LaFollette Committee). U.S. Government Printing Office, Washington, D.C., 1939.

who were on the ground and in a position to offer no show of resistance," the LaFollette Committee Report concluded (quoted in Galenson, 1960).

The "Memorial Day Massacre" at the Republic Steel Plant in Chicago was the most notorious but by no means the only violent clash in the Little Steel strike. The strike was effectively broken by these tactics. Within two weeks of the Memorial Day clash, the Republic Steel plant had resumed normal operation. Within another few weeks, other struck plants reopened as well and the strike was essentially over.

The victory of the companies was, as it turned out, only a temporary one. By the fall of 1941, all four Little Steel companies had agreed to recognize the SWOC, and in May, 1942, the Steel Workers Organizing Committee became the United Steelworkers of America. Today, the leaders of the union dine with Presidents and serve as labor spokesmen on a variety of governmental bodies. By any measure of membership of the polity, they are full-fledged and certified. In reading the bitter history of the Little Steel strike from the consciousness of today, it is difficult to credit the fact that these events occurred a mere 50 years ago, in the living memory of some readers or, at the very least, of their parents.

This particular challenger has, for better or worse, moved inside the salon. But the anterooms and corridors contain the battered hulks of less successful challengers. Their abortive careers also promise to tell us important things about the permeability of the American political system.

Take the Brotherhood of the Cooperative Commonwealth, for example. Born in the ferment of the 1890s, it was the brainchild of an obscure Maine reformer, Norman Wallace Lermond. "Its immediate and most important objective was to colonize *en masse* a sparsely inhabited Western state with persons desiring to live in socialist communities. Once established, the colonists would be in a position to capture control of the state's government and lay the foundation for a socialist commonwealth" (Quint, 1964).

Not much happened for the first year of its existence but Lermond was "a letter writing dynamo and he bombarded reformers throughout the country with appeals for assistance." He began to get some results. Imogene C. Fales, a New York reformer, "who was a charter member of innumerable humanitarian and socialist movements in the 1880s and 1890s, agreed to serve with Lermond as co-organizer" (Quint).

But the big catch for the fledgling challenging group was Eugene V. Debs. Debs had been recently released from his prison term for defying the injunction against the American Railway Union which broke the Pullman strike. He was a genuine hero of the left, who was now, for the first time, espousing socialism. Debs was a thoroughly decent person who lacked the vituperative personal style so characteristic of many leftists. Furthermore, he was an extraordinarily effective platform speaker where, as Quint describes him, "the shining sincerity of his speeches and the flowing honesty of his personality more than compensated for the lack of knowledge of the more delicate points of Marxist theory. His soul was filled with a longing for social justice and he communicated this feeling to the audiences who gathered to hear him extol the new Social Democracy."

Debs became attracted to the colonization scheme. "Give me 10,000 men," Debs told a socialist convention, "aye, 10,000 in a western state with access to the sources of production, and we will change the economic conditions, and we will convince the people of that state, win their hearts and their intelligence. We will lay hold upon the reins of government and plant the flag of Socialism upon the State House" (quoted in Quint).

Many other socialists were appalled at what they considered a diversion of energy into a thoroughly impractical scheme. However, they were gentle with Debs personally, hoping to woo him back to the true path. Even the normally vitriolic socialist leader, Daniel DeLeon, was unaccustomedly polite. "With warm esteem for the good intentions of Mr. Debs, but fully appreciative of the harm that more failures will do," he wrote, "we earnestly warn the proletariat of America once more not to embark on this chimera; not to yield out of love for the good intentions of Mr. Debs, greater respect for his judgment than it deserves" (Quint).

Gradually, Debs began relegating the colonization scheme to be one of several strategies rather than to be *the* strategy of the socialist movement. The Brotherhood of the Cooperative Commonwealth did not particularly prosper. They did establish a colony, "Equality" in Edison, Washington, and later another at Burley, Washington, but these did not thrive. "By 1902, Equality contained 105 people, living on a very plain diet in two apartment houses, four log cabins, and fourteen frame houses, earning a bare subsistence by the sale of lumber and grain" (Quint). By 1914, there wasn't anything left of the colonization plans of the Brotherhood of the Cooperative Commonwealth.

How can we account for the different experiences of a representative collection of American challenging groups? What is the characteristic response to groups of different types and what determines this response? What strategies work under what circumstances? What organizational characteristics influence the success of the challenge?

The careers of challenging groups tell us about the permeability and openness of the American political system. To know who gets in and how is to understand the central issue in competing images of the American political experience.

THE PLURALIST IMAGE OF AMERICAN POLITICS

Until the turbulence of the 1960s caused many to rethink the issue, a particular interpretation of American politics dominated the thinking of most professional observers. It remains highly influential today if perhaps not as dominant as it once was in the face of a developing body of criticism. This interpretation presents an image of a highly open system with free access for would-be competitors. Furthermore, the image has behind it a well-developed and elegant body of theoretical ideas usually presented under the label "pluralist democracy" or simply "pluralism."

A democratic political system must be able to handle two great problems if it is to continue successfully: the danger of tyranny or domination by a minority, and responsiveness to unmet or changing needs among its citizens. Pluralist theory has the virtue of explaining how a political system can handle both of these problems simultaneously. To the extent that the American political system approximates the pluralist model, it is argued, it will produce regular and orderly change with the consent of the governed.

Those who support this interpretation are not unaware of urban riots and the considerable history of violent conflict in the United States. However, they tend to view such events as abnormalities or pathologies arising from the gap between an always imperfect reality and an ideal, abstract model. In other words, the occasional, admitted failures of American democracy to produce orderly change are caused by departures from the ideal conditions of pluralism. Furthermore, even a well-functioning thermostat sometimes produces temperatures that are momentarily too hot or too cold as it goes about giving us the proper temperature.

There is a vast literature on pluralism and the American political system, and the discussion here will not attempt to do it full justice. A particularly coherent and convincing statement of the case is made in Dahl's *Pluralist Democracy in the United States* (1967). Now Dahl is no mindless celebrator of the genius of American politics; he paints his subject with all its warts and blemishes. But the important point is that this darker side of American politics is viewed as blemish and not as the essence of his subject.

Dahl suggests (p. 24) that the "fundamental axiom in the theory and practice of American pluralism is . . . this: Instead of a single center of sovereign power there must be multiple centers of power, none of which is or can be wholly sovereign." Why is this so important? Because the "existence of multiple centers of power . . . will help to tame power, to secure the consent of all, and to settle conflicts peacefully."

The brilliance of pluralist thinking is illustrated by its ability to handle multiple problems simultaneously — the prevention of dominance by a single group or individual, responsiveness to the needs of its citizens, and the prevention of extreme or violent conflict. It deals with two very different threats to the political system. The first threat is that the delicate balance of competition will be destroyed by a temporarily ascendant group that will use its ascendancy to crush its competitors. The second threat is that in the stalemate of veto groups and countervailing power there will be ineffective government, leading to an accumulation of discontent that will destroy the legitimacy and threaten the stability of the existing system.

We can examine the pluralist answer by addressing the question of how an ideal pluralist system functions. To operate properly, pluralist political institutions require an underlying pluralist social structure and values as well. More specifically, the following conditions should prevail:

Procedural Consensus

There is acceptance of the "culture" of constitutional democracy. One operates within the rules, the rules are considered generally fair, and defeats are accepted because of the strong legitimacy attached to the manner of resolving conflicts. Dahl goes even further than procedural consensus and argues for a good deal of substantive consensus as well. "In the United States, there is a massive convergence of attitudes on a number of key issues that divide citizens in other countries. As one result, ways of life are not seriously threatened by the policies of opponents" (Dahl, p. 326).

Cross-Cutting Solidarities

Individuals have strong identifications and affiliations with solidarity groups at different levels below the total society—primary group, community, formal organization, religious group, ethnic group, social class, and so forth. Furthermore, these solidarities overlap and cut across each other in a complex web which creates multiple memberships linking individuals with different sets of others.

Open Access to the Political Arena

There are no barriers to a group getting a hearing. Dissatisfied groups are encouraged to translate their dissatisfaction into political demands, to find coalition partners among other powerful groups, and to create political reforms which remedy the unsatisfactory conditions. As Dahl argues (p. 24): "Because even minorities are provided with opportunities to veto solutions they strongly object to, the consent of all will be won in the long run." The political institutions offer multiple points at which to pursue one's demands. "The institutions . . . offer organized minorities innumerable sites in which to fight, perhaps to defeat, at any rate to damage an opposing coalition" (Dahl, p. 329).

Balance of Power or Countervailing Power Operation

There is a sufficiently large number of groups that no one group can dominate. Coalitions are fluid and impermanent, being formed more or less *de novo* for each issue or, at least, for each class of issues. Furthermore, issues partition groups in different ways so that many groups not in a present coalition are potential coalition partners on subsequent issues. "Because one center of power is set against another," Dahl writes (p. 24), "power itself will be tamed, civilized, controlled, and limited to decent human purposes, while coercion, the most evil form of power, will be reduced to a minimum."

When a political system meets these assumptions, it is argued, neither tyranny nor rigidity will result. No group will become dominant for several reasons. First, it will exercise self-restraint in exploiting any temporary ascendancy for normative reasons. The institutions will "generate politicians who learn how to deal gently with opponents, who struggle endlessly in building and holding coalitions together, who doubt the possibilities of great change, who seek compromises" (Dahl, p. 329). Thus, the political process encourages a normative commitment to a set of rules which would be violated by dealing too ruthlessly with an opponent.

Second, self-restraint is encouraged by long-run self-interest. In a world of constantly shifting coalitions, it is feckless to antagonize groups which may be tomorrow's allies on some other set of issues. Third, self-restraint is encouraged by short-run self-interest. Because of the nature of cross-cutting solidarities, any temporarily ascendant group is likely to include many members who *also* belong to those groups who might be the victims of the abuse of power. In such a situation, any efforts to use power to injure or to destroy the power of opponents are automatically threats to the *internal stability* of the groups that would attempt such action. Such efforts stimulate factionalism and costly division within the ranks.

Finally, if self-restraint is not sufficient, efforts to achieve domination will encourage neutral and uninvolved groups to join an opposing coalition which controls greater resources than the temporarily ascendant group or coalition. Power which threatens to get out of hand stimulates countervailing power.

Many of the same pluralist conditions help to produce responsiveness as well. The critical element in this argument is that in the normal operation of the political system dissatisfied groups are encouraged to organize and translate their dissatisfaction into concrete political demands. Several elements in the political system lead to such encouragement. First, competitive elections assure that political parties will woo dissatisfied groups that have achieved some degree of strength, either to broaden their base of support or to prevent the allegiance of such groups to their competitors. Second, existing interest groups with similar or overlapping interests will facilitate organizations of such dissatisfied groups, seeing in them new allies. Third, multiple points of access to the political system will encourage participation by making available many sites for possible influence. Fourth, such organization and participation will be encouraged by the normative commitment of existing competitors to open access.

Thus, no group will long remain unrepresented, and it will find its entry into the political arena smoothed and facilitated by powerful allies who find it useful to do so for their own purposes. There will be no need for such groups to violate the existing rules of democratic politics to bring about the remedy of legitimate grievances.

The American political system, in this argument, approximates the underlying pluralist social structure and values quite closely. The result is an image of American politics as a contest carried out under well-defined rules. The rules prohibit the use of violence or any efforts aimed at permanently removing other contestants from the game. The essence of the competition is bargaining for relative advantage with the attendant tactics of influence trading, coalition formation, logrolling and the like.

It is a game that any number can play. The only rule of entry is that the contesting group must agree to behave itself. More specifically, this means that it must honor the rights of the existing participants by not striving to destroy them or to render them permanently impotent, and it must not be too unruly in its means. Contestants who misbehave are excluded from the contest by general agreement. Subject only to this broadest of restrictions, all are welcome to come in and try their luck.

This, then, is the essence of the pluralist image. It is the product of a subtle and persuasive argument with roots going back to James Madison and extending through an array of subsequent political theorists. In suggesting its inadequacies and in exploring an alternative image, I intend no denial of the great intellectual insights into the workings of political systems in general, and of American politics in particular, that we owe to this body of thought.

FLAWS IN THE PLURALIST HEAVEN

"The flaw in the pluralist heaven," writes Schattschneider (1960, p. 35), "is that the heavenly chorus sings with a strong upper-class accent. Probably about 90 percent of the people cannot get into the pressure system." In one form or another, this theme is present in most writing that is critical of pluralist theory.

One line of criticism of the pluralist image of American politics challenges its argument about the lack of dominance by a single center of power. This theme is given classical expression in Mills' *The Power Elite* (1956). Mills argues for the existence of a level of power operation not touched by pluralist assumptions. The pluralist model, Mills grants, is applicable to a middle level of power, but a series of really major decisions are dominated by a small group which is not subject to the constraints operating at the middle level.

Mills' argument is vulnerable at a number of points, in large part because of his emphasis on the issue of dominance rather than responsiveness. As Pilisuk and Hayden argue (1965, p. 78): "Where Mills' theory is most awkward is in his assertions that the elite can, and does, make its decisions against the will of others and regardless of external conditions. . . . What is attributed to the elite is a rather fantastic quality: literal omnipotence." Pilisuk and Hayden attempt to remedy this weakness in Mills while preserving his major insights by making the argument (p. 92) in more sophisticated, institutional terms rather than in terms of a "ruling group."

> In the United States there is no ruling group. . . . Nor is there any easily discernible ruling institutional order, so meshed have the separate sources of elite power become. But there is a social structure which is organized to create and protect power centers with only partial accountability. . . . We are describing the current system as one of overall "minimal accountability" and "minimal consent." We mean that the role of democratic review, based on popular consent, is made marginal and reactive. Elite groups are minimally accountable to publics and have a substantial, though by no means maximum, freedom to shape popular attitudes.

Having argued for the imbeddedness of a military-industrial complex in mainstream American institutions and mores, they conclude that "Our concept is not that American society contains a ruling military-industrial complex. Our concept is more nearly that American society *is* a military-industrial complex" (p. 98).

Some of this criticism can simply be accepted by pluralists by recasting it in different language. Concentration of power is necessary, it can be argued, to enjoy the fruits of leadership. Where substantial consensus exists on goals, many issues reflect technical problems. Agger, Goldrich, and Swanson write (1964, p. 76):

"Pluralists take the position, specifically or implicitly, that . . . major decisional options are not shaped by an influential ruling elite so much as they are by 'technical' factors which, assuming there is a desire for 'functional rationality,' would lead rational men to similar choice situations or decisional outcomes, regardless of socio-economic class or official positions."

If the collective interest is to be served, then the social system needs specialists in goal attainment to exercise disproportionate influence on its behalf (cf. Parsons, 1960). In this view, to see such essential leadership functions as "undemocratic" in some way is to impose an ideology on an essential fact of social life: concentration of power is necessary for efficient goal attainment. Many social scientists sympathetic to the pluralist argument probably share the view which Dahl (1961, p. 321) attributes to members of the political stratum. "Public involvement may seem undesirable . . . for alterations in the prevailing norms are often subtle matters, better obtained by negotiation than by the crudities and over-simplifications of public debate."

This defense of pluralism is, I believe, an important one, but it deals with only one part of the attack. I share the suspicions of the critics of pluralism that it is a partial truth that misses or blurs certain problems and paints an overly sanguine picture of the operation of power in American society. However, my own discomfort, like that of Pilisuk and Hayden, is not with the assertions about the absence of a small power elite or ruling group.

The pluralist interpretation seems more vulnerable and in need of modification on the issue of permeability and openness to efforts at change. "Groups provide a great deal of necessary social efficiency," Lowi writes (1971, p. 5). "They are effective means of articulating and representing interests and providing low-level social controls that reduce the need for governmental coercion. But the very success of established groups is a mortgage against a future of new needs that are not yet organized or are not readily accommodated by established groups."

From time to time, previously unorganized groups begin to find a political voice. Vague dissatisfactions begin to crystallize over some more specific claim or demand for change, be it incremental or revolutionary. These challenging groups vary in the responses they experience. Some collapse quickly without leaving a visible mark, some are destroyed by attack, some have their programs preempted by competitors, some are given the formal trappings of influence without its substance, some die and rise again from the ashes, some shove their way, yelling and screaming, into the political arena and become permanent fixtures, some walk in on the arm of well-placed sponsors, and some wander in unnoticed and remain in by fait accompli.

It is one task of any interpretation of American politics to explain the varied experience of these challenging groups. The pluralist interpretation provides one such explanation:

1.   Only those groups whose objectives leave intact pluralist social structure and values will be "successful." Participation and success is denied to those who attack and try to change the pluralist order itself.

2.   Only those groups which use institutionally provided means will be successful — in particular, the electoral system and the political pressure or lobbying system. Those who resort to the tactics of the streets will be unsuccessful.

Part of the task of this book will be to explore the adequacy of this pluralist answer. But as we attempt to understand the careers of challenging groups, we will go beyond the answer above to explore many variables where precise relevance for the pluralist argument may not be clear. Ultimately, the concern here is to make sense of the experience of challenging groups in America, not simply to evaluate the particular pluralist answer. But pluralist theory provides the logical starting point for this quest.

In Chapter Two, I will clarify what is included and excluded by the term "challenging group" and will introduce the 53 challenging groups which form the basis of this study. In Chapter Three, measures of the outcome of challenges will be discussed as we try to come to terms with the elusive concept of success or failure. In Chapter Four, the nature of the challenging group's objectives will be related to outcomes. In Chapter Five, we will explore the theory of public goods and its implications for the ability of challenging groups to mobilize their constituency. In Chapter Six, the means of influence used will become the central theme. In Chapter Seven, the focus will shift to the internal organization of the challenging group. In Chapter Eight, some assessment of the influence of different historical contexts will be attempted. Chapter Nine suggests the overall thrust of this collection of results and its implications for our image of the permeability of the American political arena. Finally, Chapter Ten, new in this edition, asks how the results apply to challenging groups since 1945.

REFERENCES

Agger, Robert; Goldrich, Daniel; and Swanson, Bert E. *The Rulers and the Ruled*. New York: Wiley, 1964.

Dahl, Robert. *Who Governs?* New Haven: Yale University Press, 1961.

_____. *Pluralist Democracy in the United States: Conflict and Consent*. Chicago: Rand-McNally, 1967.

Galenson, Walter. *The CIO Challenge to the AFL*. Cambridge, Mass.: Harvard University Press, 1960.

Gamson, William A. "Stable Unrepresentation in American Society." *American Behavioral Scientist,* 12 November/December 1968.

Lowi, Theodore. *The Politics of Disorder*. New York: Basic Books, 1971.

Mills, C. Wright. *The Power Elite*. New York: Oxford University Press, 1956.

Parsons, Talcott. "The Distribution of Power in American Society." In T. Parsons, ed. *Structure and Process in Modern Societies*. New York: The Free Press, 1960.

Pilisuk, Marc, and Hayden, Thomas. "Is There a Military Industrial Complex Which Prevents Peace?" *Journal of Social Issues,* 21 July 1965.

Quint, Howard H. *The Forging of American Socialism: Origins of the Modern Movement*. Indianapolis: Bobbs-Merrill, 1964.

Schattschneider, E. E. *The Semi-Sovereign People*. New York: Holt, Rinehart and Winston, 1960.

Sweeney, Vincent D. *The United Steelworkers of America: Twenty Years Later, 1936–1956*. 1956.

chapter two

The Challenging Group

The actor whose political career will concern us is the carrier of a challenge to the political system. It is usually a formal organization although the degree of "formality" may vary a great deal. To be a member of a challenging group may involve no more than a psychological commitment as with "membership" in the Democratic or Republican Party. With others it may involve a set of concrete acts including blood oaths and other rituals. Formal or informal, the organization has a name which it has taken for itself or been given by others.[1] Most important for our purposes, it is an entity capable of taking action — of holding meetings, planning, issuing statements, calling demonstrations, and raising money.

It will help us to understand the nature of a challenging group by distinguishing among three distinct concepts of a "target" for such groups: (1) the target of influence, (2) the target of mobilization, and (3) the target of benefits. A target of *influence* is that set of individuals, groups, or social institutions that must alter their decisions or policies in order for a challenging group to correct a situation to which it objects. Such a target is the object of actual or planned influence attempts by the group, called here the group's

---

[1] Challenging groups are similar to what Zald and Ash (1966) call "social movement organizations."

14

antagonist. In the case of the Steel Workers Organizing Committee, for example, the various steel companies were the antagonist. In the case of the Social Revolutionary Clubs (Anarcho-Communists), the national regime was the antagonist. In the case of an electoral party challenger a set of political offices or office-holders are the relevant antagonists.

The targets of *mobilization* are those individuals or groups whose resources and energy the group seeks in carrying out its efforts at change, called here the group's *constituency.* To make this clear, it is necessary to deal with an important ambiguity in the concept of political mobilization. The concept of mobilization embraces two closely related ideas, the activation of commitment and the creation of commitment. The *activation* of commitment involves efforts to move those who already possess some degree of commitment to take a specific action. For example, the American Medical Association may urge its members to get on the telephone to their Congressmen to oppose the passage of Medicare legislation, or a union may urge its members to oppose the re-election of someone they regard as antilabor.

The *creation* of commitment means a change from a low generalized readiness to act to a high generalized readiness to act collectively. A group with a high readiness to act requires a minimal amount of effort to convince them to act on a given occasion. A small precipitating event or a mere public call to action by trusted leaders is enough to produce a full response by a constituency in a high state of readiness. A group with a low readiness to act may not respond even to a much greater effort to have them engage in a specific action.

The term "mobilization" is often used to refer to both of the above processes without distinction. Here, I will use it strictly to refer to the creation of commitment, saving the term "activation" for efforts to get supporters of varying degrees of commitment to take specific actions. Mobilization is a process of increasing the readiness to act collectively by building the loyalty of a constituency to an organization or to a group of leaders. Activation is part of an influence attempt; mobilization is part of an organizing process that precedes specific efforts at influence.

The constituency of a group, then, is that set of individuals whose *readiness* to participate in collective action the group is attempting to increase. This typically takes the form of enlisting such individuals as members of an organization, but it need not require this and frequently involves more than this. For the Steel Workers Organizing Committee, the constituency consisted of those steel workers employed by plants the group was attempting to organize. For a revolutionary group, the constituency might be industrial workers or some other group whose class consciousness the group is attempting to build. In the case of an electoral challenger, the constituency is that portion of the electorate from whom the group hopes to win support.

The target of *benefits* are those individuals or groups whom the challenging group hopes will be affected positively by the changes that it seeks from its antagonist. I will call this target the group's *beneficiary*. There are many cases in which the beneficiary of the group and its constituency are identical, but this is not always true. In some cases, the changes will affect everyone more or less equally whether they are members of the group's constituency or not. In other cases, the constituency and beneficiary may have little overlap. In the case of the Steel Workers Organizing Committee, for example, the constituency and the beneficiary were identical—in both cases, the steel workers. In the case of the American Committee for the Outlawry of War, the policy changes which the group sought would not affect its middle-class reform constituency anymore than anyone else. In the case of an abolitionist group, the intended beneficiaries were the slaves, slave owners, and the society as a whole but not the nonslave holding constituency of the movement in particular.

The issue of a group's beneficiary will become relevant in Chapter Five when we explore how the relationship between constituency and beneficiary affects success. For defining a challenging group, only the antagonist and the constituency are relevant. A challenging group meets two central criteria:

1. *It must be seeking the mobilization of an unmobilized constituency.* Established interest groups are hereby excluded even though they may be seeking changes. A group is no longer a challenging group once it can call upon an already mobilized constituency whenever it decides to attempt influence. Even established groups, of course, make continued efforts to maintain the commitment of their members and express concern about membership "apathy." The practical issue, then, is a matter of a degree — whether a group faces as a central and primary task the mobilization of a constituency where it does not initially exist, or whether

this is a secondary task centered mainly on the maintenance of a commitment that threatens to decay without efforts at continual renewal. Only a group in the former situation qualifies as a challenging group.

A newly-formed group that is so rich in resources from the start that it has no need to mobilize a constituency is also excluded. For example, a group of influential citizens who formed an ad hoc group to block the passage of a treaty in the Senate would not be included unless it saw the need to draw in and mobilize an underlying constituency before it could exert effective influence. To the extent that the members hoped to rely on the persuasiveness of their arguments or the prestige of the names on their letterhead, they would lack the focus on mobilization as a primary task.

2. *Its antagonist lies outside of its constituency.* Those groups whose target of influence is a subset of their constituency are not defined as challenging groups. A utopian community, for example, attempting to mobilize a constituency to participate in a better way of life, is not included. It would be included if its plans required it to obtain new legislation or the abandonment of certain governmental policies since these objectives imply outside antagonists. Similarly, a messianic group would be excluded if it offered the members salvation by altering their own way of life without the necessity of influencing outsiders. A benevolent association, hoping to provide certain services for members, or a fraternal order, dedicated to performing acts of charity, would be similarly excluded. In short, challenging groups seek influence beyond what their constituency has the power to implement on its own; they must gain concessions or the actual offices and authority of nonmembers to achieve their goals.

Beyond these primary criteria, we have adopted a number of more or less arbitrary conventions to put practical boundaries around the universe of challenging groups we will consider in this study. Only those groups that surfaced in the United States from 1800 to 1945 are included. Contemporary groups are excluded because in many cases these challenges are still in process, and we cannot yet state what their outcome is. Because we are concerned primarily with societal power relations, we include only those challenging groups with a constituency extending beyond the borders of a single state. The group itself may be based in a single state, but its constituency cannot also be so confined. Given the dispersion of its constituency, the changes sought by the group cannot be implemented by action in a single, limited locale. This has the effect of eliminating from the universe of challenging groups considered here a vast number of small challenges directed, for example, at a single municipality or state government. It does not exclude groups with a constituency in several states whose local supporters are making essentially similar demands for change in their respective cities.

We also exclude groups whose members are neither American citizens nor striving for such citizenship. In particular, we do not include the various Indian nations, which have engaged in numerous wars and conflicts with the federal government, as challenging groups.

We also exclude groups whose constituency consists only or primarily of other organizations. Thus, many federations are excluded because they do not directly try to mobilize individuals. An association or watchdog for existing groups, designed to coordinate their efforts or monitor and influence others on their behalf, is not considered a challenging group. However, many groups which are *formally* federations in fact attempt to mobilize individuals on behalf of broader goals than their member organizations are able or willing to pursue. Such groups—the American Federation of Labor, for example—qualify as challenging groups. They have different protagonists than the member organizations and attempt to mobilize and build the loyalty of individuals to the federation by pursuit of their own, complementary objectives.

A challenging group that began as a faction or splinter from an existing group qualifies if it meets the basic criteria, but only if it establishes an independent operating structure. A faction that is challenging the leadership does not qualify unless it is both a separate organizational entity and has an antagonist outside of the organization of which it is part. Challenges by insurgent groups within an organization, aimed at changing that organization or seizing power within it, are not included here.

Satellites of other groups are excluded when they are merely a part of a parent organization. For example, a ladies' auxiliary, a vigilante protection unit, an operating committee within the group, a caucus, an advertising bureau, and the like are not treated as independent challenges when they have no separate cause and are merely providing some service or reinforcement for the parent group.

THE SAMPLE OF CHALLENGING GROUPS

The universe of groups that this book addresses are all those challenging groups that surfaced in American society between 1800 and 1945. The members of this universe meet the primary criteria: they are seeking the mobilization of an unmobilized constituency and their antagonist or target of influence lies outside of this constituency. We have restricted or clarified this universe further by adopting conventions dealing with the geographical breadth of the constituency, citizenship status, federations, splinter groups, and satellites.

There have been between five and six hundred challenging groups in American society that meet the criteria described here. We will focus on a sample of 53 of them. Shortly, I intend to defend the claim that these 53 groups are an equal probability sample of the defined universe of challenging groups in American society. But first, it will be useful if the reader has at least a general descriptive sense of the variety and nature of the members of the sample.

The 53 challengers range from the narrowest of reform groups to the most sweeping of revolutionary groups. One group, the League of American Wheelmen, aimed only at the modest goal of eliminating a series of restrictions on the use of the bicycle and winning the right to ride on public highways. Later, flushed by success, their ambitions grew to include as well the improvement of public highways as they became participants in the "good roads movement." In contrast to these most finite of goals, the German-American Bund hoped to do no less than remodel the American political system along the lines of German National Socialism.

Some groups—for example, the American Association of University Professors—have such a respectable image today that they constitute an embarrassment to a book on social protest. Others—for example, the Tobacco Night Riders of the black patch area of Kentucky and Tennessee—look more disreputable by contemporary standards than they probably did at the time. But, then, even the most reputable of groups today was usually not considered such during its period of challenge.

Some of the 53 are famous and well-remembered—for example, Father Coughlin's National Union for Social Justice. Others—for example, the League of Deliverance, a group that aimed at excluding Chinese labor from the United States—are remembered only by a handful of professional students of American labor and nativist movements.

Appendix B gives a brief description, including the period of challenge, of all 53 groups. We can divide them into four broad, descriptive categories. Twenty of the groups (38 percent) were occupationally based. The most obvious examples are unions of blue collar workers—for example, The Packinghouse Workers Organizing Committee and the American Labor Union, a forerunner of the Industrial Workers of the World or "Wobblies." But the category also includes middle-class occupational groups (The American Federation of Teachers), craftsmen (The Union Trade Society of Journeymen Tailors and The National Brotherhood of Baseball Players), and farm organizations (The Tobacco Night Riders and the Dairymen's League).

Seventeen of the groups (32 percent) were one form or another of a "reform group." Some of these groups—for example, the American Anti-Slavery Society, a leading abolitionist group—were considered very radical in their day. Some—for example, Theodore Roosevelt's Bull Moose Party and William Randolph Hearst's Independence League—were conventional political parties seeking electoral success. Some—for example, A. Philip Randolph's March on Washington Committee and the National Urban League—were civil rights groups. Some—for example, the Church Peace Union and the American Committee for the Outlawry of War—were peace groups. Some—for example, the Federal Suffrage Association and the American Proportional Representation League—sought specific institutional reforms in one area.

Ten of the groups (19 percent) were rooted in the socialist tradition. The sample includes the granddaddy of socialism in America, The International Workingmen's Association, or First International. Some of the socialist groups—for example, the National Student League—were campus-based. Some—for example, the Progressive Labor Party—were electorally oriented; while others—for example, the Revolutionary Workers League—strongly rejected the possibility of effecting change through the ballot box.

Finally, six of the groups (11 percent) were some variety of right-wing or nativist group. Electoral challengers—for example, the Native American or American Republican Party—are included here along with such classical right-wing challengers as the Christian Front against Communism and the German-American Bund. The distribution of the 53 groups is summarized in Figure 2-1.

FIGURE 2–1
Distribution of Types of Groups in the Sample

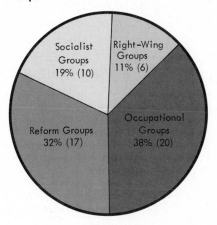

FIGURE 2–2
Distribution of Challenging Groups by Decade of Origin

The groups are also well distributed over time. A little over half (55 percent) began their careers in the 19th century, and every single decade except 1800–1810 and the 1870s is represented by at least one new challenger. Figure 2–2 shows the distribution of groups by decade and reveals the 1880s and the 1930s as the most productive of new challenges with the 1910s and 1890s not far behind. The 1830s are the major contributor in the pre-civil war period. The median length of a challenge period is about eight years, but there is great variability.

THE SAMPLING PROCEDURE

The 53 groups are a representative sample of all challenging groups, as defined here, in American society between 1800 and 1945. It is no easy matter to get an equal probability sample since no list or sampling frame exists. Such a list must be created with a considerable investment of effort and expense.

Why bother? Why not simply pick groups that are well-documented and that have various relevant characteristics? Why not pick interesting groups instead of giving such trivial efforts as the Society for the Promotion of Manual Labor in Literary Institutions the same probability for inclusion as the Ku Klux Klan or the Wobblies? Surely the resources of this study would have been more usefully allocated if these latter groups had been included at the expense of the former?

The answer is simply that we can learn a great deal more from an unbiased sample than from a biased one. The central issues concern the permeability of the political arena by new participants and how their success or failure is influenced by their strategy and organization. There are two obvious biases in picking well-documented or "interesting" groups. First, we are likely to encounter a heavy bias toward success, toward groups that lasted. Those that have made it inspire histories, indeed, sometimes even sponsor them. Those that collapse are not around to enlighten would-be chroniclers.

Of course, some groups that have "failed" do inspire historians, and this brings us to a second bias. Groups that have had an especially dramatic life, that have been involved in violent clashes and have produced martyrs, are likely to be remembered. Leftist groups, because they attract intellectuals as participants, are more likely to be written about after their demise. Thus, there is every reason to suspect that a sample of interesting failures will be quite unrepresentative of unsuccessful groups. Beyond these predictable biases, many other, more subtle biases would probably be operating as well, misleading us in our interpretations of what we might find.

By working with a representative sample of challenging groups, we minimize these biases. There are, as I will discuss later, certain problems with what is included in the *universe* of challenging groups, but at least we can be confident that the 53 groups in the sample represent this defined universe reasonably well.

Appendix C contains a detailed description of the procedure for compiling the sampling frame, and I will only summarize the main elements here. We began by compiling a *gross* list of potential sample entries. This gross list was as exhaustive as possible, but we were not concerned with how many invalid entries were included. We accepted the fact that most of the entries would, on investigation, turn out not to meet our criteria for a challenging group.

The gross list was based on the indexes of general and specialized histories. A coder turned to the index of each source used and recorded the name of each formal organization and each collective behavior episode mentioned (e.g., "Shays' Rebellion" or "The Watts Riot"). High reliabilities were achieved between independent coders using this procedure.

We began the list with general sources—for example, Louis Filler's *A Dictionary of Social Reform*—and proceeded to a bibliography of about 75 books covering different types of potential challenging groups. That our bibliographic categories overlapped was of no concern, but it was necessary that every challenging group fall into at least one of the following types: agricultural, labor, ethnic, women, religious, prohibition, nativist, reform, professional, business and commerce, conservation, black, socialist, peace, veterans, rightist, and radical left groups. Many of the sources used were quite specialized—for example, Hicks and Saloutos, *Agricultural Discontent in the Middle West*.

For each book, an index of new entries was compiled—that is, the percentage of total entries in the source not already included in the file. Initially, we established a criterion of completeness that three consecutive books from different categories should yield less than 20 percent new entries. In fact, we exceeded this substantially, and the final *dozen* sources were all below 20 percent, averaging about 10 percent new entries. The new entries were not necessarily challenging groups, of course, but were merely additional names of organizations or collective behavior episodes. It is a reasonable guess that a lower percentage of these new entries were challenging groups since many appeared to be highly localized groups—for example, chapters or branches of organizations already included. To check this possibility, we examined the final 20 new entries, and none turned out to be a challenging group (see Appendix C for details).

Once we were satisfied with the completeness of the frame, we drew a sample.[2] Each card in the gross file had 11 chances in 100 of being selected, and we ended up with a total of 467 entries. We then investigated each entry to determine whether or not it met the criteria for a challenging group. Most did not and were discarded; in fact, we were left with only 64 or 14 percent of the original cards. Note, however, that these 64 were representative of all the valid cards in the gross file even though we could not identify those that did not fall into the sample.

Of these 64 valid entries, we were able to get reasonably complete information on 53 of them, a response rate of 83 percent. Of the other 11, it is entirely possible that some would not qualify —for example, the Philadelphia Journeymen House Painters Association—but, in the absence of more conclusive evidence to question their validity, we assume that they meet the definition of a challenging group. In this sense, the figure of an 83 percent response rate is a conservative one and might turn out to be higher if we were to uncover new information on them. The 11 missing groups are described in Appendix C.

THE NATURE OF THE DATA

A series of identical questions were asked about each challenging group (see Appendix D). Instead of employing our questionnaire to interview individuals as one would on a survey, we employed it to interview books and documents. We experienced our own equivalent of the respondent who is never at home or slams the door in one's face—the group that left no record of its adventures.

Whenever possible, we relied on existing professional histories,

---

[2] The sample was actually drawn in a series of waves, but this has no importance for the discussion here.

turning to primary sources only when we were forced to by gaps in our information. Special library collections such as the University of Michigan's Labadie Collection proved very helpful in some difficult cases, particularly with left-wing groups. For most groups several different sources were used, with biases duly noted. A complete list of sources used is included in the bibliography and the reference sections of this book.

The compiler used the questionnaire to complete a "protocol" on each challenging group, a process requiring an average of 80 hours per protocol. For each question, the compiler gave a short summary of the (sometimes contradictory) answers found in the several sources used. He or she then included a photocopy of the relevant paragraphs or pages from the sources bearing on the particular question. If a section was relevant to more than one question, it was appropriately cross-referenced.

To illustrate, in response to the question, "To what extent were challenging group members subject to arrest?" the compiler of the Christian Front against Communism noted the following: "There were 233 criminal prosecutions due to racial clashes in 1939 in New York alone, and 17 Brooklyn Fronters were arrested for conspiring to overthrow the government." These comments were followed by photocopies of fairly lengthy descriptions from two sources concerning the circumstances of these arrests and indictments.

The basic questionnaire is included in Appendix D. Each question had a series of additional instructions to the compiler concerning the type of information being sought. For example, the compiler was asked to note any evidence on whether arrests were isolated and sporadic, or patterned and repetitive, and to note any evidence relating to official sanction and justification of arrests. For each protocol, the compiler established certain time reference points related to major events in the group's history and was asked to note, whenever possible, the relationship of the answers to these time points — for example, "arrests occurred from Time 1 to Time 4 but not after Time 4."

The questionnaire contained sections on the group's interaction with different institutional spheres — the law enforcement system, government agencies, mass media, political parties, legislative bodies, and private interest groups. Another section dealt with the internal characteristics of the challenging group — its leadership, organizational structure, resources, tactics, ideology, and so forth.

The final section of the questionnaire dealt with the outcome of the group's challenge, the central topic of the next chapter.

Once the protocols were completed, codes were developed for each section. Because our information was often quiet spotty, we relied heavily on quite simple codes. For example, in the case of arrests, our code basically asked whether group members were ever arrested or not.[3] Given such simple codes, it is probably not surprising that coding reliability between independent coders averaged 92 percent. Reliabilities of this order were sometimes achieved by combining categories in which independent coders were unable to make reliable distinctions. For example, if the code for arrests had included categories of "none," "a few," and "many," it might have turned out that no disagreements between coders occurred between "none" and "a few" but that several occurred between "a few" and "many." In such an instance, if reliability was below a criterion of 80 percent, we would have combined the unreliable categories to produce a 100 percent reliable code containing only the categories "none" and "some."

We also employed a variety of checks on the quality of the protocols. For several groups, protocols were completed independently by different compilers and the results checked. It was then possible to see if coders using independent versions of a protocol for the same group obtained essentially similar results.

Through these various efforts at controlling the quality of our data, we were able to keep our demands on it within reasonable limits. In many cases, we wished to measure things that were beyond what the protocols could reliably yield. Where this occurred, we learned to live with the frustration of not measuring some variable of interest rather than attempting to extract gold from inferior ore. Hopefully, the information that we were able to extract, gross as it sometimes is, is of sufficient interest in its own right to ease the frustration of not being able to satiate our curiosity.

A FINAL CAVEAT

A central purpose of this research is to gain insight into the permeability of the American political system by different types of groups using various strategies. It is important to this objective that

---

[3] It also distinguished test cases deliberately initiated by the group from ordinary arrests.

we use a low threshold to identify a challenging group, lest we be left with nothing but a sample of highly visible successes. The procedure used employed a modest threshold but a threshold nonetheless. Ultimately, a group must have reached some point of activity even to attract the notice of an historian who was interested in groups of its special type.

There may be aggregates of individuals, very much outside of the political arena and suffering some form of social disadvantage, that never organize enough to stage a hostile outburst or form a protest group. Clearly, such quasi-groups or potential groups elude our net of challenging groups. Yet, their inability to mount a challenge may be an extremely important datum for interpreting the American political experience. Some groups may be so far outside that their cries or curses never reach our ears, if indeed they are ever uttered. We will have nothing to say here about such potential challenging groups. I don't know in what numbers they exist, if at all. This book will shed no light on them. But their possible existence must be remembered in any conclusions about the openness of the American political system we hope to draw from a study of actual challenging groups.

REFERENCE

Zald, Mayer N., and Ash, Roberta. "Social Movement Organizations: Growth, Decay, and Change." *Social Forces*, March 1966, 44:327–41.

chapter three

The Meaning of Success

Success is an elusive idea. What of the group whose leaders are honored or rewarded while their supposed beneficiaries linger in the same cheerless state as before? Is such a group more or less successful than another challenger whose leaders are vilified and imprisoned even as their program is eagerly implemented by their oppressor? Is a group a failure if it collapses with no legacy save inspiration to a generation that will soon take up the same cause with more tangible results? And what do we conclude about a group that accomplishes exactly what it set out to achieve and then finds its victory empty of real meaning for its presumed beneficiaries? Finally, we must add to these questions the further complications of groups with multiple antagonists and multiple areas of concern. They may achieve some results with some targets and little or nothing with others.

It is useful to think of success as a set of outcomes, recognizing that a given challenging group may receive different scores on equally valid, different measures of outcome. These outcomes fall into two basic clusters: one concerned with the fate of the challenging group as an organization and one with the distribution of new advantages to the group's beneficiary. The central issue in the first cluster focuses on the *acceptance* of a challenging group by its antagonists as a valid spokesman for a legitimate set of interests. The central issue in the second cluster focuses on whether the group's beneficiary gains *new advantages* during the challenge and its aftermath.

Both of these outcome clusters require elaboration, but, for the moment, consider each as if it were a single, dichotomous variable. Assume a group that has a single antagonist and a single act which they wish this antagonist to perform—for example, a reform group which desires a particular piece of national legislation. We ask of such a group, did its antagonist accept it as a valid spokesman for the constituency that it was attempting to mobilize or did it deny such acceptance? Secondly, did the group gain the advantages it sought—for example, the passage of the legislation that it desired?

By combining these two questions, as in Figure 3–1, we acquire four possible outcomes: full response, co-optation, preemption, and collapse. The full response and collapse categories are relatively unambiguous successes and failures—in the one case the achievement of both acceptance and new advantages, in the other, the achievement of neither. The remainder are mixed categories: co-optation is the term used for acceptance without new advantages and preemption for new advantages without acceptance.

FIGURE 3–1
Outcome of Resolved Challenges

| | | *Acceptance* | |
		Full	None
New Advantages	Many	Full response	Preemption
	None	Co-optation	Collapse

Figure 3–1 is the paradigm for handling outcomes of challenging groups, but it requires additional complexity before it can be used to handle as diverse a set of groups as the 53 represented here. Acceptance must be given a special meaning for revolutionary groups, for example, which seek not a nod of recognition from an antagonist but its destruction and replacement. Similarly, new "advantages" are not always easy to define. We must deal with cases in which a group seeks, for example, relatively intangible value changes, shifts in the scope of authority, or a change in procedures as well as the simpler case of material benefits for a well-defined group.

THE ENDPOINT OF A CHALLENGE

The outcome measures used refer to "ultimate" outcome, to the state of the group at the end of its challenge. A given group might achieve significant new advantages at one point without receiving acceptance, but we would not consider that preemption had occurred as long as it continued to press an active challenge. Only when it eventually collapsed or ceased activity would we classify its outcome as preemption. Or, if it eventually won acceptance, its outcome would be full response instead. Similarly, the new advantages might be withdrawn and the group brutally crushed, making "collapse" the appropriate outcome. Thus, during its period of challenge, a group might appear to be in one or another cell of Figure 3–1 at different times, but the outcome measures only consider its location at the end.

A challenge period is considered over when one of the following occurs:

1. *The challenging group ceases to exist as a formal entity.* It may officially dissolve, declaring itself no longer in existence. Or, it may merge with another group, ceasing to maintain a separate identity. Note, however, that a group does not cease to exist by merely changing its name to refurbish its public image. Operationally, we consider that two names represent the same challenging group if and only if:

   a. The major goals, purposes, and functions of the two groups are the same.
   b. The constituency remains the same.
   c. The average challenging group member and potential member would agree that the new-name group is essentially the old group relabeled.

2. *The challenging group, while not formally dissolving, ceases mobilization and influence activity.* A five-year period of inactivity is considered sufficient to specify the end of the challenge. If, after such a dormant period, the group becomes active again, it is considered a new challenging group in spite of its organizational continuity with the old challenger. This occurred, in fact, with two of the 53 challengers in the sample. In each case the period of dormancy was quite a bit longer than the required five years, and, in one case, the geographical location of activity was different as well.

Marking the end of a challenge is more difficult with groups that continue to exist and be active. The line between being a challenging group and an established interest group is not always sharp. The essential difference lies in how institutionalized a conflict relationship exists between the group and its antagonists. When this conflict becomes regulated and waged under some standard operating procedures, the challenge period is over. Operationally, this can be dated from the point at which the group is accepted. Hence, for continuing groups, the challenge period is over when:

　3. *The challenging group's major antagonists accept the group as a valid spokesman for its constituency and deal with it as such.* In the case of unions, this is indicated by formal recognition of the union as a bargaining agent for the employees. In other cases, the act of acceptance is less clear, and, even in the case of unions, different companies extend recognition at different times. Issues such as these are dealt with in the discussion of measures of acceptance below.

　With continuing groups, then, there is some inevitable arbitrariness in dating the end of a challenge. The compiler was instructed to err, in ambiguous cases, on the side of a later date. Thus, where acute conflict continues to exist between the group and important antagonists, the challenge is not considered over even when some other antagonists may have begun to deal with the challenger in a routinized way. Furthermore, by extending the challenge period, we include new benefits that might be excluded by using a premature termination date.

MEASURING OUTCOMES

Acceptance

　Did the relationship between the challenging group and its antagonists change from the beginning to the end of the challenge? Although more than 75 percent of the groups here are more complicated, we will begin the discussion of this question with the simplest case of a group with a single antagonist. This antagonist necessarily begins with a relationship of active or passive hostility toward the challenging group or, at best, indifference. Acceptance involves a change from hostility or indifference to a more positive relationship.[1]

---
　[1] If acceptance existed from the very beginning, the group would not qualify as a challenging group.

There are four indicators of this more positive relationship:

1. *Consultation*. This must involve some degree of initiative by the antagonist. For example, if a legislative body has opened hearings on a matter of importance to the challenging group, the antagonist might invite representatives of the group to testify. On the other hand, if the group asks to testify and is permitted, this would not by itself be considered consultation. Similarly, if the antagonist issues a subpoena to force the group to testify, no consultation would be coded because the group is not being treated in such an instance as a legitimate spokesman for a constituency.

2. *Negotiations*. If the antagonist is willing to enter into negotiations with the group on a continuing basis, not simply at the height of a particular crisis, this also implies acceptance of the group as a spokesman for a constituency. To be coded as acceptance, the negotiations must imply that the antagonist is dealing with the challenging group's negotiators as representatives of a constituency. The outcome of the negotiations is not relevant here; the two parties may fail to reach an acceptable settlement. But the mere fact of a continuing negotiating relationship implies acceptance.

3. *Formal recognition*. This form of acceptance is characterized by the antagonist making explicit, typically in writing, that it recognizes the challenging group as a legitimate spokesman for a designated constituency. This is the functional equivalent of diplomatic recognition of a government in international politics. Nothing needs to be implied about general mutuality of interests or approval of the challenging group and its actions.

4. *Inclusion*. This form of acceptance is characterized by the inclusion of challenging group leaders or members in positions of status or authority in the antagonist's organizational structure. It is essential, however, that the included challenging group members maintain their status, formally or informally, as group members. If serving in the antagonist's organization requires repudiating membership in the challenging group as a condition of office, it is not coded as acceptance through inclusion.

Special definitions of some of the above terms are needed to deal with certain types of groups. Consider, for example, revolutionary groups that have no desire for conventional acceptance by authorities they are attempting to overthrow. In such a case, only inclusion is a relevant measure of acceptance unless the group abandons its revolutionary ambitions. Inclusion, in this case, means self-inclusion. If the revolutionary group is successful, its members will be included at the expense of existing incumbents. In addition, the authority structure may be radically reorganized with old positions abolished and new ones created. Thus, acceptance does not imply psychological acceptance by the antagonist. A similar line of reasoning applies to electoral challenges. Here, the target is the set of offices being sought, and, again, only acceptance through inclusion is meaningful. Winning elections leads to such inclusion.

For a certain number of groups, the antagonist is not a circumscribed set of authorities but the general public. This is especially true with respect to groups that aim at changing values or aggregated individual practices. Many such groups—for example, the American Birth Control League—may also seek actions from targets such as a legislature or courts. But, when the "public" or "public opinion" is one target of change, how can acceptance be defined? The major consideration here is that acceptance refers to a response to the challenging group itself rather than to its issues or program. Thus, in the American Birth Control League example, the relevant consideration is not a change in attitudes toward contraception but toward the League that is promoting the change. There is an issue of acceptance only when the challenging group is initially regarded as deviant in some sense, either as subversive or as excessively eccentric. Acceptance in such a case is reflected by a change to the view that the organization is no longer deviant— that is, that a reasonable man or woman could belong to such a group and not be considered a crack-pot or worse.

Finally, we must consider the common situation of multiple antagonists. To handle this, targets are first grouped by types—for example, legislatures, steel companies, city governments, and so forth. Then, each type of antagonist is separately coded for a challenging group, allowing for distinctions in response within a given type between all, some, only one, and none. Thus, many groups have several types of antagonists and multiple codes for different kinds of acceptance for each.

This complex set of measures of acceptance must be reduced to some summary measures to be useful for analysis. I have explored several but will rely mostly on one very simple dichotomous one: the existence of a minimal acceptance relationship with *any* antagonist at the end of the challenge period. Such a relationship exists if there is a positive code on any of the measures of acceptance (consultation, negotiation, formal recognition, or inclusion) with any of the antagonists. Or, to put it the other way, a group without acceptance is one which has no type of acceptance from any antagonist.

I have chosen such an apparently minimal measure of acceptance because it it both unambiguous and, hence, highly reliable and also divides the sample quite neatly. Slightly more than half of the groups (28) never achieved even this minimal degree of acceptance; the other half (25) received one or another kind with some or all antagonists. In four cases, this involved nothing more than consultation, but, in the other 21, it involved one of the stronger forms of acceptance.

New Advantages

Did the potential beneficiaries of the challenging group receive what the group sought for them? No assumption is made that the challenging group necessarily caused the benefits. We asked only whether desired results were forthcoming, for whatever reason, during and immediately after the period of challenge.

In assessing the achievement of benefits, the group's own perspective and aspirations are the starting point. There are several cases in which I personally regarded the group's efforts at change as a form of false-consciousness. I do not believe, for example, that Father Coughlin's monetary nostrums would have actually helped the workers and farmers who were the alleged beneficiary of the National Union for Social Justice. There are even cases where a group began to question its own aspirations as it began to achieve them. The Grand Eight Hour Leagues, for example, successfully sought the passage of eight-hour legislation, but these laws turned out to be useless. And certainly many women today question the successful achievements of the Federal Suffrage Association, finding them a less meaningful accomplishment than the advocates of the time had expected. Similarly, the passage of the prohibition amendment failed to realize its advocates' hopes.

These reflections are intended as a caution in the interpretation of the achievement of new advantages. We leave it to the reader to judge whether the benefits were or would have been "real" benefits. They are benefits as defined by the challenging group. Some people, according to the challenging group, will improve their lot in life if certain things can be made to happen. If these desired changes occurred, then we regarded new advantages as having been realized, adopting the group's perspective on what constitutes a benefit.

Many of the 53 groups do not seek a specific material benefit but some broader change in institutions or values. Since no revolutions have occurred in American society during the period covered, it would appear that revolutionary groups are doomed to fail on this outcome measure. But it is not always clear just which group is or isn't revolutionary. It is consistent with some revolutionary ideologies, for example, to adopt immediate goals which are seen as providing benefits in their own right, as well as bringing one a step closer to Armageddon. If a so-called revolutionary group devotes energy and resources to the achievement of such an immediate goal, then different outcomes are possible as with any other group. The National Student League, for example, had general socialist goals, but it also concerned itself with a number of immediate campus issues, including the elimination of compulsory R.O.T.C. and the achievement of a free student press. If a group rejects all changes short of revolution and devotes its energy entirely to the mobilization process, then in this place and era, it will not have achieved new advantages.

For third-party challengers, new advantages are not measured by electoral success, which is used to measure acceptance, but by program enactment. Thus, a group may win some elections but fail to pass any significant legislation or otherwise influence policy (a case of co-optation); or it may fail to elect its own members but gain new advantages through the adoption of policy changes and programs by those who are elected (a case of preemption).

Similar reasoning applies to the challenging group that wishes to alter values or some aspect of public behavior. New advantages for the American Birth Control League, for example, meant a change in practice by Americans—increased usage of contraceptive techniques.[2] New advantages for the North Carolina Manumission Society are measured by their success in persuading individual plantation owners to grant freedom to their slaves. Note that in each of these cases, the target is still a target of change, not of mobilization.

How is the achievement of new advantages actually measured? First, consider the simplest case of a group with a single goal or area of concern. Four perceptions of goal achievement were

---

[2] New advantages can also come through changes in the legal status of birth control, another relevant goal of this particular challenging group.

coded: the perception of degree of achievement (1) by historians, (2) by the challenging group, and (3) by its antagonist, and (4) the challenging group's level of satisfaction with its achievement at the end of the challenge. In many cases, we were unable to get sufficient information on one or more of these perceptions, in which case we coded what we could. The codes covered changes both during the period of the challenge and in the following 15 years.[3]

Since many groups had multiple goals and since sources sometimes disagreed on how well the goals were achieved, each group had multiple measures of new advantages. To reduce this complexity for analysis, a summary measure was essential. We ended up using the following four categories:

1. *Twenty groups (38 percent) received no new advantages.* These groups had minuses and zeroes on all clusters.

2. *Twenty-six groups (49 percent) received new advantages.* These groups had at least one positive field (i.e., pluses, no more than two zeroes, and no minuses) in a majority of their areas of concern. In other words, on most of their goals, these groups received a positive response on at least one major aspect.

3. *Four groups (7 percent) received peripheral advantages.* These were groups that had some positive fields but did not meet the full definition of a group receiving new advantages.

4. *Three groups (6 percent) received equivocal advantages.* These were groups with mixed fields (some pluses and some minuses concerning the same goal). In other words, these were groups on which disagreement existed among different observers on whether goals had been realized or not.

The seven groups in the last two categories will be combined with the no-advantage group for analysis purposes. Figure 3–2 shows the distribution of the 53 groups in the four outcome categories described above. In many analyses, we will examine each summary measure separately as we explore the relative influence

---

[3]Since most groups had multiple goals and multiple areas of concern within each goal cluster, a challenger's goal achievement was covered by a code consisting of many columns. We first broke goals down into specific clusters for separate evaluation. Then, for each cluster, we gave a challenger a plus for each source (that is, an historian, challenging group, or antagonist) who agreed that at least half of the relevant targets had responded in the desired fashion. We recorded a minus when a source asserted that less than half of the targets responded as desired or the group was no more satisfied at the end of the challenge than when it began. If there was insufficient information on the perceptions of one or another source, a zero was recorded.

FIGURE 3–2
Outcomes for the Sample of Challenging Groups Based on Summary Measures of Acceptance and New Advantages

		Minimal Acceptance Relationship	
		Yes	No
New Advantages	Yes	Full response = 20 38%	Preemption = 6 11%
	No (or equivocal and peripheral)	Co-optation = 5 9%	Collapse = 22 42%

$$n = 53$$

of some variable of interest on these different measures of outcome. Henceforth, when I use the term "success," it will refer to either or both outcome measures in those contexts in which there is no need to differentiate between them.

chapter four

The Strategy of Thinking Small

There is a certain absurdity in comparing a group that seeks a modest change and threatens no major redistribution of power with one that seeks to sweep aside the old order and all its supporting institutions. For modesty of aspiration, few challenging groups can compete with the Society for the Promotion of Manual Labor in Literary Institutions. This quaint effort of the 1830s was one of several reform efforts supported by the Tappan brothers. The group's mobilization effort consisted primarily of lectures by its paid general agent, Theodore Weld. No state militias were necessary to hold back the crowds aroused by Weld's impassioned pleas. In fact, Weld, who was apparently a skillful speaker, frequently found it expedient to build his audience by advertising his topic as temperance, then using the occasion to make an additional pitch on educational reform.

Weld invoked an image of the college student and seminarian that 150 years has not seriously dated. His portrait depicted the typical collegian "with his feet elevated upon a mantelpiece as high as his head, body bent like a halfmoon or a horseshoe, lolling, stretching, yawning, smoking, snoring." Strong physical labor was recommended for this shiftless lot, to "tone the body, stimulate the intellect, safeguard the student's morals by occupying his spare time, teach him useful skills, promote industry, originality, and manliness. By cheapening the cost of education, it would broaden the country's intellectual base, and by demonstrating the compatibility of physical and intellectual endeavor, it would do away with absurd social distinctions between those who work with their brains and those who produce with their hands" (Thomas, 1950).

In contrast, although in a way equally quaint, consider the Communist Labor Party. This was the name taken by the so-called Benjamin Gitlow-John Reed, left-wing faction of the Socialist Party when they broke away in the summer of 1919. It was a period of considerable hysteria, stimulated by the success of the Bolshevik revolution and the substantial labor unrest in the United States. Nineteen nineteen was the year of the Seattle general strike, the Lawrence textile strike, the Boston police strike, the national coal strike and a large steel strike involving 365,000 workers.

The fledgling and ineffectual Communist Labor Party was a natural target of the various organs of the antired hysteria. First, in November, 1919, many of its members, including Gitlow, were arrested in raids growing out of the New York State Senate's Lusk Committee and its investigations of "seditious activity." There was considerable competition among anticommunist entrepreneurs of the day; group members were also arrested in large numbers in raids initiated by the District Attorney of Chicago and U.S. Attorney General Mitchell Palmer. Gitlow also reports a great deal of additional harassment (Gitlow, 1940), and he personally was sentenced and jailed for more than a year. John Reed once faced three indictments at the same time. Most of the leaders "lived in a half-world of indictments, trials, defense committees, convictions, sentences, and appeals" (Draper, 1957).

What were the goals of this beleaguered group? "The Communist Labor Party of America declares itself in complete accord with the principles of Communism as laid down in the Manifesto of the Third International formed at Moscow."[1] This included the organization and training of the working class for the capture of state power and the establishment of new, working class, government machinery. The new working class government would "transfer

---

[1] From the "Party and Labor Program," reprinted in the *Report of the Joint Legislative Committee Investigating Seditious Activities*, (Lusk Committee), April 24, 1920, Senate of the State of New York.

private property in the means of production and distribution to the working class government, to be administered by the workers themselves. It shall nationalize the great trusts and financial institutions. It shall abolish capitalist agricultural production" (ibid). In short, their aim was a classical revolutionary set of goals.

The revelation that the Communist Labor Party was unsuccessful will come as a surprise to no one. Organizationally, it gave up its existence in less than a year, uniting with the Ruthenberg faction of the Communist Party to form the United Communist Party. Both groups were heavily depleted by the devastating and effective arrests and deportations to which their members were subjected. The United Communist Party, in turn, went through several more fusions and fissions with no noticeable positive response on any outcome measure.

The Society for the Promotion of Manual Labor in Literary Institutions had the more complicated fate of preemption but did not live much longer as an organization. By 1833, Arthur and Lewis Tappan and Theodore Weld were becoming interested in other causes, especially abolitionism. With Weld's resignation to pursue a career in the ministry, the Society essentially ceased to function. During its existence, the manual labor system was adopted in some form by many colleges, theological seminaries, several medical schools, and several hundred academies. Many of the changes were short-lived, however, and, with no one pressing the challenge, "the system declined nearly as rapidly as it arose and had been abandoned by most institutions before 1840" (Anderson, 1913).

What meaning can there be in comparing the fate of groups as different as the Society for the Promotion of Manual Labor in Literary Institutions and the Communist Labor Party? Very little, if we are able to discover nothing more than the half-truth that the less one tries to get, the more likely he is to get it. Clearly, many groups have incommensurate tasks. The challenge is to discover two things about the goals these groups have undertaken:

1.   Is differential success related to aspects of group goals that are less obvious than the magnitude of the group's ambition?

2.   When we compare groups with more or less commensurate tasks, do we still find major differences in their rate of success?

The second of these questions is really the concern of later chapters. We will need to constantly reassure ourselves that any apparent difference in outcome due to strategies of mobilization, influence, or internal organization are not due simply to differences in underlying goals[2] or type of group. The remainder of this chapter explores the first question. We will examine the "think small" formula for success in more detail to see how well it fits the 53 groups here.

THREE CHOICES

Roberta Ash (1972), like a number of other observers before her, notes the failure of radical movements in America which have "functioned mainly to impress elites with the relative mildness of reform movement demands." Although not intended as a reproach to radical groups with which she has much sympathy, her interpretation of the past supports the "think small" formula for success. "The broader the goals of a social movement, the more central its focus, and the greater its threat to class structure," she writes, "the less likely it will be to succeed" (Ash, p. 12).

Magnitude of goals is a multidimensional concept, and Ash is helpful in suggesting three aspects. "All movements must make a series of choices:

Between single issue demands and multiple demands.

Between radical demands and demands that do not attack the legitimacy of present distributions of wealth and power.

Between influencing elites (or even incorporating movement members into the elite) and attempting to replace elites" (Ash, p. 230).

DISPLACING THE ANTAGONIST

Some 30 percent (16) of the 53 challenging groups had goals requiring the removal of at least some of their antagonists. It is misleading, however, if this conjures up the guillotine. Although sev-

---

[2] It is useful to think of a goal as an *internal justification* for collective action planned by the group. It is internal in the sense that it is considered a justification by group members themselves and is not simply trotted out on public occasions to impress outsiders. It is a justification in the sense that X is a goal if group members agree that the statement "Action A will lead to X" is *if true* a positive reason for doing A. They may, of course, think that Action A will not really lead to X but this does not affect the status of X as a desirable end-state. Since a group can have multiple goals, a member might argue that A will lead to X but will detract from Y and Z. If this is generally accepted by members as a valid argument against A, if true, this implies that Y and Z are also goals of the group.

Among goals defined in this way, there are two types: external goals and organizational goals. The latter refer to the enhancement of the strength and ability of the challenging group rather than to the realization of new advantages for the group's beneficiary. The discussion here focuses on external goals.

eral fully expected to use force to overcome resistance, most wanted less to destroy antagonists than to retire them to peaceful pastures.

Only half of these groups were left-wing, and some of these were nonviolent in both ideology and practice. The Brotherhood of the Cooperative Commonwealth, for example, hoped to displace the government of the state of Washington by means of a rather implausible colonization scheme (see pp. 3–5). Socialists, migrating to Washington and establishing colonies there, would achieve political power through constitutional means, "call a constitutional convention, inaugurate public ownership of all the means of production and distribution, and solve the money question through use of labor exchanges. . . . Other states would be inspired by the success of the first, and soon the entire nation would be socialist" (Kipnis, 1968).

Likewise, the eight nonsocialist groups did not necessarily foresee bloody battles in replacing their antagonist. While the Christian Front against Communism was not averse to extralegal means, the American Party of the 1880s was a straightforward electoral challenger. Of the 16 groups that hoped to displace their antagonist, only six made no actual use of the electoral system in their influence attempts, and even some of these accepted some role for it in theory.

How successful are the groups that aim to displace one or more antagonist compared to the 70 percent that merely wanted to change its policies or organization in some way? Note that acceptance here must mean one of two things, either self-acceptance or acceptance by an antagonist other than the one being potentially displaced. Self-acceptance means some degree of successful displacement—for example, winning offices by a third party.

Figure 4–1 indicates a dismal success rate by either criteria. Two of the groups (12 percent) achieved some minimal acceptance, but only one, the League of Deliverance, achieved new advantages as well. The Bull Moose Party (Progressive Party) failed to elect Theodore Roosevelt president but had some success in congressional and state elections, most notably in electing Hiram Johnson and Robert LaFollette. As for new advantages, we quote from Amos Pinchot, one of the party's major protagonists:

> The party had an aspiration instead of an issue, a most creditable aspiration, but one for whose accomplishment its platform provided no

understandable means. Social and industrial justice! The square deal! Destruction of invisible government! The dawn of a new day! But how realize these ends? The answer of the Progressives was, "Make Roosevelt president." And when it became clear that they could not do that, the Progressives disbanded and the country knew them no more (Pinchot, 1958).

The League of Deliverance won both acceptance and new advantages, but there is some reason to question whether displacement of its antagonist was a true goal. This nativist group of the 1880s tried to prevent the employment of Chinese labor by boycotting those businesses that continued to employ Chinese. "Don't patronize Grass or Butterfield; they sell Chinese-made boots and shoes. Avoid them! They are traitors to their race," said one of the League's leaflets. However, destruction of such businesses was really more means than goal—that is, not a justification in its own right. By getting rid of its Chinese workers, a business could buy peace with the League and many did just that. Ira Cross (1935)

FIGURE 4-1
Success Rate by Displacement of Antagonists

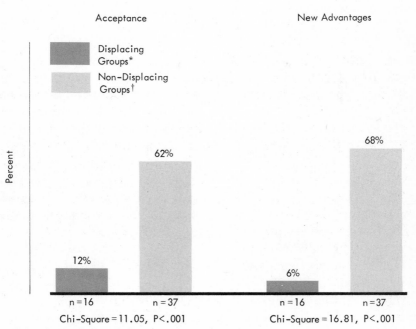

* Groups that hoped to displace one or more antagonists.
† Groups that hoped only to change the policies or organization of antagonists.

describes how "one factory which had from 500 to 600 Chinese on its payroll replaced them with white workers, as did many other employers."

With the possible exception above, then, no group that attempted to displace its antagonist, even by peaceful means, was successful in winning new advantages. In contrast, two-thirds of the remaining groups achieved this success.

MULTIPLE-ISSUE GROUPS

There is a fundamental ambiguity in the concept of "issue" that makes it difficult to address the question of whether groups with multiple-issue demands are more or less successful than those with a single demand. Is abolishing capitalism a single- or multiple-issue demand? Is a group that wants to both raise wages and better working conditions for a group of laborers making a single-issue demand or two separate ones? It is not difficult to formulate any group's demands as either single or multiple. If a group has several issues, the level of generality can be raised so that they are seen as aspects of a single, larger issue, or any larger issue can be subdivided into different aspects.

Ideologies group issues differently. A Marxist does not see American intervention in the Dominican Republic and Vietnam and the neglect of domestic poverty as separate issues but as part of a single, larger issue. A non-Marxist participant in the antiwar movement might see these as separate issues that should not be aggregated.

To ask whether a group has multiple-issue demands is to assume a clarity in the unit one is counting that simply does not exist. I have made several attempts to reformulate this question in a more useful way, but even the one I will describe here contains a considerable element of arbitrariness. Whether a group formulates an overarching demand (e.g., "establish National Socialism in the U.S.") or a more specific demand (e.g., "adopt proportional representation" or "lower the tariff") is irrelevant. It is considered to have multiple goals only if it gives programmatic attention to distinct subgoals in different institutional spheres. Thus, two socialist groups might have similar general demands, but one might never get to the point of subdividing these for separate action. The Brotherhood of the Cooperative Commonwealth and the Communist Labor Party, described above, are both considered "single-issue" groups under this definition. One focused its energy on a single program, colonization, and the other was so busy with constant defense that it scarcely had the luxury of initiating any action program, let alone several.

The National Student League, on the other hand, was equally Marxist in orientation but adopted a number of specific causes as its own. It had a series of campus-oriented concerns such as ending compulsory ROTC and compulsory chapel and gaining equal educational opportunities for women and blacks. It cooperated with other groups in the early 1930s in sponsoring antiwar strikes and involved itself in the bitter struggle of the coal miners in Harlan County, Kentucky. No doubt, many National Student League participants saw these separate struggles as part of the process of building "consciousness" for the larger struggle, but they became goals in their own right as well. Since they involved different antagonists in different institutional spheres, we classify such a group as having multiple issues.

About one-sixth of the groups (9) have multiple-issue demands in the above sense. Five of these are political parties, making an appeal to the electorate on different issues. These five, incidentally, include all of the pure third parties, pure in the sense that they were created to contest elections. They vary in political orientation with two nativist, two reform, and one socialist group among their number.

There are two reasons why we might expect a greater degree of success for these multi-issue groups. First, only a group that has managed to survive for a little while can be expected to begin the process of differentiating action programs in different areas. The very idea of multiple issues seems to imply some strength and stability. Second, with many hooks in the water, it seems that one would be more likely to catch a fish or two.

Figure 4–2 indicates no support for these expectations. A couple of the groups manage to achieve a minimal acceptance relationship, but none win new advantages. The Bull Moose Party is one of the exceptions on the basis of a few electoral victories below the level of the Presidency. The other exception, the American Student Union, was a "popular front" group of the middle and late 1930s. It grew from a merger between the socialist-dominated Student League for Industrial Democracy and the communist-dominated National Student League, described above. During its convention in 1938, the delegates received a letter of greetings from President

FIGURE 4-2
Success Rate by Multi-Issue Demands

Acceptance   New Advantages

Multi-Issue
Groups
Single-Issue
Groups

Percent

                                                                    59%

                        52%

        22%

                                            0%

    n = 9   n = 44   n = 9   n = 44
Chi-Square = 2.71, P<.10   Chi-Square = 10.44, P<.01

Roosevelt, as well as messages from the mayor of New York, the president of CCNY, and the women's director of the Democratic National Committee. As one former member and critic writes, "The student movement was now completely respectable, completely pro-administration, and completely emasculated" (Hal Draper in Simon, 1967). For even this group, however, co-optation rather than full response was its fate. Despite the many hooks these multi-issue groups had in the water, the fish apparently weren't biting.

RADICAL GOALS

If the idea of multiple issues presented us with problems of ambiguity, the idea of radical demands is even more formidable. There are, of course, some clear cases. No one would have any difficulty classifying the Communist Labor Party and the Society for the Promotion of Manual Labor in Literary Institutions. Assume that we mean by "radical," the degree of threat to existing distributions of wealth and power. In judging a group, we immediately confront a danger of tautology. It is tempting to judge threat by the response of the threatened. If an antagonist reacts with rage and horror, marshalling all his forces in defense, we would appear to be dealing with a severe threat. If he ignores the challenger or responds benignly, the threat presumably cannot be too great. But these responses of the antagonist are essential parts of our outcome measures, and to use them also to measure radicalness involves us in circularity. If a radical group is defined as one that is fiercely and stubbornly resisted, then, in examining success, we can only find that radical groups are fiercely and stubbornly resisted. The problem becomes one of defining radicalness of goals independently of response.

Common sense language here is a source of considerable confusion. Groups that were once called "radical" are now seen as mild and accommodating. Was the Federal Suffrage Association radical? It was certainly considered so by many, and one could easily argue that it challenged "the legitimacy of present distributions of wealth and power." But, today, few would claim that it fundamentally altered the position of women in society. Not long ago, the setting of wages and working conditions and the right to hire and fire workers were seen as fundamental and exclusive management prerogatives; the demand that such prerogatives be shared with worker representatives was highly threatening to many employers and their allies. With a handful of exceptions, all of our groups appeared to their antagonists to be making radical demands.

If the term "radical" is hopelessly unclear, perhaps we can gain a purchase on this question by a more oblique approach. We coded a number of specific questions about the concerns of the challenging group. Specifically, we asked whether in its influence attempts, the group was concerned with (1) altering the scope of authority of all or some of its antagonists, (2) altering the procedures used by these antagonists, (3) altering the personnel of its antagonists, and/or (4) destroying or replacing all or some of its antagonists. If the answer to these four questions for a group is uniformly negative, we can call its goals "limited"; they are concerned simply with changing the content of some specific policy. If the answer to any one of these questions is positive, we will call its goals "more-than-limited."

More-than-limited is somewhat less than what many would mean by radical, but presumably it includes, among others, what most people mean by the term. It includes the Communist Labor Party and the Anarcho-Communists, but it also includes many unions, engaged in challenges to management authority and hiring procedures. It includes the Federal Suffrage Association and the American Proportional Representation League, both bent on altering electoral procedures. It includes, in fact, about two-thirds of the sample.

By definition, none of the 18 groups with limited goals include the replacement of the antagonist as part of their objective. We already know that groups which aim to displace their target do poorly. Thus, we need to make sure that differences between those with limited and those with more-than-limited goals are not due simply to the presence among the latter of a good many groups that aim to displace their target. In Figure 4–3, we subdivide those with more-than-limited goals to distinguish the displacing groups from the rest.

It is apparent that having limited or more-than-limited goals

FIGURE 4–3
Success Rate by Limited Goals

* These groups have more-than-limited goals, but their goals do not involve the destruction or replacement of antagonists.
† These groups have more-than-limited goals *including* the destruction or replacement of antagonists.

makes no difference in its own right. Once we remove the displacing groups with their low rate of success, the success rate for the others is indistinguishable. While about two-thirds of the groups with limited goals achieve new advantages, about two-thirds of the others do also as long as they do not try to replace or destroy their antagonist as well.

THINKING SMALL REEVALUATED

It appears that there is some modest advantage in setting one's sights low. There are 18 groups with the combination of limited goals, a single-issue area, and no displacement of antagonists; two-thirds of them gain new advantages and 56 percent gain some minimal acceptance.

But lack of ambition is neither necessary nor sufficient for success. Even groups with modest aims often fail. Furthermore, we can identify more precisely what it is about the goals of the more ambitious groups that is most closely associated with failure.

First, having limited goals makes little difference in the fate of a group as long as those with more-than-limited goals do not try to displace their antagonist. Second, while groups with multiple-issue demands do poorly, it turns out that eight of the nine also are attempting to displace their antagonist. The one exception here is the American Student Union, which may account for its partial success on the criterion of acceptance. Thus, there is no clear evidence for an *independent* effect of multiple-issue demands on the fate of these groups; their low success rate may be due simply to the fact that they also aim to displace their antagonist. On the other hand, there are eight single-issue groups that have displacement as an objective, and with the exception of the League of Deliverance (the anti-Chinese group discussed above, pp. 43–44) they are uniformly unsuccessful in spite of their more concentrated focus.

It appears then, perhaps not too surprisingly, that what really stands in the way of success for the ambitious challenger is not diffuse objectives but targets of change who are unwilling to cooperate in their own demise. It is not that these antagonists would rather fight than yield half-a-loaf but rather that no half-loaf exists that will give these particular challenging groups what they seek. The antagonist must resist or give up the ghost. An antagonist begins with resources while the challenging group usually starts from scratch. Thus, it is not surprising that a challenging group attempting to displace it has a bad time of it, regardless of the means employed or the narrowness or broadness of its goals.

A NOTE ON GROUP SIZE

We know now what it is about group goals that we must consider in interpreting subsequent results. Should we also be concerned about group size? Although it is not theoretically interesting in its own right, if size has an important influence on success, we will need to control its effects in interpreting other relationships.

Group size is a very crude variable for two reasons. First, there are great differences among groups in the definition of membership. For many groups, the line between supporter and member is not sharp, and "membership" is more psychological than formal. To be a member of the Bull Moose Party involved no more than psychological identification; in contrast, the Communist Labor Party required a formal application, including a pledge renouncing membership in any other party, and each application was approved or disapproved at a formal meeting. The Tobacco Night Riders required a blood oath of new members. However, more than one-fourth of the groups (15) did not even maintain an official membership list.

Second, it is not uncommon for groups to inflate membership claims to impress outsiders. Father Coughlin, for example, claimed over seven-and-a-half million members for his National Union for Social Justice, but some outside observers were willing to grant only that the group had well over a million members at its height. When such discrepancies occurred, the more conservative figure was used here, usually that of an outside observer.

The measure of size, then, is a gross one, the estimated peak membership during the period of challenge. The 53 groups vary from under 1,000 to many millions and are divided here into classes differing by orders of magnitude (i.e., 10^3, 10^4, 10^5, 10^6). About half the groups had less than 10,000 "members" at their peak and about half had more.

Do groups that think small grow big? The answer is, not any more so than others. The 16 displacing groups are well-distributed over the size categories — three are under 1,000, four are over 100,000 and the rest are in between. The same lack of relationship holds for groups with multiple-issue demands.

One might expect that larger groups would be more successful in

general. First, larger groups should have larger amounts of resources at their disposal. Numbers, one might think, mean power
for a challenging group. Second, size might be a symptom as well as
a cause of success. A group in the process of succeeding ought to
find it easier to get partisans than would an apparent lost cause.[3]

The relationship between size and success is somewhat complex,
as Figures 4–4 and 4–5 indicate. There is only a negligible difference between groups of different size in gaining new advantages.
Larger groups are not much more likely to achieve the changes
they desire than smaller ones. There is, however, a more substantial difference in gaining acceptance. Here, bigness seems to help;
only 30 percent of the groups with under 10,000 members win
some minimal acceptance, while almost two-thirds of those over
10,000 are successful on this measure.

That size has a different relationship to acceptance than it does to
new advantages indicates that there is something interesting here
concerning co-opted and preempted groups. Preempted groups
tend to be small—only one of six is over 10,000; co-opted groups
tend to be large—only one of five is under 10,000.

What conclusions can we draw about size? Overall, it is essentially irrelevant with respect to a group's gaining new advantages.
However, there is a complex interaction between size and gaining
acceptance which we can see in Figure 4–6. Among those groups
that gain new advantages, if they are over 10,000, they are almost
certain to gain acceptance as well; only one in 14 fails to achieve
this additional form of success. Of those under 10,000, only 58 percent achieve both measures of success. Among those groups that
fail to gain new advantages, large size is a help in at least gaining
some minimal acceptance. For those under 10,000 only one in 15
gains some minimal acceptance while one-third of the larger groups
gain at least this form of success.

Preemption serves as an incomplete form of full response.
Among the groups that achieved new advantages, some grew large
and gained acceptance as well; some remained small and a substantial minority of these never achieved acceptance. Perhaps their
success came too easily and early. It is worth noting that five of the
six preempted groups gained new advantages within the first five
years of their challenge. In a few cases, there seemed to be no par-

---

[3] This argument, as we will see in the next chapter, is based on premises that are called
into question by the "theory of public goods."

FIGURE 4–4
Acceptance by Size of Group

FIGURE 4–5
New Advantages by Size of Group

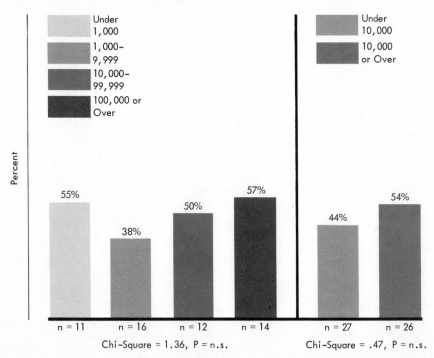

FIGURE 4-6
Acceptance and Size Controlling for New Advantages

ticular desire for acceptance, once gains had been achieved. The Tobacco Night Riders, for example, were a clandestine group and never anticipated or sought acceptance for themselves. But they were allied with the Planter's Protective Association, and this partner came to control 90 percent of the tobacco market and was dealt with by all of the major tobacco companies. In some other cases — for example, the Society for the Promotion of Manual Labor in Literary Institutions — partial success seemed to spoil the appetite, as key activists turned to other issues. In any event, a certain number of groups won new advantages but never became sufficiently established and formidable to win acceptance. Such groups tended to be relatively small.

Co-optation, by a similar argument, is an alternative to collapse. A group that not only failed to achieve new advantages, but failed to grow as well, ended up collapsing without acceptance. But others got large and some, developing a stake in the maintenance of the organization, made their peace with their antagonists at the expense of their supposed beneficiaries. Thus, a certain number of groups never won new advantages but became sufficiently established and formidable to win acceptance. Such groups tended to be relatively large.

REFERENCES

Anderson, L. F. "The Manual Labor School Movement." *Educational Review*, 1913, 46.

Ash, Roberta. *Social Movements in America*. Chicago: Markham, 1972.

Cross, Ira B. *A History of the Labor Movement in California*. Berkeley: University of California, 1935.

Draper, Hal. "The Student Movement of the Thirties." In Rita Simon, ed. *As We Saw the Thirties*. Urbana: University of Illinois Press, 1967.

Draper, Theodore. *The Roots of American Communism*. New York: Viking Press, 1957.

Gitlow, Benjamin. *I Confess: The Truth about American Communism*. New York: E. P. Dutton, 1940.

Kipnis, Ira. *The American Socialist Movement, 1887–1912*. New York: Greenwood Press, 1968.

Pinchot, Amos. *History of the Progressive Party, 1912–1916*. New York: New York University Press, 1958.

Thomas, Benjamin P. *Theodore Weld: Crusader for Freedom*. New Brunswick, N.J.: Rutgers University Press, 1950.

chapter five

The Limits of Solidarity

"It is often taken for granted," Mancur Olson writes, ". . . that groups of individuals with common interests usually attempt to further those common interests. Groups of individuals with common interests are expected to act on behalf of their common interests much as single individuals are often expected to act on behalf of their personal interests" (1965, p. 1).

In his seminal work, *The Logic of Collective Action*, Olson calls this underlying assumption into question with highly provocative results. "It does *not* follow, because all of the individuals in a group would gain if they achieved their group objective, that they would act to achieve that objective, even if they were all rational and self-interested." Indeed, except under certain special conditions, "rational, self-interested individuals will not act to achieve their common or group interests" (p. 2).

This apparent paradox arises from the nature of the common interests that are pursued through collective action.

> The basic and most elementary goods or services provided by government, like defense and police protection, . . . are such that they go to everyone or practically everyone in the nation. It would obviously not be feasible, if indeed it were possible, to deny the protection provided by the military services, the police, and the courts to those who did not voluntarily pay their share of the costs of govern-

ment, and taxation is accordingly necessary. The common or collective benefits provided by governments are usually called "public goods" by economists. . . . A common, collective or public good is here defined as any good such that, if any person X_i in a group $X_l, \ldots X_i, \ldots X_n$ consumes it, it cannot feasibly be withheld from the others in that group" (Olson, p. 14).[1]

It is important to note that a collective good is defined for a particular group. A given social change, for example, may affect only some people and leave the lot of others unchanged. Assuming that if produced, all members of the first group will be affected, it is a collective good for them. If it is also feasible to supply the benefits to others on an individual basis, it is a private good for these others. Olson illustrates this point with the example of a parade to which one can buy tickets. It is a private good for those who must purchase seats but a public good for those who live in houses overlooking the parade route.

The word "feasible" in Olson's definition should be understood broadly. Even if it is technically feasible to supply the goods privately, the definition holds if it is impractical or inconvenient to do so. In the example above, a high wall might be erected to block the view of those who did not purchase tickets, but the economic and political costs of such action would undoubtedly make it impractical.

The changes sought by challenging groups are collective goods for those who are affected by such changes. This is true whether they approve of the group's program or not, for, as Albert Hirschman (1970) puts it, "He who says public goods says public evils. . . . What is a public good for some — say, a plentiful supply of police dogs and atomic bombs — may well be judged a public evil by others in the same community" (p. 101). The distinguishing characteristic of collective goods, then, is that one receives the "benefits," dubious or real, whether one has paid for them and wants them or not.

Now if we suppose a group large enough that the contribution or efforts of any one member would not make a difference in

---

[1] This definition emphasizes a property of collective goods called "nonexclusiveness." There is a second property, called "nonrivalness of supply," meaning that the consumption by one member of the group does not reduce the supply available to others. The social changes sought by challenging groups are "pure" public goods, meeting both properties, and we will not need to distinguish between the properties here.

whether the group achieves its goals, why should a given member contribute? If he is not conscious of the value of the goals sought, clearly he will have no motive to contribute, but, even if he values their achievement a great deal, he still will have no self-interested reason to help. It is against his individual interests to pay any costs since *he will enjoy the benefits produced by the group whether or not he has helped to support it.* He will be individually better off pursuing his personal interests and taking an effortless, free ride while others make sacrifices for his group interests.

Olson applies his analysis to Marxian class theory, arguing that the critics of Marx are wrong in thinking that he overestimated rationality in expecting people to pursue their class interest. On the contrary, Olson argues, Marx underestimated it "for class-oriented action will not occur if the individuals that make up a class act rationally. If a person is in the bourgeois class, he may well want a government that represents his class. But it does not follow that it will be in his interest to work to see that such a government comes to power. If there is such a government, he will benefit from its policies, whether or not he has supported it, for by Marx's own hypothesis, it will work for his class interests." It follows that the rational thing for an individual bourgeois to do "is to ignore his *class* interests and to spend his energies on his *personal* interests" (Olson, pp. 105–6).

It cannot be taken for granted, then, that individuals will tend to organize to pursue their collective interests. On the contrary, they will not, except under special conditions that will be examined in detail below. I accept the basic premise—that when individuals sometimes unite to pursue their collective interest, this requires an explanation. It cannot be taken for granted as something "natural."

Although Olson does not use the term, the groups face a problem of internal social control. There are three basic ways of handling such a problem: through constraints, inducements, or persuasion. Constraints and inducements involve the use of negative and positive sanctions, respectively (cf. Gamson, 1968). Persuasion works on the orientation of the actor rather than his situation.

> There is an interesting variety of words used to describe this social control technique—some of them highly pejorative and others complimentary. The approving words include education, persuasion, therapy, rehabilitation, and, perhaps more neutrally, socialization. The disapproving words include indoctrination, manipulation, prop-

aganda and "brainwashing." The choice of words is merely a reflection of the speaker's attitude toward [the group doing the controlling] (Gamson, p. 125).

There is in Olson's argument a strong bias or skepticism about the effectiveness of "internalized" social control or persuasion. Olson can see readily enough how a group can induce members to join by means of selective, private rewards given only to those who participate. Similarly, he can understand readily enough that members can be constrained to join by threat of personal harm for not participating. But he really does not view group loyalty or solidarity as a meaningful form of control. He grants the usefulness of "social incentives." The social approval that comes from participating or the ostracism that comes from remaining aloof may be quite important in mobilizing individuals. But these remain social *sanctions,* rewards and punishments analogous to material sanctions, and not a form of persuasion.

Clearly, it is possible to argue for the effectiveness of normative appeals as well. James Coleman (1973), for example, addresses the general problem of why individuals are willing to surrender so much freedom to corporate actors. He recognizes selective incentives as part of the process. "When a person joins a guild, union, or professional association, he yields control over certain actions (as well as monetary fees) expecting to gain thereby." But there are more subtle examples as well involving "those corporate actors which persons invest in and sacrifice for with no tangible returns. These range from the sports team in an elementary school, to the nation for which men may give their lives. Such investments pay intangible but directly experienced rewards in the sense of pleasure a person experiences in being on a winning team or the sense of . . . well-being he experiences when his nation does well."

The psychological processes involved in this pleasure are centered on identification and the investment of part of oneself in collective actors. To reap the rewards of such identification requires commitment. The greater the sacrifice and effort involved, the greater is the investment of self, and, hence, the greater the personal satisfaction (or disappointment) with the achievements of the collective actor. Note that there is no contradiction of Olson's basic premise here, since I refer to a form of private personal satisfaction over and above any collective benefits produced by the group. In this sense, it is still a kind of selective incentive, but not one that is mediated by the group as a sanction. It is not useful to treat it as simply another form of inducement in the same category as a private good or service that the group provides to its members. Rather, it is an alternative, internalized means of overcoming the free-rider problem.

Olson makes some effort to address the point above. He grants that "the theory developed here is . . . not very useful for the analysis of groups that are characterized by a low degree of rationality, in the sense in which that word is used here. Take for example the occasional band of committed people who continue to work through their organizaitons for admittedly lost causes. Such a labor of love is not rational, at least from the economic perspective, for it is pointless to make sacrifices which by definition will be ineffective" (Olson, p. 161).

But why speak of "lost causes"? By Olson's own argument, the statement should apply as well to the occasional band of committed people who make sacrifices for causes that have some chance of success. He notes Lenin's insight in *What Is to Be Done?* (Lenin, 1929) for the "need to rely on a committed, self-sacrificing, and disciplined minority rather than on the common interests of the mass of the proletariat." Some members of the vanguard might be motivated by the personal benefits of their organizational position should the challenge succeed; it would make sense for them to invest energy for an essentially personal benefit. But commitment and self-sacrifice imply a willingness to continue when a cost-benefit analysis yields a negative expected value. One doesn't speak of self-sacrifice when personal interest dictates support. For most challenging groups, the vanguard is distinguished by its larger risks and investments in pursuit of little more than the promise of achieving collective goods. They are as irrational in Olson's terms as the pursuers of a lost cause.

Implicit in Olson's argument, then, is a belief in the insufficiency of ideological appeals except for a special category of "mass movements" about which he purports to say little. However, many of the groups he uses to illustrate his argument do make heavy use of appeals to solidarity. "Oh, you can't scare me, I'm sticking to the Union" says one of the many songs of the labor movement in its period of challenge. Many groups seek an enlarged notion of self — an identification of self and group interest such that an individual experiences personal pleasure from the achievement of a collective good.

There can be little doubt that such "irrational" loyalty is highly functional for a group, and, in fact, it may be absolutely vital. If it is too much to ask of members in general, at least it is necessary for a core of dedicated activists to have it. Although Olson gives little importance to loyalty, we turn to another political economist, Albert Hirschman (1970), for an argument in which loyalty plays a central role.

Hirschman is addressing a somewhat different problem—the conditions under which dissatisfied members of an organization will choose to leave or to stay and attempt to change it. Loyalty, he argues, "is at its most functional when it looks most irrational, when loyalty means strong attachments to an organization that does not seem to warrant such attachment because it is so much like another one that is also available. Such seemingly irrational loyalties are often encountered, for example, in relation to clubs, football teams, and political parties." Why is such loyalty so important? Because, "it can neutralize within certain limits the tendency of the most quality-conscious . . . members to be the first to exit. . . . Thus, loyalty, far from being irrational, can serve the socially useful purpose of preventing deterioration from becoming cumulative, as it so often does when there is no barrier to exit" (Hirschman, pp. 79 and 81).

It is not difficult to extend this argument to challenging groups. It is especially in large groups where one individual can hardly hope by his sacrifices to make a real difference in the group's achieving its goals that loyalty is needed. Terms like "irrational" obscure the issue. This loyalty remains "irrational" in the individual sense in which Olson uses it, even while it is functional and even necessary for the group to succeed. But an individual, imbued with a sense of responsibility to the group, might recognize the necessity of personal sacrifice, not in spite of, but *because of* the full force of Olson's argument. And he may appeal to others on this basis rather than on the basis of personal interest. "Ask not what your challenging group can do for you but what you can do for it," he might intone.

The thrust of this discussion is that Olson's argument must be evaluated in empirical terms. It does not follow *logically* from the theory of collective goods that loyalty or solidarity will be insufficient as a means of social control. What does follow logically is only that, to be successful, groups must find *some* way of overcoming the free-rider problem. It is Olson's hypothesis that, because of the overwhelming claim of personal interests, appeals to solidarity will not do the job adequately. Granted that it may be sufficient for some few committed loyalists, a group that asks voluntary sacrifices from all its members will not succeed. Stating the issues in these terms, we can examine the sufficiency of this form of social control for the 53 challenging groups studied here.

UNIVERSALISTIC GROUPS

Olson attempts to state some of the limits of his argument. While the theory is not limited to situations where only monetary or material interests are at stake, "it is true that this theory, like any other theory, is less helpful in some cases than in others. . . . The theory is not at all sufficient where philanthropic lobbies, that is, lobbies that voice concern about some group other than the group that supports the lobby, or religious lobbies, are concerned. In philanthropic and religious lobbies, the relationships between the purposes and interests of the individual member, and the purposes and interests of the organization, may be so rich and obscure that a theory of the sort developed here cannot provide much insight" (Olson, pp. 159–60).

This is a particularly unfortunate form of special pleading because one of the strengths of Olson's argument is the central insight it gives about these groups. It suggests that they are, in fact, *no different* than supposedly self-interested groups because self-interested groups face an identical problem—how to get members to work for something that they will receive or not receive independently of their individual efforts. In this sense, *all* large groups are "philanthropic," in that support cannot be explained by personal interest.

For Olson to make the distinction is faint-hearted, given the implications of his own argument. For the older group theorists whom he criticizes, the distinction is relevant. They see it as entirely reasonable that individuals with common interests usually attempt to further their common interests while it requires an explanation that individuals should attempt to further someone else's interest or the interests of everybody. But in rejecting the "naturalness" of pursuing one's common interests, Olson shows the distinction to be irrelevant. It is no more in one's personal interest to make sacrifices to achieve the goal of his *particular* group than it is for him to make sacrifices to achieve the good of the whole world

FIGURE 5-1
Success Rate by Universalistic Goals

or of some disadvantaged group to which he does not belong. All require an explanation.

Ten of our 53 groups fit what Olson means by "philanthropic" groups, although I find myself very uncomfortable applying this term to the likes of the German-American Bund. I will use, instead, the term *universalistic*. Universalistic groups are defined by a special relationship between their constituency and their beneficiary (see Chapter Two, pp. 15–16). For most of our groups, the constituency is either exclusively or especially affected by the changes that the group seeks. Thus, the major beneficiary and the constituency are identical. For universalistic groups, this is not true. Either everyone will be affected by the changes, the constituency no more or less than others, or some group other than the constituency – for example, some group seen as the victim of special injustice – will benefit more than the constituency. In either case, the major beneficiary and the constituency are not identical, the defining characteristic of universalistic groups.

In Olson's argument, there is no logical reason why universalistic groups should have more difficulty in succeeding than others. Both types must overcome the free-rider problem. Both may need to make use of selective incentives. And if one must appeal to personal loyalty and demand sacrifices, it does not follow that appeals to subgroup loyalties are more effective than universalistic appeals to nation, brotherhood, or social justice. If, in fact, narrower appeals turn out to be more effective, the explanation lies outside of Olson's theory.

The ten universalistic groups in the sample include three abolitionist groups, two right-wing groups, two peace groups, two reform groups, and a religious group that was part of the social gospel movement. Figure 5–1 indicates a slight but insignificant tendency for these groups to be less successful. The three abolitionist groups and the two right-wing groups were unsuccessful for reasons that seem to have little to do with the universalistic nature of their goals. Most of the others achieved some sort of success. It is hard to draw conclusions with confidence on the basis of so few cases, but, in line with Olson's theory, there is no real reason to see the distinction between universalistic and nonuniversalistic groups as an important one in understanding success.

PRIVILEGED GROUPS

Olson's argument applies with full force only to large groups, groups in which one member's contribution will not significantly affect the achievement of the collective goal. Certain smaller groups may be what Olson calls "privileged" groups: "A group such that each of its members, or at least some one of them, has an incentive to see that the collective good is provided, even if he has to bear the full burden of providing it himself" (p. 50). It will not necessarily be provided in the optimal amount, but the general argument against personal interest does not apply where the benefits to an individual are worth more than the total cost. These privileged groups have no need to rely on ideology or personal loyalty to produce the needed contributions because a personal interest, not simply a collective one, already exists for at least some people.

Note that this argument actually applies to the size of the constituency rather than the size of the challenging group itself. None of the 53 groups could really be considered small in this sense. Even those that failed to mobilize many were aiming at a substantial group. But size is, anyway, only a rather crude indicator of a privileged group and not a defining characteristic. Some large groups may have individuals who value the change sought by the group enough to pay the full cost or, at least, to make up any deficit not provided by the constituency. Many smaller groups may lack such individuals.

Not all of the challenging groups in this study began life friendless. About one-fourth of them (14) enjoyed the patronage of some individual or group with significant power or wealth. Although these groups, by definition, were also attempting to mobilize a constituency, they were not as completely dependent on this constituency for resources as an unsponsored group was. The American Committee for the Outlawry of War, for example, enjoyed the patronage of an energetic and well-connected lawyer, Salmon O. Levinson. In many ways, the committee was a vehicle for Levinson's crusade. He made sporadic efforts to raise money from others but without much success. At one point, he "tried charging a small price for printed material that he had been sending out gratis, especially when large batches were called for. But when Amy Woods of the Women's International League for Peace and Freedom asked for fifty thousand pamphlets and insisted that there was no money to pay for them, he made an exception. In point of fact, exceptions were made in nearly every case, so that very little money was raised from that source" (Stoner, 1942, p. 108). Levinson did not have unlimited personal funds and made plaintive pleas for help from rich angels but without success.

Engrossed as he was in the campaign, Levinson "really never made any but scattered and sporadic attempts to raise money. He much preferred to give what was needed out of his own pocket rather than be distracted from his main object. . . . He began to pay more than 95 percent of the expense of the campaign out of his own pocket, and he continued to do so even when it was costing upward of fifteen thousand dollars annually" (Stoner, pp. 108–110).

In addition to this kind of personal sponsorship, there is organizational sponsorship. The fledgling Steel Workers Organizing Committee did not have to depend on its nascent membership for the resources it needed to carry on its battles with the steel producers. The CIO was ready to lend its help. "[John L.] Lewis had given us a check for $25,000," David McDonald explained, "[but] that barely got our office open. The task of putting together an effective group of organizers was the heart of our effort. It was also expensive, and Lewis knew it. Within a few weeks, he sent us a second check, this time for $500,000" (McDonald, 1969, p. 91). When it came time to select quarters, McDonald chose a suite "on the thirty-sixth floor of the Grant Building — Pittsburgh's tallest at that time — [which] looked out splendidly over the industrial heart of the city. It also topped by several floors offices of some of the steel companies we hoped to organize and left no doubt of our permanence and stability. . . . The word got around quickly in the right places that this was no fly-by-night effort but a well-financed movement of labor union professionals who knew what they were about and meant business" (McDonald, p. 91).

Sponsorship, then, is an indicator of a privileged group. Someone or some organization has a special concern for the cause and resources to back up their concern. Such a challenger is no happier with free-riders than anyone else and is anxious to draw needed resources from its constituency. But it can tolerate a greater number of free-riders given the presence of a few highly committed, well-paying passengers.

Figure 5–2 indicates that privileged groups are only very slightly more successful than the others — 57 percent against slightly less

FIGURE 5–2
Privilege or Sponsorship by Outcome

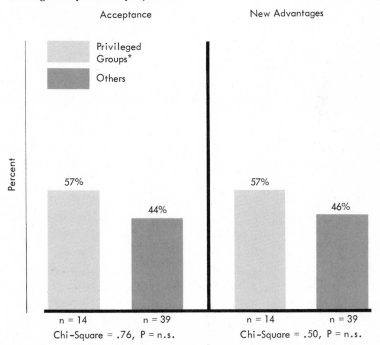

* Privileged groups are those with rich and/or powerful patrons. To be included, resources of the patron or sponsor must have existed prior to the challenge and not have resulted from the challenge itself.

than half of the rest. There is, however, some indication of an interaction between sponsorship and size in determining success. Overall, privileged groups are no different in size from the rest — half are over 10,000 and half are under. But the successful privileged groups tend to be a little smaller than the others. Only one of the eight successful ones grew to over 100,000 (the Steel Workers Organizing Committee) while half of the six unsuccessful privileged groups achieved this size. There is at least a suggestion here that sponsorship has more of an impact with groups of smaller size, but that its effects are dissipated when the group is beyond a certain magnitude.

SELECTIVE INCENTIVES

The core of Olson's argument for overcoming the free-rider problem is the "by-product" theory of the production of collective goods.

> The common characteristic which distinguishes all of the large economic groups with significant lobbying organizations is that these groups are also organized for some *other* purpose. The large and powerful economic lobbies are in fact the by-products of organizations that obtain their strength and support because they perform some function in addition to lobbying for collective goods.
> The lobbies of the large economic groups are the by-products of organizations that have the capacity to "mobilize" a latent group with "selective incentives." The only organizations that have the "selective incentives" available are those that (1) have the authority and capacity to be coercive, or (2) have a source of positive inducements that they can offer the individuals in a latent group (Olson, pp. 132–33).

Challenging groups are, by definition, organized for the purpose of producing a collective good and not for some other purpose. If a group organized for the purpose of providing some benefit or service to members and, once well-established, took on a new cause, it would not be included here. I suspect that Olson has an important insight in recognizing the advantage that such groups possess in separating the problems of mobilization and social influence. Challenging groups, in contrast, face the problems simultaneously; they seek changes from an antagonist and support from a constituency at the same time.

We cannot compare challenging groups with groups organized

for other purposes because we have no sample of the latter. But we can examine the use of selective incentives among challenging groups and compare those that used them with those that did not. Challenging group leaders were not unaware of the need for selective incentives, and one of them formulated the issues 75 years ago in a form not very different from Olson's argument. Henry Crowther, of the League of American Wheelmen, addressed the question "How to Increase the League Membership" in an article in *Good Roads Magazine* in the 1890s.

> It will, I think, be universally admitted that the average man (and it has not yet been discovered that the average wheelman is built on a different plan from the ordinary citizen) in nowise attempts to conceal his anxiety to know what he gets out of anything he is solicited to "go into," whether it be a real estate deal, stock-jobbing operation, secret society, or beneficial or fraternal organization—and justly so. The quid pro quo obtains in all our dealings from the cradle to the grave. . . . During a period extending over something like ten years of League work, my experience has almost invariably been . . . that the first question broached by a rider, when requested to join the L.A.W., is "What do I get out of it?" And, mind you, he is usually quite deaf to any sentimental arguments. The benefits of fellowship with the thirty-odd thousand of us who go to make up the elect have no weight with him. He wants—and justly so, again—to see paid down to him in hand the material benefits. . . . This being the case, what is to do? Why, give it to him, of course. Herein lies, in a nutshell, the secret of that future growth of the organization which can make the League of American Wheelmen that power in the land which it can become under properly directed effort. . . . Pennsylvania owes no small measure of her growth to the fine road books which are furnished to her members free . . . in addition to the weekly paper which each one of them receives.

The League of American Wheelmen was not the only group to offer private inducements to its members as selective incentives for joining. Eight others did also, including some unions that emphasized private benefits as well as collective ones. The Sons of Vulcan, for example, emphasized "aid to sick and distressed members." The Amalgamated Association of Street and Electrical Railway Employees of America maintained a death and disability benefit system, as did the United Brotherhood of Carpenters and Joiners of America.

In addition to these nine that offered selective inducements to members, two more made use of selective incentives of a negative sort. David McDonald describes the early problems of making the emerging steelworkers union solvent. "In the first glow of the U.S. Steel and J&L [Jones and Laughlin] victories, it seemed that our financial problems were finally at an end. Dues from our new members in these companies would make us solvent and perhaps even permit us to put a little aside to apply on our debt to the United Mine Workers. All of this would have been true if the steelworkers had paid their dollar-a-month dues. But once in, the great majority of them simply ignored their dues. We were suddenly rich in members and starved for funds" (McDonald, 1969, p. 108).

While dues check-off offered an ultimate answer, McDonald judged it impossible to gain agreement from the steel industry at that point in the struggle. The technique adopted to collect dues was something "we called . . . visual education, which was a high-sounding label for a practice much more accurately described as dues picketing. It worked very simply. A group of dues-paying members, selected by the district director (usually more for their size than their tact) would stand at the plant gate with pick handles or baseball bats in hand and confront each worker as he arrived for his shift" (p. 121).

While steelworkers confronted the pick handle, tobacco growers who resisted the Night Riders faced the whip or worse. Holdouts were terrorized by activities that "included the writing of threatening letters; the destruction of plantbeds; the burning of barns and other buildings; whippings; night visits to farmers to warn them or leave threatening notes; shooting scrapes; and the destruction of such other property as farm machinery, grain, hay, livestock, steam engines, sawmills, and wheat-threshing outfits. . . . The majority of growers . . . who received notes or night visits from the Night Riders, obeyed their orders as soon as convenient" (Nall, 1939, pp. 115–17).

All 53 groups attempted persuasion as a means of mobilization. All attempted to appeal to values or group loyalty to recruit potential members. The 11 groups that make use of selective incentives differ from the others, not in ignoring appeals to solidarity but in going beyond such appeals. Thus, we are contrasting groups that rely *only* on some form of persuasion with those that make use of some form of inducement or constraint as well.

Figure 5–3 provides clear support for the Olson hypothesis. All but one (91 percent) of the selective incentive groups won acceptance, and all but two (82 percent) won new advantages contrasted with, respectively, 36 percent and 40 percent of the others. The only exception to acceptance was the Night Riders, and, as indicated earlier, the allied Planters Protective Association achieved this in their stead. The exceptions to winning new advantages were two co-opted groups, the Dairymen's League and the Seamen's Union. Both of these groups developed cozy relationships with their "antagonists" and continued to exist after the end of the challenge and to maintain or, in one case, even increase their membership. That they were able to do this at the same time they were failing to deliver any real collective benefits to their constituency may well have been due to their use of selective inducements to membership.

There is another relevant fact about the selective incentive

FIGURE 5–3
Selective Incentives by Outcome

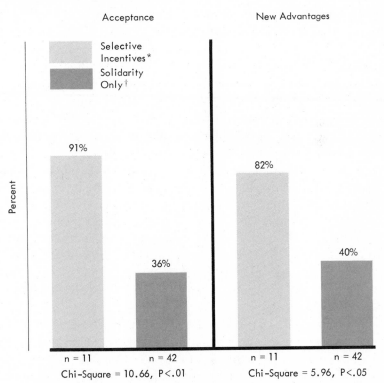

* Groups that provide selective incentives to members in addition to attempting mobilization on the basis of loyalty or solidarity.
† Groups that rely only on appeals to loyalty or solidarity.

groups—they tended to be large. Seventy-three percent of them reached a membership of over 100,000 while only 16 percent of the remainder did so. Put another way, large groups were not notably successful without selective incentives. Of those over 100,000, only two of seven won new advantages without selective incentives, and only three of seven won acceptance. For groups of this size with selective incentives, six of eight won new advantages and all won acceptance. In short, groups may grow large without the use of selective incentives, but, in their absence, they have difficulty converting size into success.

SUMMARY

There is much in this chapter to suggest the relevance of the theory of public goods for understanding challenging groups. The logic of collective action suggests that those groups that appeal to members in terms of their common interest have the same fundamental problem as universalistic groups. The data here provide no particular reason to doubt this.

Privileged groups, in the theory, should have at least a partial immunity to the free-rider problem. Overall, these privileged groups do not fare much better than the others, but there does seem to be some effect when the privileged group remains small. Even though many potential members fail to join these smaller groups, the intense support of a few is apparently able to compensate for lack of numbers. With the larger groups who have managed somehow to overcome the problem of free-riders, the help of rich or powerful sponsors is largely irrelevant in determining outcome.

In lieu of sponsors, large groups do particularly well when they employ selective incentives, and selective incentives help a group to grow large. Eight of 11 groups employing selective incentives gained more than 100,000 members, and, whether large or moderate in size, all 11 achieved at least one form of success. Large groups that relied only on loyalty or solidarity were considerably less successful.

Selective incentives and sponsorship serve as alternative means of meeting the basic problem suggested by the theory of collective action. Only one group, the Steel Workers Organizing Committee, had both. There were 29 groups that had neither, and only about one-third of these (10) were able to win new advantages with even fewer (8) winning acceptance. Thus, it is not impossible to succeed with only loyalty and solidarity as one's mobilization weapon, but the reduced success rate of such groups supports the usefulness of the theory of collective goods in understanding the careers of these challengers.

REFERENCES

Coleman, James S. "Loss of Power." *American Sociological Review,* February 1973, 38:1–17.

Gamson, William A. *Power and Discontent.* Homewood, Ill.: Dorsey, 1968.

Hirschman, Albert. *Exit, Voice, and Loyalty.* Cambridge, Mass.: Harvard University Press, 1970.

Lenin, V. I. *What Is to Be Done?* New York: International Publishers, 1929.

McDonald, David J. *Union Man.* New York: E. P. Dutton, 1959.

Nall, J. O. *Tobacco Night Riders of Kentucky and Tennessee, 1905–1909.* Louisville, Ky.: Standard Press, 1939.

Olson, Mancur, Jr. *The Logic of Collective Action.* Cambridge, Mass.: Harvard University Press, 1965.

Stoner, John E. *S. O. Levinson and the Pact of Paris.* Chicago: University of Chicago Press, 1942.

chapter six

The Success of the Unruly

It is a happy fact that we continue to be shocked by the appearance of violence in social protest. Apparently, frequency is no great cushion against shock for, at least in America, social protest has been liberally speckled with violent episodes. One can exaggerate the frequency — a majority of challenges run their course without any history of violence or arrests. But a very substantial minority — more than 25 percent — have violence in their history. The fact that violence is a common consort of social protest in the United States is not a matter of serious contention.

The consequences of violence are at issue. It is commonly believed to be self-defeating. Evaluating the validity of this belief is made elusive by a tendency that we all have, social scientists and laymen alike, to allow our moral judgments to influence our strategic judgments and vice versa. Kaplowitz has suggested the following general hypothesis. If strategic rationality does not clearly specify a course of action as desirable but normative criteria do,

Earlier versions of this chapter were presented at the annual meeting of the Israel Sociological Society at Bar Ilan University, January, 1973, and the American Sociological Association in New York, August, 1973.

people will tend to believe that the normatively desirable course of action is also strategically rational.[1]

Violence is relatively unambiguous morally. At most, it is regarded as a necessary evil which may be justified in preventing or overcoming some even greater evil. And for many, the situations in which it is justified are scant to nonexistent. The issue depends on one's image of the society in which violence takes place. In a closed and oppressive political system that offers no nonviolent means for accomplishing change, the morality of violence is not as clear. But when it is believed that effective nonviolent alternatives exist, almost everybody would consider these morally preferable.

In the pluralist image of American society, the political system is relatively open, offering access at many points for effective non-violent protest and efforts at change. With this premise, the use of violence by groups engaged in efforts at social change seems particularly reprehensible. The above reasoning should apply not only to violence as a means of influence but as a means of social control as well. The use of violence and other extralegal methods for dealing with protestors is also morally reprehensible.

While the moral issues may be clear, the strategic ones are ambiguous. There is no consensus on the set of conditions under which violence is a more or less effective strategy, and the issue has been seriously analyzed only in the international sphere. The Kaplowitz hypothesis, if correct, explains the strong tendency for people to believe that something so immoral as domestic violence is not a very effective strategy in domestic social protest. It also helps us to recognize that the fact that many people regard violence as self-defeating is no evidence that it is actually futile.

The pluralist view, then, acknowledges that collective violence has taken place in the United States with considerable frequency but argues that it is effective neither as a strategy of social influence when used by challenging groups nor as a strategy of repression when it is used by the enemies of such groups. We treat this view here as an hypothesis. It would be comforting to find that moral and strategic imperatives coincide, but the evidence discussed below suggests that they do not.

---

[1] Kaplowitz has explored the interaction between normative and strategic criteria experimentally (1977, 1979). He also argues for the complementary hypothesis to the one stated above: If normative criteria do not clearly specify a course of action while strategic criteria do, people will tend to believe that the strategically rational choice is the more normative one.

VIOLENCE USERS AND RECIPIENTS

I mean by the term "violence" deliberate physical injury to property or persons. This does not embrace such things as forceful constraint—for example, arrest—unless it is accompanied by beatings or other physical injury. It also excludes bribery, brainwashing, and other nasty techniques. To use the term violence as a catch-all for unpleasant means of influence or social control confuses the issue; other unpopular means need to stand forth on their own for evaluation, and we will explore some of these as well.

Among the 53 groups, there were 15 that engaged in violent interactions with antagonists, agents of social control, or hostile third parties. Eight of these groups were active participants; they themselves used violence. It is important to emphasize that these "violence users" were not necessarily initiators; in some cases they were attacked and fought back, and in still others the sequence of events is unclear. No assumption is made that the violence users were necessarily the aggressors in the violent interaction that transpired.

Whether they initiate violence or not, all of the violence users accept it, some with reluctance and some with apparent glee. Wallace Stegner (1949, pp. 255–56) describes some of the actions of Father Coughlin's Christian Front against Communism. "In Boston, a *Social Justice* truck went out to distribute the paper without benefit of the mails. When a *Boston Traveler* photographer tried for a picture, the truck driver kicked his camera apart while a friendly cop held the photographer's arms." In another incident in the Boston area, a printer named Levin was approached by Christian Fronters who handed him *Social Justice* and told him, " 'Here, you're a Jew, Levin. You ought to read about what your pals have been doing lately. Take a look how your investments in Russia are coming.' . . . One morning, . . . Levin came down to his shop to find it broken open and its contents wrecked." In New York, as Stegner describes it (p. 252), Christian Fronters would start fights with passing Jews, would beat up one or two opponents, and then vanish. Another source, Charles Tull (1965, p. 207) writes, that "it was common for the Coughlinite pickets . . . to be involved in violence with their more vocal critics. . . . Street brawls involving Christian Fronters and Jews became frequent in New York City. . . ." Now these accounts are at best unsympathetic to the Christian Front. Some of the clashes may well have been initiated by opponents of the group. For example, Tull points out that the "most notable incident from the standpoint of sheer numbers occurred on April 8, 1939, when a crowd of several thousand people mobbed ten newsboys selling *Social Justice*." Although the Christian Fronters may have been passive recipients of violence in this particular case, on many other occasions they clearly played the role of active participant or more.

The active role is even clearer in the case of the Tobacco Night Riders. Earlier (Chapter Five, p. 68), I discussed violence directed against their constituency, but much of their violence was directed at the tobacco trust as well. "The Tobacco Night Riders were organized in 1906 as a secret, fraternal order, officially called 'The Silent Brigade' or 'The Inner Circle.' Their purpose was to force all growers to join the [Planters Protective] Association . . . and to force the [tobacco] trust companies to buy tobacco only from the association" (Nall, 1942).

The violence of the Night Riders was the most organized of any group studied. They "made their first show of armed force at Princeton [Kentucky], on the morning of Saturday, December 1, 1906 when shortly after midnight approximately 250 armed and masked men took possession of the city and dynamited and burned two large tobacco factories. . . . Citizens in the business district opened windows and looked out on bodies of masked men hurrying along with guns on their shoulders. They saw other masked and armed men patrolling the sidewalks and street corners and they heard commands: 'Get back!' And if they did not obey, bullets splattered against the brick walls near by or crashed through the window panes above their heads. . . . Several squads of men had marched in along the Cadiz road and captured the police station, the waterworks plants, the courthouse, and the telephone and telegraph offices. They had disarmed the policemen and put them under guard, shut off the city water supply, and taken the places of the telephone and telegraph operators. . . . Within a few minutes the city was in control of the Riders and all communication with the outside was cut off." With their mission accomplished and the tobacco factories in flames, the men "mounted their horses and rode away singing 'The fire shines bright in my old Kentucky home' " (Nall, 1942, p. 69).

About a year later, the Night Riders struck again at the town of Hopkinsville, Kentucky. It is worth noting, since the argument here views violence as instrumental rather than expressive, that the

Hopkinsville raid was twice postponed when it appeared that the town was prepared to resist. "The Night Riders were not cowards," Nall writes, "but their cause and methods of operation did not demand that they face a resistant line of shot and shell to accomplish their purposes." The Night Riders made heavy use of fifth columnists in the town to assure that their raid could be successful without bloodshed. As in the Princeton raid, they carried out the operation with precision, occupying all strategic points. During this raid, they "shot into the . . . residence of W. Lindsay Mitchell, a buyer for the Imperial Tobacco Company, shattering electric lights and windowpanes. A group entered the house and disarmed him just in time to keep him from shooting into their comrades. He was brought into the street and struck over the head several times with a gun barrel, sustaining painful wounds. The captain of the squad looked on until he considered that Mr. Mitchell had 'had enough' then rescued him and escorted him back to his door" (Nall, p. 78). After the raid, they reassembled out of town for a roll call and marched away singing. The sheriff and local military officer organized a small posse to pursue the raiders and attacked their rear, killing one man and wounding another before the posse was forced to retreat back to Hopkinsville. One might have thought that the Night Riders would have retaliated for the attack made on them by the posse, and, indeed, Nall reports that "some of the Riders considered a second raid to retaliate . . . but such was not considered by the leaders. They had accomplished their purpose" (p. 82).

The Native American, or American Republican Party, a nativist group of the 1840s, was heavily implicated in less organized violence directed against Catholics. "Traversing the Irish section [of Philadelphia], the [nativist] mob was soon locked in armed conflict with equally riotous foreigners. The Hibernia Hose Company house was stormed and demolished; before midnight, more than thirty houses belonging to Irishmen had been burned to the ground. . . ." A few nights later, "roaming the streets, the rioters finally came to Saint Michael's Catholic Church. A rumor that arms were concealed within the building proved sufficient grounds for attack, and while the presiding priest fled in disguise, the torch was applied. . . ." The mob also burned St. Augustine's Church and "throughout the city, priests and nuns trembled for their lives" (Billington, 1963, pp. 225–26). Party leadership repudiated much of this mob action but especially deplored and emphasized the counterattacks: "the killing of natives by foreign mobs." The central involvement of American Republicans was, however, substantial and well-documented.

The other violence users were all labor unions involved in clashes with strikebreakers or police and militia called out to assist and defend the strikebreakers. Among the violence users, then, the challenging group is sometimes the initiator but not always; sometimes the leadership openly defends and advocates the practice but not always. To be classified as a violence user, it is only necessary that the group be an active participant in the violent interactions in which it is involved.

The recipients of violence were passive recipients — they were attacked and either did not or, because they had insufficient means, could not fight back. The International Workingmen's Association, the First International, is one example. In September, 1873, a major financial panic occurred in the United States, resulting in subsequent unemployment and economic dislocation. A mass demonstration was called for January 13, 1874, in the form of a march of the unemployed in New York City. To quote John Commons (1966, p. 220), "It was the original plan of the Committee that the parade should disband after a mass meeting in front of the city hall but this was prohibited by the authorities and Tompkins Square was chosen as the next best place for the purpose. The parade was formed at the appointed hour and by the time it reached Tompkins Square it had swelled to an immense procession. Here they were met by a force of policemen and, immediately after the order to disperse had been given, the police charged with drawn clubs. During the ensuing panic, hundreds of workmen were injured."

Abolitionists were frequent recipients of violence in the form of antiabolitionist riots. The object of the violence was primarily the property and meeting places of abolitionists rather than their persons, although there were frequent threats and some physical abuse as well. The National Female Anti-Slavery Society was victimized on various occasions, although the women themselves were never attacked. Once, when the hall in which they were scheduled to hold a meeting was set on fire by an antiabolitionist mob, the women sought refuge in the home of Lucretia Mott. "As the rioters swarmed through nearby streets, it seemed as if an attack on the Mott house were imminent but a friend of the Motts joined the mob, and crying, 'On to the Motts' led them in the wrong direction" (Lutz, 1968, p. 139). William Lloyd Garrison was attacked at one of the meetings and dragged through the streets. The American Anti-Slavery Society was similarly abused. Eggs and stones were thrown at the audience of several of their meetings. In Cincinnati, rioters attacked the shops and homes of abolitionists, particularly Englishmen. An abolitionist printer in Illinois, Elijah Lovejoy, was killed when he attempted to resist an antiabolitionist mob destroying his shop. Lovejoy's resistance was isolated and provoked a controversy in the fervently nonviolent Society. Lovejoy had had his printing presses destroyed three times, "his house was invaded, and his wife was brought to the verge of hysterical collapse. When a fourth new press arrived, Lovejoy determined that he would protect it. . . . When his press was attacked he raised his pistol but was quickly gunned down by one of the mob." Even under such circumstances, "abolitionists in the American Anti-Slavery Society and elsewhere were divided on whether or not to censure Lovejoy's action" (Sorin, 1972, p. 91). They did not censure Lovejoy but reasserted their commitment to nonviolent means of achieving the end of slavery.

Members of the National Student League were attacked in the familiar manner of northern civil rights workers going south in the 1960s. In one instance, the cause was the bitter struggle of coal miners in Harlan County, Kentucky. "At Cumberland Gap, the mountain pass into Kentucky, the full impact of Kentucky law and order descended. The road was almost dark when the bus turned the corner over the boundary; out of the approaching night the scowling faces of a mob of more than 200 people greeted the visitors. Cars drove up and surrounded the bus; most of the throng were armed, wearing the badges of deputy sheriffs. . . . There were derisive cat-calls, then the ominous lynch-cry: 'String 'em up' " (Wechsler, 1935). Students were shoved and some knocked down, but none seriously injured on this occasion.

The recipients of violence, then, unlike the users, play essentially passive roles in the violent episodes in which they were involved. The success or failure of the violence users will enable us to say something about the effectiveness of violence as a means of influence; the success or failure of the violence recipients will help us to evalute the effectiveness of violence as a means of social control.

THE RESULTS

What is the fate of these groups? Are the users of violence crushed by adverse public reaction and the coercive power of the state? Do the recipients of violence rouse the public sympathy with their martyrdom, rallying to their cause important bystanders who are appalled at their victimization and join them in their struggle?

FIGURE 6–1
Violence and Outcome

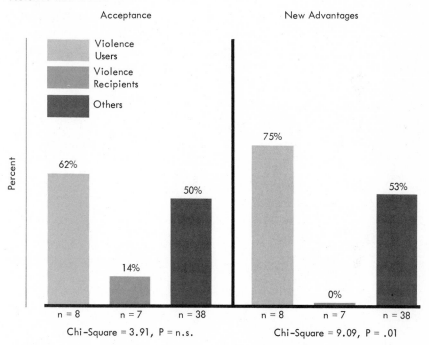

Figure 6–1 gives the basic results. The violence users, it turns out, have a higher-than-average success rate. Six of the eight won new advantages, and five of these six established a minimal acceptance relationship as well. Of course, some paid their dues in blood in the process as we have seen in the descriptions above. The seven recipients of violence also paid such dues but with little or nothing to show for it in the end. One, The Dairymen's League, established a minimal acceptance relationship with its antagonist, but none of them were able to gain new advantages for their benefi-

ciary. With respect to violence and success, it appears better to give than receive.

It is worth asking whether the different goals of these groups might account for the difference. The most relevant variable, as we learned in Chapter Four, is whether the displacement of the antagonist is part of the goals. Two of the eight violence users have displacement goals, and two of the seven violence recipients do also. Figure 6–2 makes the same comparison as Figure 6–1 but only for those groups that are not attempting to replace their targets. It reveals that every violence user with more limited goals is successful, although the Night Riders were not accepted; every violence recipient was unsuccessful, although the Dairymen's League won minimal acceptance. The earlier result is, if anything, sharpened.

FIGURE 6–2
Violence and Outcome Excluding Displacing Groups

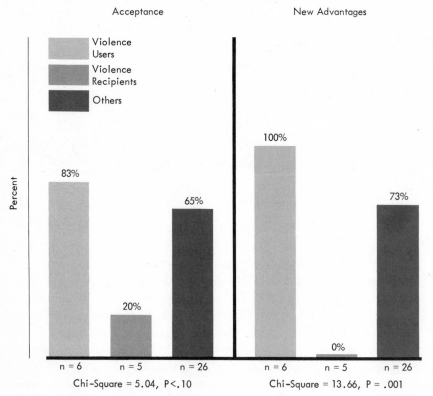

DOES VIOLENCE PAY?

Am I ready to conclude then that violence basically works? Not quite, or at least not in any simple fashion, and my caution is not due simply to the small number of cases involved and the real possibility of sampling error. It is easier to say what these data refute than what they prove.

Specifically, the data undermine the following line of thinking: violence is the product of frustration, desperation, and weakness. It is an act of last resort by those who see no other means of achieving their goals. In this view, the challenging group, frustrated by its inability to attract a significant following and gain some response from its targets of influence, turns to violence in desperation. However, this merely hastens and insures its failure because its actions increase the hostility around it and invite the legitimate action of authorities against it.

When authorities use violence against challenging groups, there are similar dynamics in this argument. Frightened by the growing strength of the challenging group and unable to halt its rising power by legitimate means, tottering on their throne and unwilling to make concessions, the threatened authorities turn to repression. But this attempted repression simply adds fuel to the fire, bringing new allies to the cause of the challenging group and increasing its chances of ultimate success.

However compelling these images may be, they clearly do not fit the data presented here. The interpretation I would suggest is almost the opposite. As Eisinger (1973) puts it in discussing protest behavior in American cities, one hypothesis is that protest is as much a "signal of impatience as frustration." Violence should be viewed as an instrumental act, aimed at furthering the purposes of the group that uses it when they have some reason to think it will help their cause. This is especially likely to be true when the normal condemnation which accompanies its use is muted or neutralized in the surrounding community, when it is tacitly condoned by large parts of the audience. In this sense, it grows from an impatience born of confidence and rising efficacy rather than the opposite. It occurs when hostility toward the victim renders it a relatively safe and costless strategy. The users of violence sense that they will be exonerated because they will be seen as more the midwives than the initiators of punishment. The victims are implicitly told, "See how your sins have provoked the wrath of the fanatics and have brought this punishment upon yourselves."

The size of the violence users and recipients supports this interpretation. The violence users tend to be large groups, the recipients small ones. Only one of the eight violence users is under 10,000 (the Night Riders) while five of the seven violence recipients are this small. Such growth seems more likely to breed confidence and impatience, not desperation.

I am arguing, then, that it is not the weakness of the user but the weakness of the target that accounts for violence. This is not to say that the weakness of a target is sufficient to produce violence but that, in making it more likely to be profitable, it makes it more likely to occur. As Figure 6–2 showed, many challenging groups are able to gain a positive response without resorting to violence, and many collapse without the added push of repression. But groups that are failing for other reasons and authorities that are being forced to respond by rising pressures generally do not turn to violence. This is why, in my interpretation, violence is associated with successful change or successful repression: it grows out of confidence and strength and their attendant impatience with the pace of change. It is, in this sense, as much a symptom of success as a cause.

It is worth noting that, with the exception of the Night Riders, none of the groups that used violence made it a primary tactic. Typically it was incidental to the primary means of influence—strikes, bargaining, propaganda, or other nonviolent means. It is the spice, not the meat and potatoes. And, if one considers the Night Riders as merely the striking arm of the respectable Planters Protective Association, even this exception is no exception.

The groups that receive violence, with one exception, are attacked in an atmosphere of countermobilization of which the physical attacks are the cutting edge. They are attacked not merely because they are regarded as threatening—all challenging groups are threatening to some vested interest. They are threatening *and* vulnerable, and most fail to survive the physical attacks to which they are subjected.

OTHER CONSTRAINTS

This argument can be further evaluated by extending it to other constraints in addition to violence. "Constraints are the addition of new disadvantages to the situation or the threat to do so, regardless of the particular resources used" (Gamson, 1968). Violence is a special case of constraints but there are many others.

Twenty-one groups (40 percent) made use of constraints as a means of influence in pursuing their challenge. We have already considered eight of them, those that used violence, and we turn now to the other 13. The most common constraints used by these groups were strikes and boycotts, but they also included such things as efforts to discredit and humiliate individual enemies by personal vituperation. Discrediting efforts directed against "the system" or other more abstract targets are not included, but only individualized, ad hominem attacks attempting to injure personal reputation.

Included here, for example, is A. Philip Randolph's March on Washington Committee, designed to push President Roosevelt into a more active role in ending discrimination in employment. A mass march in the spring of 1941 to protest racial discrimination in America would have been a considerable embarrassment to the Roosevelt administration. America was mobilizing for war behind appeals that contrasted democracy with the racism of the Nazi regime. Walter White of the NAACP described "the President's skillful attempts to dissuade us" (Quoted in Garfinkel, 1969). The march was, from the standpoint of the administration, something to be avoided, a new disadvantage which the committee was threatening.

William Randolph Hearst's Independence League made liberal use of personal vituperation against opponents. "Most of Hearst's energy was devoted to pointing out the personal inequities of boss Charles F. Murphy. He found himself obliged to go back to the time of Tweed to discover any parallel in political corruption. . . . 'Murphy is as evil a specimen of a criminal boss as we have had since the days of Tweed' " (Carlson and Bates, 1936, pp. 146–47).

The League of Deliverance made primary use of the boycott weapon, employing it against businesses that hired Chinese labor. They threatened worse. The League's executive committee proposed to notify offenders of their desires and if not complied with, "after the expiration of six days it will be the duty of the Executive Committee to declare the district dangerous . . . . Should the Chinese remain within the proclaimed district after the expiration of . . . thirty days, the general Executive Committee will be required to abate the danger in whatever manner seems best to them" (Cross, 1935). The League, however, never had call to go beyond the boycott tactic.

Among the 13 nonviolent constraint users are three groups that were considered earlier as violence recipients. Including them makes it more difficult to interpret the relationship of success to the use of constraints since this is compounded by physical attacks on the group. Therefore, in Figure 6–3, we include only those ten groups that employed constraints but were not involved in violent interactions as either user or recipient. The advantage again goes to the unruly. Four-fifths of the constraint users and only two-fifths of the others are successful.

Constraints other than violence can also be used as a means of social control. In particular, many groups experience arrest and imprisonment or deportation of members which can be equally as devastating as physical attack, if not more so. Almost two-fifths of

FIGURE 6–3
Constraints and Outcome

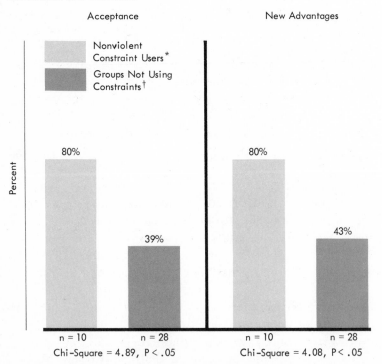

* This includes only those groups making use of constraints as a means of influence that were not involved in violent interactions as either users or recipients.

† This excludes groups that did not use constraints if they were also violence recipients.

the sample (20 groups) had members arrested at some time or another during the period of challenge. These twenty included all eight of the violence users and four of the seven recipients, leaving only eight groups that were not involved in violent interactions but were subjected to arrests.

The Young Peoples Socialist League had people arrested during both its periods of challenge. " 'You're under arrest' " began an article in *The Challenge,* the YPSL paper. "This was not the first time members of the Young Peoples Socialist League had heard this pronouncement by officers while they were peacefully demonstrating against injustice." During its period of challenge in the World War I era, the national secretary of the group, William Kruse, was arrested, tried, convicted, and sentenced to 20 years imprisonment but ultimately won on appeal.

The German-American Bund was subject to arrests on a number of occasions. Fritz Kuhn, the group's major leader, was convicted of embezzling Bund funds, income tax evasion, and forgery. Other members were indicted on more political charges such as espionage. Some were tried in New York State under a rarely invoked statute passed in 1923 as a measure against the Ku Klux Klan, but Bundists won on appeal (Rowan, 1939, p. 178).

The American Birth Control League also experienced its share of official harassment. Soon after its organization, Margaret Sanger arrived at Town Hall in New York with her featured speaker, Harold Cox, editor of the *Edinburgh Review.*

> She found a crowd gathered outside. One hundred policemen, obviously intending to prevent the meeting, ringed the locked doors of the hall. When the police opened the doors to let people already inside exit, those outside rushed in, carrying Mrs. Sanger and Cox before them. Once inside, Mrs. Sanger tried several times to speak, but policemen forcibly removed her from the platform. . . . Cox managed only to blurt, "I have come across the Atlantic to address you," before two policemen hauled him from the stage. The police arrested Mrs. Sanger and led her out of the hall while the audience sang, "My country, 'Tis of Thee."

A few weeks later, with evidence of complicity of the Catholic Church in the raid emerging, Mrs. Juliet Barrett Rublee, a friend of Mrs. Sanger, was arrested "while she was in the act of testifying at an investigation into the charge of church influence behind the [earlier] raid" (Kennedy, 1970, pp. 95–96).

Figure 6–4 considers the eight groups subjected to arrest, again

FIGURE 6-4
Arrests and Outcome

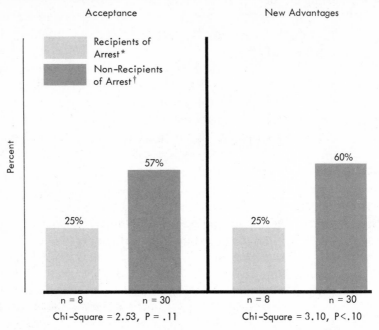

* This excludes 12 groups that were involved in violent interactions and experienced arrests.

† This excludes 3 groups that were involved in violent interactions but did not experience arrests.

excluding all groups involved in violent interactions.[2] Only two of the eight groups were successful while nearly 60 percent of the remainder were. The results seem even clearer when we examine the two exceptions. Only two of the eight groups made use of non-violent constraints — the League of Deliverance used the boycott and the United Brotherhood of Carpenters and Joiners of America used strikes and boycotts. These two groups were the only successes among the eight groups considered in Figure 6-4. In other words, groups that used neither violence nor any other form of constraint and yet experienced arrest were uniformly unsuccessful. In the absence of offsetting tactics by challenging groups, arrest seems to have the same connection with outcome as receiving violence, both are associated with failure for the receiving group.

---

[2] Only three of the 15 groups involved in violent interactions escaped arrests, all violence recipients. The violence in these cases came from hostile third parties — for example, anti-abolitionist mobs — and the perpetrators of violence also escaped arrest.

There is another interesting fact about the six groups in Figure 6–4 that experience both arrests and failure. Five out of the six were attempting to displace antagonists as part of their goals, and three of the six advocated violence in principle even though they never actually employed it. Eisinger points out that "as long as protestors do not manipulate the threat of violence explicitly, they enjoy a slim legality, even, occasionally, legitimacy. Once they employ the threat openly, however, they open the way for authorities to suppress their movement or action" (1973, p. 14).

Groups like the Communist Labor Party, the Revolutionary Workers League, and the German-American Bund put themselves in the position of advocating or accepting violence as a tactic without actually using it. One might call this the strategy of speaking loudly and carrying a small stick. These groups seem to pay the cost of violence without gaining the benefits of employing it. They are both threatening and weak, and their repression becomes a low-cost strategy for those whom they attempt to displace.

SUMMARY

The results on arrests and other constraints seem to parallel those on violence very closely. Unruly groups, those that use violence, strikes, and other constraints, have better than average success. Of the 21 groups that use some form of constraint, fully two-thirds win new advantages and 71 percent win acceptance. Among the ten groups that use no constraints but receive either violence or arrests, none are successful on either criterion. The 22 groups that neither experience nor use constraints fall in the middle, 54 percent (12) win new advantages and half win acceptance.

Virtue, of course, has its own, intrinsic rewards. And a lucky thing it does too, since its instrumental value appears to be dubious. If we cannot say with certainty that violence and other constraints are successful tactics of social influence or social control, we must at least have greater doubt about the proposition that they lead to failure. When used by challenging groups, there is no evidence that they close doors that are open to those who use only inducements and persuasion. When used against challenging groups, there is no evidence that such tactics bring allies and sympathetic third parties to the effective aid of the beleaguered groups, allowing them to gain what would have been impossible acting alone.

Perhaps it is disconcerting to discover that restraint is not rewarded with success. But those who use more unruly tactics escape misfortune because they are clever enough to use these tactics primarily in situations where public sentiment neutralizes the normal deviance of the action, thus reducing the likelihood and effectiveness of counterattack.

REFERENCES

Billington, Ray Allen. *The Protestant Crusade, 1800–1860.* Gloucester, Mass.: P. Smith, 1963.

Carlson, Oliver, and Bates, Ernest S. *Hearst, Lord of San Simeon.* New York: Viking Press, 1936.

Commons, John R., et al. *History of Labor in the United States.* Vol. 2. New York: A. M. Kelley, 1966.

Cross, Ira B. *A History of the Labor Movement in California.* Berkeley: University of California Press, 1935.

Eisinger, Peter K. "The Conditions of Protest Behavior in American Cities." *American Political Science Review*, March 1973, 67:11–28.

Gamson, William A. *Power and Discontent.* Homewood, Ill.: Dorsey Press, 1968.

Garfinkel, Herbert. *When Negroes March.* New York: Atheneum, 1969.

Kaplowitz, Stan. "An Experimental Test of a Rationalistic Theory of Deterence." *Journal of Conflict Resolution*, September 1973, 17:535–72.

Kennedy, David M. *Birth Control in America.* New Haven: Yale University Press, 1970.

Lutz, Alma. *Crusade for Freedom—Women of the Antislavery Movement.* Boston: Beacon Press, 1968.

Nall, J. O. *The Tobacco Night Riders of Kentucky and Tennessee, 1905–1909.* Louisville, Ky.: Standard Press, 1942.

Rowan, Richard W. *Secret Agents against America.* New York: Doubleday, Doran, 1939.

Sorin, Gerald. *Abolitionism: A New Perspective.* New York: Praeger, 1972.

Stegner, Wallace. "The Radio Priest and His Flock." In Isabell Leighton, ed. *The Aspirin Age, 1919–1941.* New York: Simon & Schuster, 1949.

Tull, Charles J. *Father Coughlin and the New Deal.* Syracuse, N.Y.: Syracuse University Press, 1965.

Wechsler, James A. *Revolt on the Campus.* New York: Covici, Friede, 1935.

chapter seven

Combat Readiness

"The modern party," Robert Michels wrote more than 70 years ago, "is a fighting organization in the political sense of the term, and must as such conform to the laws of tactics. Now the first article of these laws is facility of mobilization" (1949, p. 41[1]). There is a basic asymmetry in the contest between a challenging group and its antagonist. On the one hand, we have a nascent organization without established member commitment or internal control over members. A challenging group starts with no willing agents at its command; at best, it has sympathizers, some fervent and some easily distracted. It faces organized antagonists who possess all the control over members that established bureaucracies possess. The antagonists typically have available to them full-time professionals who can be deployed and redeployed at the will of the organizational hierarchy.

One way of overcoming the asymmetry is for the challenging group to adopt the organizational pattern of established groups. It can create an apparatus of internal control that enables it to deal on more equal terms with its antagonist. Every challenging group faces the problem that Philip Selznick has addressed in *The Orga-*

---

[1] First published in 1915.

89

nizational Weapon, "transforming a voluntary association into a managerial structure. . . . Put most simply, the process referred to is one which changes *members* into *agents,* transforms those who merely give consent into those (at an extreme, soldiers) who do work as well as conform" (Selznick, 1960, p. 21).

To fight effectively, a challenging group must solve two related problems that are frequently confounded. The transformation of a voluntary association into a managerial structure involves more than the creation of a high willingness of members to act as agents of the group. Even when challenging groups have a committed membership that can be quickly activated, they may lack unity of command. Competing voices, each with its plausible claim to legitimate authority, are often heard—one saying "March!" another "Wait!" Who speaks for the group? It is not enough to have agents if the problem of who directs these agents is left unresolved. One may convert members into soldiers, but soldiers fight civil wars as well as foreign ones.

Put in somewhat different language, two separate functional problems must be solved for the group to operate effectively in conflict situations. On the one hand, the group must be able to maintain a series of commitments from members that can be activated when necessary—essentially a problem of pattern maintenance. Pattern maintenance exists when the members of a group carry around their membership in latent form even while not actively participating in collective action. When they convene, the individuals are ready to begin functioning immediately as group members again. In this sense, the group continues to exist even while individual members are scattered about and not in direct interaction with each other.

On the other hand, the group must be able to solve problems of internal conflict so that power struggles within the group do not paralyze its ability to act—essentially a problem of integration. Only if both of these functional problems are solved will the group have achieved the necessary combat readiness by marrying the willingness to obey and the right to command.

Of course, all this military language exaggerates. The challenging group remains a voluntary association, and the good soldiers, if they get fed up, desert without facing the firing squad. Claims to authority are not buttressed by any apparatus of legal coercion or by long-established tradition but must be established *de novo.* But the military analogy is a useful one because it alerts us to certain features of the internal organization of challenging groups that are associated with successful outcomes.

BUREAUCRACY

Bureaucratic organization helps a group with the problem of pattern maintenance. By creating a structure of roles with defined expectations in the place of diffuse commitments, a challenging group can better assure that certain necessary tasks will be routinely performed. It gives the challenging group a higher readiness for action.

It is sometimes supposed that challenging groups go through stages, becoming increasingly bureaucratic as they grow older. For the groups in this sample, the reality is considerably more complex. Many groups sprang up as full-blown bureaucracies with more rules and procedures than they had members. Others never assumed the essential characteristics of bureaucratic organizations even after a number of years. Still there is a kernel of truth in the hypothesis of increasing bureaucratization: none of the groups grew less bureaucratic over the years.

Three minimum characteristics are used here to define bureaucratic challenging groups:

1. The group possesses a written document, a constitution or charter, that states both the purposes of the organization and its provisions for operation. A written document stating only purposes — for example, a manifesto — is insufficient if it contains no provisions for how the group will conduct its business.

2. The group maintains a formal list of members, thus distinguishing members from mere supporters and sympathizers.

3. The group possesses three or more levels or internal divisions — for example, officers or executive committee; division, committee, or chapter heads; and rank and file. Groups that have only officers and rank and file do not meet this criterion.

Forty-five percent of the groups (24) met all three criteria of bureaucratic organization at some point during the period of challenge. Are these groups more successful than their more loosely organized counterparts? Figure 7–1 indicates that they are, but only moderately so. The difference is stronger for acceptance (71 percent vs. 28 percent) than for new advantages (62 percent vs. 38 percent). Four of the five co-opted groups, but only two of the six

FIGURE 7-1
Bureaucracy and Outcome

Acceptance   New Advantages

Bureaucratic

Nonbureau-
cratic

71%

Percent

62%

38%

28%

n = 24   n = 29   n = 24   n = 29
Chi-Square = 9.86, P<.05   Chi-Square = 3.17, P<.10

preempted groups are bureaucratic. Apparently imitating the form of one's antagonist eases the development of some sort of working relationship.

It appears also to enhance the group's ability to win new advantages, but here bureaucracy is clearly only part of the story. There are nine bureaucratic groups out of 24 that gain no new advantages in spite of the hypothesized benefits of this form of organization. Why are they unsuccessful?

CENTRALIZATION OF POWER

Our theoretical argument above suggests an answer. Bureaucratic organization aids with the problem of keeping an organization in a state of readiness to act — that is, with the problem of pattern maintenance — but it guarantees nothing with respect to the problem of internal conflict. Now one might well include hierarchy of command in the definition of bureaucratic organization, but it has not been included in the operations used here. Formality of procedures, record keeping, and some complexity of role differentiation are the defining elements, and their relationship to centralization of power remains to be determined.

A challenging group is coded as having a centralized power structure if there is essentially a single center of power within the organization, whether or not this is formally sanctioned. As a matter of fact, the single center of power is frequently associated with personal leadership, with a central figure around whom the organization revolves and with whom it is identified. In some cases, the group is essentially a personal vehicle for such a leader and could hardly be said to exist independently of its core figure.

Slightly over half of the groups (28) have a centralized power structure, and two-thirds of these (19) have a dominant personal leader. The other nine have some form of collective leadership, frequently vested in an executive committee or national board. The executive committee or individual leader may be accountable to the membership and may be responsive to their influence, but we would not code a group as centralized if there were branches or chapters that enjoyed substantial autonomy to act without the formal or informal approval of the center.

Decentralized groups lack such a single center of power. In a few cases, mostly quite small groups, power is diffused through the membership at large. More typically, there are chapters or divisions of the organization that maintain substantial autonomy and the freedom to decide whether or not to support collective action by the group as a whole. Such challenging groups are coalition-like; the elements that make up the group as a whole maintain a separate identity and importance.

Centralization of power, I am suggesting, is the way in which challenging groups deal with the problem of internal conflict and through which they are able to achieve unity of command. Figure 7–2 indicates that, like bureaucracy, centralization of power is also associated with success. Again the relationship is a modest one, but, unlike bureaucracy, it is stronger for gaining new advantages than it is for acceptance. Five of the six preempted groups but only two of the five co-opted groups are centralized.

The argument that bureaucracy and centralization solve two separate functional problems implies that they are making independent contributions to the success of challenging groups. That this is indeed the case can be seen from two pieces of additional evidence. First, there is no relationship between bureaucracy, as measured

FIGURE 7–2
Centralization of Power and Outcome

FIGURE 7–3
Bureaucracy and Centralization of Power

here, and centralization of power. In Figure 7–3, we see that half of the bureaucratic groups had centralized power structures as did approximately half (55 percent) of the nonbureaucratic groups.

That each variable has a modest relationship to success is to be expected if each is solving only one of the problems of combat readiness. Together, the relationship ought to be stronger. Groups that had both bureaucratic structures and centralization of power should have done especially well; those that had neither should have done especially poorly. Figure 7–4 presents these results.

The combination is especially potent with respect to gaining new advantages. Three-fourths of the groups that had both gained new advantages while only 15 percent of those which had neither were successful in this respect. Both variables are relevant for gaining acceptance also, but here bureaucracy is clearly making the

FIGURE 7–4
Bureaucracy and Centralization of Power by Outcome

stronger contribution. A group that had neither bureaucratic structure nor centralized power had very little chance of gaining acceptance.

It is worth taking a closer look at some of the deviant cases in Figure 7–4. Two groups, lacking both bureaucracy and centralized power structures, defied the odds against success although only one of these won both acceptance and new advantages. The double-winner was the Federal Suffrage Association. The FSA was but one, and not the most important, carrier of the successful women's suffrage challenge. It began in 1892 and fought for many years but was less prominent than the National American Woman Suffrage Association in the vigorous activity period of 1916 to 1920, preceding the ratification of the constitutional amendment. The group achieved its major objective, but it was neither alone nor always in the center of the struggle. Its organizational strengths or weaknesses may not have been as relevant as for many other groups.

The other exception, the American Free Trade League, was a post-civil war group pursuing tariff reform. They argued that high tariffs placed a heavy burden upon wage earners and farmers and aimed their mobilization efforts at these groups. The League established branches in a number of areas and, with the support of a number of influential newspapers, spread their message throughout the country. During the years of peak activity, they circulated more than half a million of their pamphlets annually. The Free Trade League served as a rallying point for a loose coalition of liberal forces concerned not only with tariff revision but other issues — for example, civil service reform — as well. They were credited with the defeat of a number of protectionist Republican congressmen in the 1870 election. Their new advantages came in the form of small rate reductions in 1870 and 1872, but these were short-lived victories. Although the League was the most active and influential element in the Liberal Republican third-party movement to defeat President Grant in 1872, the Liberal Republican convention went on to nominate a staunch protectionist, Horace Greeley. The Free Trade League went into a state of disarray and ceased to be an active force while Grant was re-elected with ease. It was not long before the limited gains of 1870 and 1872 were removed in the Tariff Act of 1875. The earlier, short-lived successes qualify the League for preemption rather than collapse as an outcome, but its success was both partial and temporary.

There are also exceptions in the opposite direction — groups that had the proper organizational credentials but were unsuccessful. Only two groups that had both centralized power and bureaucratic structures failed to gain at least one form of success although both of them left an important legacy for the future.

The International Workingmen's Association (the First International) was one such group. The I.W.A. was founded in London in 1864 by British trade unionists together with Karl Marx. John Commons suggests that "its starting point was the practical effort of British trade union leaders to organize the workingmen of the continent and to prevent the importation of continental strikebreakers. That Karl Marx wrote its Inaugural Address was merely incidental. It chanced that what he wrote was acceptable to the British unionists. . . . His Inaugural Address was a trade union document, not a Communist Manifesto" (Commons, 1966, p. 205).

The I.W.A. in America was beset by a sharp ideological split from its inception. "The philosophy of the International . . . was based on the economic organization of the working class in trade unions and cooperative societies. These must precede the political seizure of the government by labour. . . . This conception differed widely from the teaching of Ferdinand Lassalle." In Lassallean socialism "there was but one means of solving the labour problem — political action. When political control was finally achieved, the labour party, with the aid of State credit, would build up a network of co-operative societies into which eventually all industry would pass. In short, the distinction between the ideas of the International and of Lassalle consisted in the fact that the former advocated economic organization prior to and underlying political organization, while the latter considered a political victory as the basis of economic organization" (Commons, p. 206).

The International in America reflected this difference; to make matters worse, ideological differences were merged with differences in social background, making the cleavage even sharper and more difficult to manage. The American I.W.A. contained two distinct groups, German wage earners and native American intellectuals. "The most important German forerunner of the International was the General German Workingmen's Union (Der Allegemeine Deutsche Arbeiterverein), which became subsequently known as Section 1 of New York of the International" (Commons, p. 207).

In addition to the immigrants, there was a group of native American radicals who affiliated with the International, with Section 12 becoming the most prominent representative of this group. Section 12 was headed by two sisters, Victoria Woodhull and Tennessee Claflin, "notorious (sic) advocates of woman suffrage and 'social freedom' " (Commons, p. 211).

Now the I.W.A. in America had a Provisional Central Committee dominated by Frederich A. Sorge, the leader of the immigrant sections. Section 12, it appears, was not easy to bring under this central control. Sorge complained repeatedly to the central committee about the activities of the maverick section. "The manifesto signed by William West and published in a certain 'Weekly' in behalf of Section 12 . . . was published and issued *without* the authority or consent of the Central Committee," he wrote. Later, he reported to London, with disapproval, about the activities of Section 12. "The Woodhull-Claflin Section (No. 12) issued a call to the 'citizens of the union' full of empty phraseology. Section 1 protested against it—in vain so far. The right of women to vote and to hold office, the freedom of sexual relations, universal language, pantarchy were preached by Section 12 and slanders were thrown against all opponents" (quoted in Commons, pp. 211–12).

By late 1871, a split between the German immigrant and American elements was imminent. Section 12 was expelled but fought back, organizing the American confederation of the International at a convention in July, 1872, with several other English-speaking sections represented. The split paralleled the Marx-Bakunin split that was rocking the International in Europe at the same time. At the Congress of the Hague in 1872 at which Bakunin was eventually expelled, Bakunists supported the representative of the American intellectuals, William West, while the Marxists supported Sorge.

On returning to New York, Sorge did a rather remarkable job of holding the faction-scarred organization together and active for four more years. During this period, the power centralization lacking earlier was consolidated under Sorge, although internal disharmony remained a problem. The organization never did solve the problem of internal conflict. Perhaps its bureaucratic structure and power centralization enabled it to survive as long as it did, in spite of lack of success and external attack (see the earlier description, p. 77, of its victimization in the so-called Tompkins Square Riot in 1874). Nevertheless, they did not bring it any favorable outcomes.

The other exception, the American Anti-Slavery Society, also suffered from acute factional strife, and, interestingly, the issue of women's rights again played a role. The AASS was dominated by its executive committee in New York under the leadership of Theodore D. Weld, Henry B. Stanton, and James G. Birney. There is historical disagreement about the causes of factionalism in the American Anti-Slavery Society, much of it centering around the historian's view of William Lloyd Garrison. Garrison was the leader of the radical faction within the AASS and confronted the organization with a continuing dilemma. He was given the essentially powerless post of Secretary for Foreign Correspondence, but, even in this apparently innocuous position, he was not trusted to follow the lead of those who controlled the organizational apparatus. "The Executive Committee ordered all letters written by him as Secretary for Foreign Correspondence to be first submitted to the committee for approval. Garrison, chafing at this restraint, resigned the position within a month" (Nye, 1955, p. 73).

But the centralization of power in the American Anti-Slavery Society never really subdued the growing internal differences. As the movement grew in size and importance, the division became increasingly acute. "The struggles that occurred within the AASS before the split at the annual convention in May, 1840 — struggles over the role of women in the movement and over religious and political questions — were . . . manifestations of the more basic radical-conservative conflict" (Kraditor, 1969, p. 10).

Both the International Workingmen's Association and the American Anti-Slavery Society had power centralization and bureaucratic structure without gaining any form of success. They both experienced factional splits. Of the ten successful groups with centralization and bureaucratic structure, only three experienced such factional splits. It is worth looking more closely at this whole issue of factionalism and its relationship to both internal organization and relations with outside groups.

FACTIONALISM

Internal division is a misery that few challenging groups escape completely — it is in the nature of the beast. Men and women of the best intentions, sharing common goals, will disagree on strategy and tactics. They will differ in the priorities they give to different subgoals and in their emphasis on the pursuit of short-range or long-range solutions. And they may compete for control of the organizational apparatus with power as an end in itself, using particular ideological postures as means of gaining support over rivals.

In fact, the content of internal disputes seems to offer very little promise for understanding why factional splits develop and with what effects. There is really no end to the issues that imaginative antagonists can use as a *casus belli,* especially if they happen to be on the political left. "We do not envy the future historian of the American revolutionary movement when he faces the problem of tracing the course of the ephemeral sects," wrote a considerate socialist, "M.S." in *The New International* in December, 1938. He attempts to make the task easier by describing in some detail Trotskyist splinter groups. One such splinter fell into our sample, the Revolutionary Workers League (Revolt), a factional split from a factional split.

The original faction, the "Oehler-Stamm group broke from the then Trotskyist Workers Party around November, 1935, because of chaste opposition to our proposal to enter the Socialist party and unite with its revolutionary wing," writes this spokesmen for the parent group. The group they formed was called the Revolutionary Workers League, but Oehler and Stamm soon had their own falling out. "A furious struggle broke out between Oehler and Stamm," writes M.S.,

> perhaps the greatest dispute since the churchmen gathered for the Council of Nicaea in 325 A.D. to work out what became the Nicene Creed of Catholicism. One faction held that the description of Christ or God the son should read *homo'ousias* or a being of identical substance with God the Father; the other faction held that the Greek word in question properly had another letter, making it read *homoi'ousias* or a being of similar substance with God the Father. Result: the split between the Roman Catholic and the Eastern (Greek Orthodox) churches. Of no less importance was the fight between Oehler and Stamm.

One contended that Trotskyism had degenerated in 1934 while the other claimed that the degeneration had already occurred by 1928. "It seems that Oehler won, after assailing the rebels for their 'false position on democratic centralism [which] has its leader in Stamm, who combines errors of bourgeois democracy with bureaucracy,' to say nothing of his 'ultra-left and false evaluation of Marxism.' " Stamm, however, was not prepared to accept banishment quietly. Not only did he form a rival group, but he chose to call it by the same name, the Revolutionary Workers League, adding still another pitfall for the hapless historian. One small kindness: the new group established its own newspaper, *Revolt,* allowing one to identify them as Revolutionary Workers League (Revolt) to avoid confusion with the Oehler group.

Sometimes, of course, divisions concern more than a single iota. Certainly, to the participants, they seem to involve fundamental differences in principle, however trivial the dispute appears in historical perspective. But given the infinite possibilities of division, it seems more fruitful to approach the issue of factionalism by asking why groups do not split rather than why they do.

The measure of factionalism used here is formal schism. Many challenging groups have vigorous internal opposition, sometimes leading to the expulsion or resignation of individual members. If these disgruntled former members proceed to set up a rival challenging group, the original challenging group is classified as factional; if, like good soldiers, they accept their fate and slowly fade away, the group has escaped factionalism as defined here.

Factional splits were part of the history of 43 percent of the groups in the sample. Sixteen of these experienced splits during their period of challenge; seven others were themselves born of factional disputes — that is, they were created by dissident members of another challenging group as in the case of the Revolutionary Workers League (both versions). Although there might be theoretical arguments for separating these two categories, they are similar empirically and are combined here for convenience of comparison with the 30 groups that experienced no formal schism in their history.

Figure 7–5 indicates that the sorry reputation of factionalism is a deserved one. It is especially related to the achievement of new advantages; less than one-fourth of the groups that experience it are successful, in contrast to 70 percent of those that escape it. For reasons that will become clearer when we examine the relationship between factionalism, bureaucracy, and power centralization, it is less sharply related to gaining acceptance.

Factional splits, I am arguing, are the primary manifestation of the failure of the group to solve the problem of internal conflict. All groups experience internal disagreement but only some divide. That factional splits are a concomitant of failure is clear enough, but the causal status of factionalism is far from clear. It is possible that it makes an important contribution to failure. No one would

FIGURE 7–5
Factionalism and Outcome

Acceptance   New Advantages

Groups with
Factionalism
Groups without
Factionalism

Percent

70%

57%

35%

22%

n = 23   n = 30   n = 23   n = 30
Chi–Square = 2.50, P = .11   Chi–Square = 12.13, P<.001

suggest that a group, well-launched on the road to success, is suddenly and capriciously struck down by this malady, but a strong argument can be made that it is an essential link in a chain of events that leads to failure. In this view, groups that lack mechanisms for dealing with internal division become crippled by factionalism and succumb when they might have succeeded.

An alternative line of argument minimizes the importance of factionalism, viewing it primarily as an epiphenomenon. In this view, factionalism is merely a manifestation of failure and not a cause. It develops in moribund groups, and, while it may hasten their collapse, it helps very little in understanding the dynamics of success or failure.

A reasonable guess is that there is some degree of two-way causality between factionalism and failure. Groups that are not doing well are prone to defection by dissident leaders with their own following. The exit of part of the group deprives it of a major source of energy and skill that might have allowed it either to persevere until its strategy bore results or to correct its course to a more successful one (cf. Hirschman, 1970).

But to acknowledge mutual influence does not imply that it is equal in both directions. By examining the sources and consequences of factional splits, we can gain some purchase on the issue of causality.

STIMULATING AND CONTAINING FACTIONALISM

I have argued that natural heterogeneity provides sufficient cause for a factional split if a group lacks adequate mechanisms for managing internal conflict. But perhaps these internal differences are helped along by hostile outsiders. Gary Marx (1972) discusses a series of documented cases of the use of agents provocateur in contemporary challenging groups. Many had the explicit purpose of promoting discord and distrust. The FBI has subsequently admitted a systematic program aimed at disrupting militant black and leftist groups. Political sabotage of the sort so extensively revealed during the Watergate scandal frequently had a similar objective.

Conceivably, such shadowy figures were present among some of the challenging groups in this historical sample, but there is no evidence of anyone later revealed as an agent of outside groups playing a role in any of the splits that occurred. Unfortunately, we can never be certain that such dirty tricks were absent, but there is no positive evidence suggesting it.

Open attacks on the group by its enemies can be evaluated more easily. In particular, we can ask if factional splits were usually preceded by external attacks upon the group, implying that it broke up under outside pressure. In contrast, we can speculate that internal division advertises weakness and invites attack by antagonists looking for a safe opportunity; thus attacks might tend to follow rather than precede a factional split.

By external attack, I mean the application of violence, arrest or other constraints to group members by outsiders. Of the 23 groups with factionalism, 17 experienced no attack either in the two years before or the two years after a factional split.[2] The other six did experience attack, half before the factional split and half afterwards. In other words, only three of the 23 groups experienced factionalism following attacks, and, even in these three cases, there is ample evidence of sharp internal divisions before the attack. If ex-

---

[2] For groups that were born of a factional split, this refers to attacks on the predecessor from whom they issued.

ternal pressure hastened the ultimate disintegration in these cases, this still occurred in less than 15 percent of the groups.

In general, then, challenging groups seem to contain the seeds of internal division within themselves. They find ample basis for fratricide in the natural frictions of cohabiting a common cause, independently of any contribution from those outsiders who would encourage their disharmony. The critical question remains, not why internal division arises, but how it is contained and managed. What mechanisms help a group to keep internal divisions from resulting in formal schism?

If we are correct in arguing that centralization of power is a device for managing internal division, then we ought to find that it is related to factionalism. Figure 7–6 indicates a substantial relationship: only 25 percent of the groups with centralization of power experienced factional splits, while this was the lot of almost two-thirds of the decentralized groups.

FIGURE 7–6
Centralization of Power and Factionalism

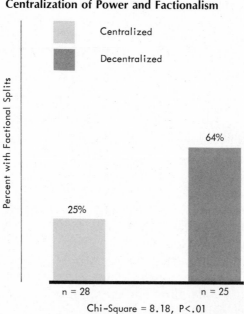

There is some suggestive evidence that factionalism is connected with failure independently of its connection with decentralization. Decentralized groups are not only more likely to develop factional splits to begin with but are *more likely to be hurt by them if they develop*. Of the 25 decentralized groups, 16 developed factional splits. As Figure 7-7 shows, only one-eighth of those which developed factionalism were able to gain new advantages, but two-thirds of these decentralized groups that somehow escaped factionalism were successful in winning new advantages. Decentralized groups, then, have a reduced ability to avoid factional splits, but, if they are able somehow to manage their internal differences, they do quite well in spite of their lack of centralized power. One reason that they do well is that they have another organizational attribute that promotes success — bureaucratic organization. Only eight decentralized groups were able to win new advantages, but six of these were bureaucratic.

FIGURE 7-7
Factionalism and Outcome for Decentralized Groups

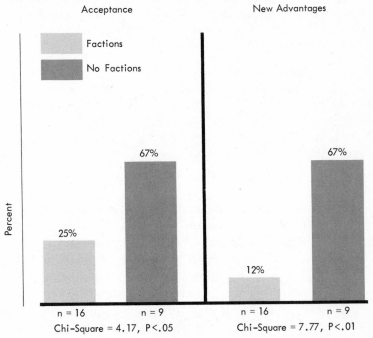

Bureaucracy has its effect on success independently of factionalism. One can make a plausible theoretical case that bureaucracy either helps to control factional splits or encourages them. A group that subjects members to tight organizational discipline ought to be able to suppress dissent and thus avoid factionalism, but Zald and Ash (1966) make exactly the opposite argument, relying on a distinction between "inclusive and exclusive" organization.

> The inclusive organization requires minimum levels of initial commitment – a pledge of general support without specific duties, a short indoctrination period or none at all. On the other hand, the exclusive organization is likely to hold the new recruit in a long "novitiate" period, to require the recruit to subject himself to organization discipline and orders. . . . Inclusive and exclusive challenging groups differ not only in recruitment procedures and requirements, but they also differ in the amount of participation required. The inclusive [group] typically requires little activity from its members – they can belong to other organizations and groups unselfconsciously, and their behavior is not as permeated by organization goals, policies, and tactics. On the other hand, the exclusive organization not only requires that a greater amount of energy and time be spent in movement affairs, but it more extensively permeates all sections of the members' life, including activities with non-members (Zald and Ash, pp. 330–31).

In spite of the greater ability of exclusive organizations to make demands on members, Zald and Ash suggest that it will be more faction prone. "The inclusive organization with its looser criteria of affiliation and of doctrinal orthodoxy is more split-resistant than the exclusive organization. The inclusive organization retains its factions while the exclusive organization spews them forth" (p. 337).

The vast majority of challenging groups in this study are inclusive organizations by almost any criterion. The one used here to define exclusiveness is the presence of a probationary period or investigation after which a would-be member is formally inducted.

Only five groups in the sample meet this minimal measure of exclusiveness, but they were neither more nor less likely to experience factionalism than their inclusive counterparts. Two of the five had factional splits while 44 percent of the inclusive groups did also. Another two of the five also gained new advantages – but these were groups that managed to escape factionalism.

The Zald-Ash hypothesis remains a suggestive one and does not deserve to be dismissed on the evidence of five cases. But the result is consistent with our explanation that individual member commitment — an issue of pattern maintenance — tells us little about the ability of the group to handle internal conflict.

Further evidence on this is provided by the absence of any substantial relationship between bureaucratic organization and factionalism. In Figure 7–8, 50 percent of the bureaucratic organizations experienced factional splits, but only 38 percent of the nonbureaucratic groups had this malady. If anything, bureaucracy is associated with more rather than less factionalism. Bureaucracy and factionalism are independently associated with outcome. When bureaucratic groups avoid factional splits, 83 percent win new advantages (10 of 12); when they experience factional splits, only 42 percent are successful in this regard (5 of 12). Put another way, groups that succeed in spite of factional splits are bureaucratic. Only five groups with factionalism won new advantages but all were bureaucratic; eight factional groups won acceptance and all but one was bureaucratic.

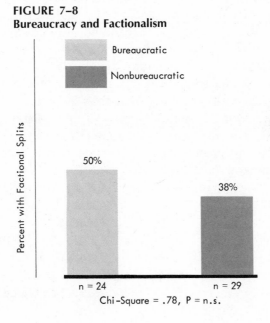

FIGURE 7–8
Bureaucracy and Factionalism

Bureaucratic

Nonbureaucratic

Percent with Factional Splits

50%

38%

n = 24   n = 29
Chi-Square = .78, P = n.s.

SUMMARY

Challenging groups are involved in political conflict. They are ready for such combat if they maintain a structure of specific commitment on the part of members that enables them to conduct routine tasks between battles so that they are ready for action when necessary. Bureaucratic organization provides a solution to the first problem of combat readiness — a cadre of reliable workers with coordinated tasks. Its contribution to the management of internal dissent is minimal; bureaucratic groups are at least as likely to experience factional splits as nonbureaucratic ones. But their ability to act quickly also depends on their having solved the problem of internal division. Centralization of power is an organizational device for handling the problem of internal division and providing unity of command. It has much to do with preventing factionalism, but sometimes (25 percent of the time), such centralized groups experience factional splits anyway. Furthermore, decentralized groups are able to escape factionalism in a substantial minority of cases.

Each of these variables — bureaucracy, centralization of power, and factionalism — makes a contribution to success, and there is a substantial interaction between centralization and factionalism. A centralized, bureaucratic group that escapes factional splits is highly likely to be successful; so, in fact, is a decentralized, bureaucratic group that escapes factionalism, but it is less likely to escape than its centralized counterpart.

A decentralized, nonbureaucratic group that experiences factionalism is doomed to failure; but, if it somehow manages to escape factionalism, it still has a modest possibility of success. Its chances of escaping a split are considerably enhanced if it has a centralized power structure. There are, then, definite advantages for a challenging group, inevitably engaged in conflict with an organized antagonist, to organize itself for facility in political combat.

REFERENCES

Commons, John R., et al. *History of Labor in the United States.* Vol. 2. New York: A. M. Kelley, 1966.

Hirschman, Albert O. *Exit, Voice, and Loyalty.* Cambridge, Mass.: Harvard University Press, 1970.

Kraditor, Aileen S. *Means and Ends in American Abolitionism.* New York: Pantheon Books, 1969.

Marx, Gary T. "Thoughts on a Neglected Category of Social Movement Participant: The Agent Provocateur and Informant." Paper delivered at the American Sociological Association meetings, New Orleans, 1972.

Michels, Robert. *Political Parties*. Glencoe, Ill.: Free Press, 1949.

Nye, Russell B. *William Lloyd Garrison and the Humanitarian Reformers*. Boston: Little, Brown, 1955.

Selznick, Philip. *The Organizational Weapon*. Glencoe, Ill.: Free Press, 1960.

Zald, Mayer N., and Ash, Roberta. "Social Movement Organizations; Growth, Decay, and Change." *Social Forces*, March 1966, 44:327–41.

chapter eight

The Historical Context of Challenges

The United States has changed immensely from that summer day in 1816 when the North Carolina Manumission Society held its first general meeting to the winter day in 1941 when A. Philip Randolph proposed that 10,000 black people march on Washington to demand an end to racial discrimination in defense employment. We have treated all 53 challenging groups as part of the same society, but the predominantly rural, pre-industrial America of the early 19th century can hardly be considered the same society as the urban, industrial giant poised on the edge of World War II.

There is no research method without its costs. In searching for patterns in the careers of a sample of diverse challenging groups, we have ripped each from its historical context. Each challenge has a thousand unique features that have been studiously ignored. It would be an idle conceit to pretend that this chapter will somehow rectify past neglect. My intention at this point is not to restore the challenging groups to their special setting but to render the setting itself amenable to the same type of generalization that earlier chapters have pursued.

Three related questions about historical context will concern us:
1. Are certain kinds of historical periods especially profitable

for launching challenges? For example, are turbulent or quiet periods more conducive to success? How does a major crisis such as war or economic collapse affect the chances of a challenging group succeeding?

2. Have there been significant shifts in what it takes for a challenging group to succeed in the 125 years between the first and last challenger in the sample? More specifically, did groups find it easier or more difficult to mount successful challenges in an earlier age? Have their strategies and characteristics changed over the years? Did they become more or less bureaucratic and centralized? Were violence and other constraints more or less frequent in earlier periods? What long term trends exist, if any?

3. Do the relationships discovered earlier hold generally or only for certain historical periods? More specifically, does success have the same connection with challenging group goals, strategy, and organization at different times?

CRISIS AND SUCCESS

In quiet times, a challenging group faces a political system well-equipped to deal with would-be troublemakers. There is reserve capacity or slack resources that can be mobilized to control a challenging group if necessary. In system-wide crisis periods, this state of affairs no longer holds because there is little slack that can be diverted for social control purposes.

This is true for both external or internal crises. In an external crisis – for example, a foreign war or natural disaster – the ability of the system to achieve collective goals is on trial. It is a crisis precisely because the reserve capacity of the political system must be employed to deal with the problem and its effects. In quiet times, it may be cheaper to devote resources to controlling a demanding challenging group rather than giving it what it wants, but this balance is shifted in crisis. It frequently becomes more convenient to yield than to divert precious resources from an already strained system for purposes of social control.

Internal crises produce the same effect. As with external crises, the reserve capacity is employed, in this case to deal not only with the conditions of crisis but also with the many challengers pressing their demands simultaneously. Resources are not available to control all of the challengers at once, and it becomes more convenient to come to terms with some of them. This argument, then, suggests a hypothesis: challenging groups should enjoy relatively greater success in times of general crisis than in quiet times.

Are challenges initiated during times of crisis more successful than those launched in quiet times? With respect to wars, the question is moot: none of our 53 challenging groups began during a major war.[1] This is not surprising. As Ash (1972, p. 179) observes, "A national war effort can be understood as a movement phenomenon . . . in which an elite mobilizes a large portion of the population, exciting them ideologically and deroutinizing them." When the government enters the mobilization arena in a major way, it is difficult for any mere challenging group to compete successfully for the same constituency; in any event, no group in our sample initiated a challenge in these circumstances.

We can, however, compare challenges launched in periods of social unrest with those started in quiet times. Almost three-fourths of the groups (39) began during relatively turbulent periods, periods characterized by major social movements and many new and diversified challenges. In particular, the 1830s, the period from 1880 until the eve of World War I (including the populist and progressive eras), and the 1930s are treated here as turbulent times. Any challenging group beginning during these periods had very substantial competition for center stage. The effect of the competition, I have hypothesized, is to benefit all by making it more difficult to control any.

Figure 8–1 indicates no support for this hypothesis. The 14 challenging groups that began their challenge in quiet times with relatively little competition do neither better nor worse than their brethren in turbulent times. One gets a similar result in looking at a more direct measure of competition. About three-fifths (30) of the challenging groups were operating in a situation in which another group existed at the same time, attempting to appeal to the same constituency. Again it can be argued that multiple challengers, especially when they offer a division of labor between more radical and moderate alternatives, enhance each other's effectiveness. Or more precisely, the existence of a radical challenger in the field helps the cause of the more moderate challenger.

---

[1] That is, the Civil War, World War I, or World War II. The Mexican War, the Spanish-American War, and the various Indian wars could not really be considered general crisis occasions. The War of 1812 might be considered major, but the first challenging group in the sample emerged in 1816.

FIGURE 8–1
Turbulent Times and Outcome

I am unable to discover any evidence that such competition makes a difference. Overall, as Figure 8–2 shows, having a competitor has no effect on success. Figure 8–3 subdivides the competitive groups into three parts: those with a more moderate competitor (10 groups), those with a more radical competitor (7 groups), and those with no consistent difference from their major competitor in militancy of tactics or goals (13 groups). Included in this last category are, for example, unions engaged in jurisdictional disputes with rivals or any group that claims its rival is less effective on grounds unrelated to degree of militancy or radicalness. Again, little or no difference is revealed in Figure 8–3. There is a suggestion that having a radical competitor makes it easier for a group to win acceptance than having a moderate competitor, but the differences with respect to new advantages are negligible.

It is obvious that if the rate of success is the same in turbulent and quiet periods, a larger number of groups will be winning new advantages and success when many are making challenges. But we have found no evidence that these turbulent periods are associated

FIGURE 8–2
Competition and Outcome

with relative success. However, before abandoning the quest for a relationship completely, there is an additional, more subtle argument to consider.

In this argument, crisis is an aid to those challengers who have already launched their effort and have sustained it, although without results, up to the time of the crisis. Such challenges are not part of the crisis itself and are seen as merely a distraction from the effort needed to manage the immediate more general challenge. The result is that challenging groups will be under pressure to postpone their demands in exchange for the promise of future advantage, and antagonists will be pressed to normalize their relationships with the challenging group. In war, for example, the national effort is provided as justification for sacrifices by both management and labor. Unions are asked to postpone wage demands and avoid strikes for higher wages, management to extend recognition to unions—all in the interest of industrial stability for war production.

This process is not as clear for groups that launch their challenge during the crisis. They are pressing new demands at a time when the system is having trouble meeting existing ones. They may be seen as aggravating an already strained situation and having picked an especially unpropitious time to initiate a challenge. That we find no new challenges launched during wars is consistent with this argument — would-be challengers find it impossible to even surface, let alone succeed. Implicit in this argument is a view of an important third-party or audience role (cf. Schattschneider, 1960 and Lipsky, 1970). The challenging group and antagonist are pressured to make peace — the one by accepting a promissory note for future delivery, the other by giving such a promissory note with acceptance, and a continuing relationship implied.

To explore this argument, we will make two comparisons, one focusing on the role of major wars and the other on the Great Depression. About two-fifths (22) of the groups had challenges in progress when the country became involved in a major war. One of these, the United Sons of Vulcan, started in 1858 and spanned the Civil War, 14 more spanned World War I, and another seven lasted into World War II. The remaining 31 groups carried out their challenge entirely in peacetime.

FIGURE 8–3
Nature of Competitor and Outcome

Figure 8–4 shows that there is a greater success for challenging groups when a war occurs during their challenge period. This is especially true for acceptance, where 77 percent during wartime are successful while only about one-quarter of the all peacetime challengers gain acceptance. The result is less dramatic with respect to winning new advantages (64 percent vs. 39 percent) but still suggestive.

FIGURE 8–4
Wars and Outcome

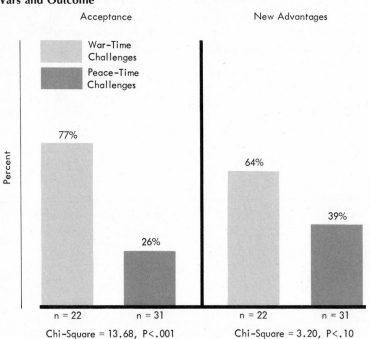

Chi-Square = 13.68, P<.001   Chi-Square = 3.20, P<.10

* Challenges begun before a war but still in progress when a major war started.
† Challenges begun and settled during peacetime periods.

The difference between new advantages and gaining acceptance suggests that co-optation is a wartime danger for challenging groups. War occurred during the period of challenge in only one of the six preempted groups but in four of the five co-opted groups. It appears that, at least with a few groups, the pressure to normalize relations with the antagonist produces acceptance, but the deferred concessions are never delivered, at least not within the 15 years following the end of the challenge.

In Figure 8–5, we focus on the effect of the Great Depression. Here we can directly compare those groups that launched a challenge prior to the depression — a challenge that was still unresolved when the depression came — with those who began their challenge while the country was in the throes of this national crisis. The nine pre-depression groups are markedly more successful, this time especially with respect to gaining new advantages. While only 30 percent of the depression-born groups were eventually successful in gaining new advantages, 89 percent of the pre-depression groups achieved this form of success eventually.

Before we can conclude that crisis gives a boost to groups that started their challenge earlier, we must consider an important contaminating variable — having target-displacement goals. As we will see shortly, the results in Figure 8–5 (concerning the depression) turn out to be largely spurious, but the results in Figure 8–4 (concerning war) hold up under this control. One of the effects of the

FIGURE 8–5
The Great Depression and Outcome

* Challenges initiated before 1929 but still in progress when the depression occurred.
† Challenges begun from 1929 to 1940.

depression was to stimulate challenging groups with goals of replacing their antagonist; in fact, six of the ten depression-spawned groups were of this type. In contrast, none of the nine pre-depression groups had such goals. Several of them (five of nine) were unions that had been struggling for many years and were finally able to consolidate their position under New Deal legislation and support.

Those groups born during the depression that did not attempt to displace their antagonist were as successful as their pre-depression counterparts. All four of these challengers won acceptance, and three of the four gained new advantages also. The three double-successes were all militant unions – Harry Bridges' West Coast Longshoremen, and the CIO-backed Steel Workers Organizing Committee, and Packinghouse Workers Organizing Committee. Although launched in the depression, it took World War II to provide the needed boost for these three challengers. Controlling for target-displacement goals does not eliminate the effect of war on success. In Figure 8–6, we repeat Figure 8–4 only for those groups that do not have target-displacement goals. If anything, the effects of war are sharpened rather than diminished. Only one of 18 wartime challengers fails to gain acceptance while less than one-third of all peacetime challengers gain this form of success. As in the figure for all groups, the differences are much smaller for gaining new advantages, indicating again that co-optation is much more likely to be an outcome for wartime groups than for their peacetime counterparts.

The hypothesized mechanism for success is third-party pressure on the antagonist. Although antagonists have not accepted the challenging group, its ability to survive has convinced many bystanders that the group is a permanent fixture. In noncrisis times, these third parties do not become involved in what they see as someone else's quarrel, but in times of crisis it is everyone's quarrel and they are less tolerant. While they do not necessarily support the particular demands of the challenging group, they are likely to be a strong force for institutionalizing the conflict. This means that they pressure antagonists to bargain and negotiate and, hence, to extend implicit or explicit recognition to the challenging group. In many cases, but not always, the resultant negotiating relationship eventually produces new advantages.

This process is nicely illustrated by the settlement between the Steel Workers Organizing Committee (SWOC) and its most bitter antagonist, the Little Steel companies. "What happens to labor-management relations when a war starts?" David McDonald of the United States Steelworkers asks (1969, p. 152). "Usually, they're frozen, and in the case of the steel industry in the United States in December, 1941, that wasn't a very satisfactory state of affairs. We were in the midst of our first negotiations with Little Steel. Nothing had yet been resolved and — for the moment, at least — it appeared nothing would be. . . . President Roosevelt immediately called upon organized labor and business to forget their differences and unite to provide the material needed to prosecute the war."

FIGURE 8–6
Wars and Outcome for Nontarget-Displacement Groups Only

Eventually, President Roosevelt created the National War Labor Board to mediate whatever disputes might arise. The deadlocked Little Steel negotiations were taken to this board and the NWLB issued its famous "Little Steel Formula" in July, 1942, providing a 5½ cent cost-of-living increase in pay, checkoff of union dues, and a maintenance of membership provision that required every man signed up by the union to continue his membership and dues checkoff during the life of the agreement. Nobody was satisfied. The companies didn't like the union security provisions and the union felt the pay raise was totally inadequate. [Philip] Murray called a meeting of the SWOC district representatives and explained the decision to them, making no specific recommendation as to whether or not they should approve it. They were confused and undecided and, while they debated among themselves, R. J. Thomas, president of the United Automobile Workers and a member of the NWLB, cornered Murray and me. He had been listening to the proceedings as an invited guest.

He shifted a massive chew of tobacco from one side of his mouth to the other as he told us: "You fellows don't seem to understand that you got something a lot more important than wages. You got the union security you wanted and the checkoff. These things will really make your union grow. What the hell else do you want?"

On impulse, Murray introduced Thomas to the delegates and he told them what he had just told us. Murray then repeated his denouncement of the wage provisions but stressed the importance of union security. I spoke last, taking the position that the advantages of the security provisions more than offset the disappointing wage scale, and moving that the NWLB recommendations be accepted. They were, and at last we had moved permanently into the ranks of Little Steel (McDonald, pp. 153–54).

If the union had doubts, the Little Steel companies were unambivalently negative toward the Little Steel Formula. The president of Bethlehem Steel

characterized the decision as one which ignored "the basic principles upon which our government was founded and the result . . . will be harmful to our national economy and to the war effort." A statement by the president of Republic Steel said in part: "In *normal times* the company would exercise its right to appeal to the courts to test the legality of [the] directive orders [emphasis added]." Frank Purness of Youngstown Sheet and Tube also characterized the WLB decisions as contrary to the national interest but indicated acquiescence for patriotic reasons (Galenson, 1960, p. 118).

Tom Girdler, the leader of the Little Steel opposition to the Steel Workers Organizing Committee, gave the clearest indication that industry acceptance resulted only from external pressure by the government. "In our private discussions, my associates and I find ourselves unreconciled. We can't help but feel that if the checkoff, which is now a fact in the steel industry, had been resisted by business generally as effectively as we and our employees resisted it in that so-called strike in Little Steel, everybody in the country would have been the gainer" (quoted in Galenson, p. 119).

Wartime challengers are, in many cases, long-time challengers. They manage to stay alive and active in spite of not having stabilized their relationship with their antagonists, and when a war or other system-wide crisis finally comes along, they are able to cash in. Sixteen groups had a challenge period lasting longer than 20 years, and all but three of these were eventually successful. These long-timers had some interesting characteristics. They were, as Figure 8–7 shows, more bureaucratic than the others (75 percent vs. 29 percent), but, if anything, they had less power centralization (44 percent vs. 58 percent).

Figure 8–7 helps to explain an earlier result. We noted in Chapter Seven (see p. 93) that bureaucracy had a stronger re-

FIGURE 8–7
Length of Challenge by Bureaucracy and Power Centralization

* These groups had a period of challenge lasting 20 years or more.
† These groups had a period of challenge of less than 10 years.

lationship to one measure of success—acceptance—while centralization was more strongly related to the other—new advantages. Now we note that long-term challengers tend to be more bureaucratic than short-timers but not more centralized and, further, that groups with a challenge in progress when a crisis arrives have a clear advantage in winning acceptance but a more equivocal one in gaining new advantages. Putting these results together suggests that third-party pressure in a crisis may be a mechanism that connects bureaucracy and acceptance. Bureaucracy helps a group to survive for a longer period in the absence of tangible results; a system-wide crisis then occurs and outside pressures push the group's antagonist to make some accommodation with it. The result is a higher rate of acceptance for bureaucratic groups.

Long-time challengers were also much less likely to seek to displace their antagonist. In fact, only one of the 16 groups that sought to replace its antagonist managed to remain active for over 20 years but without gaining success. This group, the venerable Young People's Socialist League (YPSL) began in 1915 and still surfaces from time to time in one or another incarnation.

In summary, a crisis seems to help only certain kinds of challenging groups. If a group does not aim to displace its antagonist, and if it organizes itself so that it is able to survive and persist, it is in a position to benefit by outside pressures on its antagonist in a national crisis. Being handy, the group is available to exploit the opportunity provided. Its immediate reward, however, is not the ripened fruit of new advantages but the seedlings of acceptance. Eventually, when the crisis is past, the group is usually able to reap a satisfactory harvest, but sometimes the plants prove barren.

TRENDS IN OUTCOME

What long term trends are there in the success of challenging groups? Eight "early" groups began their challenge before the Civil War; 27 "middle" groups began their challenge in the period between the Civil War and the eve of World War I (1865–1913); and the remaining 18 "recent" groups began their challenge in the period from 1914 to the U.S. entry into World War II.

Overall, there is very little indication of change in the success rate of challenging groups in these different periods. As Figure 8–8 shows, there is no difference in the rate of acceptance between middle and recent groups—about half of each are successful in this

regard. The early groups had more difficulty with acceptance—only 25 percent were successful.

There might appear to be some modest difference with respect to
gaining new advantages, but this result is completely accounted for
by the higher frequency of groups with target-displacement goals
in recent times. The depression, in particular, bred a large percentage of these groups, and, when one compares only the other kind,
there is no advantage for the middle groups over the more recent
ones. More precisely, 70 percent of the recent groups and 75 percent of the middle groups gain new advantages when we consider
only those without target-displacement goals.

Incidentally, preemption as an outcome does not appear among
recent groups; none of the six preempted groups began a challenge
after 1914. Co-optation, in contrast, is a more modern phenomenon; none of the five co-opted groups began its challenge before

FIGURE 8–8
Trends in Outcome

* Began challenge 1800–1860.
† Began challenge 1865–1913.
‡ Began challenge 1914–1945.

1880, and this outcome extends to some recent groups. But this is an isolated strand of evidence based on a handful of cases. We must leave this potential will-o-the-wisp as a lure for some future scholar.

Figure 8–9 explores trends in other characteristics of these groups. One might have expected recent groups to be more bureaucratized, but, if anything, they were less so. Only one-third of the post-1914 groups had bureaucratic structures compared to more than half of the remainder. With power centralization, there is no

FIGURE 8–9
Trends in Characteristics of Challenging Groups

trend at all except for slightly less concentration among the eight pre-civil war groups.

Nor are recent groups more unruly in means than middle and early groups. Only one-third of the post-1914 challengers made use of violence, strikes, or other constraints as a means of influence while a slightly higher percentage of the remainder (43 percent) utilized such means.

But while challenging groups have not become more unruly, their enemies may have. In Chapter Six, we noted the low success rate of groups that use no constraints but are subjected to violent attack or arrest of leaders and members. Only two of 27 middle groups (7 percent) but one-third of the recent groups were the passive victims of such measures.

These victimized groups in the recent period were, with one exception, target-displacement groups. While in earlier periods, some of the groups were victimized primarily by mobs of hostile private citizens or privately hired "detectives" and security forces, all of the recent victims were subjected to arrest by governmental authorities.

Figure 8–9 also shows a decline from middle groups to recent groups in the percent that make use of selective incentives. One-third of the middle groups used such incentives to supplement ideological appeals, but only one recent group among 18 (6 percent) employed this means of mobilization.

The trend that emerges here is a slight increase in groups of the following type: they sought the displacement of their antagonist, with some advocating violence to achieve this goal, but none ever got around to using it; they relied on ideological appeals without supplementing them with selective incentives for individual members; they lacked an organizational structure that produces combat readiness; and they were subjected to arrest and other constraints by hostile authorities. It is not a formula that makes a challenger prosper in American society.

HISTORICAL CONTEXT CONTROLLED

In earlier sections of this chapter, we have explored the relevance of particular historical contexts for the outcome of challenges and the extent to which challenging groups have changed through the years. In this final section, our concern is with the historical period as a limit on the validity of the relationships reported earlier. We found success to be related to certain strategies of mobilization and influence and to certain characteristics of goals and internal organization. But perhaps these relationships were only true during certain periods and not generally. Power centralization, for example, was found to have some relationship to success. Is the relationship as true in recent times as in earlier days?

FIGURE 8–10
Bureaucracy and New Advantages by Historical Period

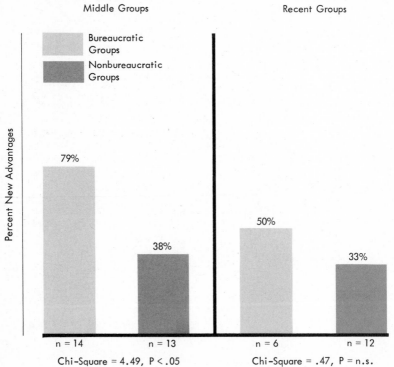

We are handicapped in answering this question by the small number of cases. First, we must ignore the eight early groups since once we begin subdividing them into bureaucratic vs. non-bureaucratic and the like, the numbers are too small for any meaningful comparison of success rates. Hence, we will only contrast the 27 middle groups with the 18 recent ones. Second, we cannot control for time period unless the variable in question is distributed in reasonable quantity over both middle and recent periods. This limits our focus to the first three variables in Figure 8-9: bureaucratic structure, power centralization, and the use of constraints. Finally, to simplify presentation, we will focus on the relationship of these variables to new advantages rather than using both outcome measures.

FIGURE 8-11
Centralization of Power and New Advantages by Historical Period

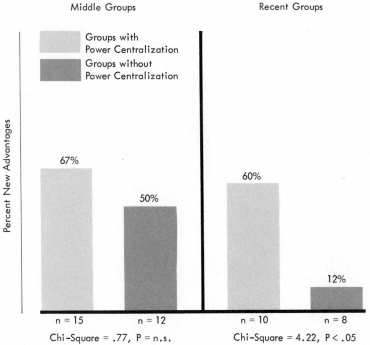

Figures 8-10 to 8-12 compare the relationship of the three variables above with success for middle and recent groups. Basically, the direction of the relationships found earlier hold for both historical periods. Groups that were bureaucratized, that had centralized power structures, and used constraints were more successful than nonbureaucratized, noncentralized, nonconstraint users in both historical eras. One suggestive difference emerges: bureaucratic organization is more sharply related to success than is power centralization for middle groups, but this order is reversed for recent groups.

FIGURE 8-12
Constraints and New Advantages by Historical Period

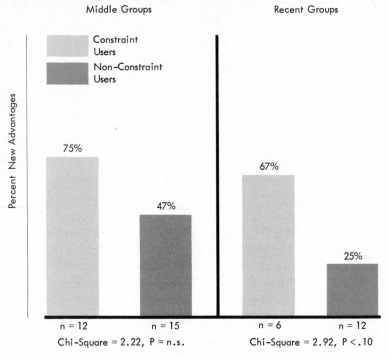

Middle Groups   Recent Groups

Constraint Users

Non-Constraint Users

Percent New Advantages

75%

47%

67%

25%

n = 12   n = 15   n = 6   n = 12
Chi-Square = 2.22, P = n.s.   Chi-Square = 2.92, P < .10

SUMMARY

The historical context adds something to our understanding of the dynamics of success and failure of challenging groups but does not force us to reconsider any earlier conclusions. Having many other challenging groups in the field at the same time does not seem to have much effect on the probability of success of any given challenger. However, a major crisis such as war or economic collapse can aid those challengers who have established their presence before the crisis occurs. A group that is not attempting to displace its antagonists and has organized itself for a long battle is in a position to exploit the opportunity presented by a crisis.

The internal organization of challenging groups has not changed greatly over the years, but there is a tendency in recent times for a particular type of unsuccessful group to appear with greater frequency. This group seeks to displace its antagonist and relies on ideological appeals without selective incentives, it lacks bureaucratic organization, and, although not itself a user of constraints as a means of influence, it experiences attack by hostile authorities.

REFERENCES

Ash, Roberta. *Social Movements in America*. Chicago: Markham, 1972.

Galenson, Walter. *The CIO Challenge to the AFL*. Cambridge, Mass.: Harvard University Press, 1960.

Lipsky, Michael. *Protest in City Politics*. Chicago: Rand-McNally, 1970.

McDonald, David J. *Union Man*. New York: E. P. Dutton, 1969.

Schattschneider, E. E. *The Semi-Sovereign People*. New York: Holt, Rinehart and Winston, 1960.

chapter nine

The Limits of Pluralism

The study of social protest has only recently emerged from the straightjacket of collective behavior. Under this stultifying tradition, the questions addressed in this book have been largely ignored by American social science. The classical perspective is one in which organized groups seek goals, mobilize resources, and employ strategies, but social movements merely express reactions by the victims of social pathology. Their cries and emotional expressions are viewed as signals of the stresses and strains of society. They react, frequently violently, sensing, without really understanding, the larger social forces which buffet them.

Social movements, in this view, are one product of social disorganization; other products include suicide, criminal behavior, and additional symptoms of a social system in trouble. The participants in social movements are the uprooted. Aminzade (1973, p. 4), a critic of this view, summarizes it for purposes of contrast with an alternative.

> The disrupting effects of large-scale social change, such as migration and urban population growth, involve a breaking apart of social bonds due to the uprooting of persons from traditional communities, which disorients individuals and leads them into disorderly, and sometimes violent, political action. The focus is upon the social disorganization and disintegration produced by the rapid pace of struc-

tural change, which leads to deviant behavior, such as crime, suicide, and political violence. . . . Implied in the model is the mass society notion that the most alienated and disoriented individuals are most likely to join the ranks of the revolution and that collective political violence is essentially an anomic phenomenon.

The collective behavior tradition has produced its prophets such as Eric Hoffer (1951) as well as its serious theorists. Hoffer's treatment has helped to spread many of the basic ideas, albeit in a simplified form, to a large and receptive audience. His central theme is the fundamental irrationality of participation in mass movements. "For men to plunge headlong into an undertaking of vast change, they must be intensely discontented yet not destitute. . . . They must also have an extravagant conception of the prospects and potentialities of the future. Finally, they must be wholly ignorant of the difficulties involved in their vast undertaking. Experience is a handicap" (Hoffer, p. 7).

Mass movements, in Hoffer's argument, offer a substitute for individual hope. They attract the frustrated, those whose present lives are irremediably spoiled. "A man is likely to mind his own business when it is worth minding. When it is not, he takes his mind off his own meaningless affairs by minding other people's business." Participants deal with the frustrations of their present lives by dwelling on what are essentially fantasies about the future. The content of the fantasies is of secondary importance. "The frustrated follow a leader less because of their faith that he is leading them to a promised land than because of their immediate feeling that he is leading them away from their unwanted selves. Surrender to a leader is not a means to an end but a fulfillment. Whither they are led is of secondary importance" (Hoffer, p. 116).

Hoffer is an extreme representative of the collective behavior tradition; he virtually ignores the social conditions that produce the behavior he describes. But other more sophisticated proponents still rely on such psychological states as loss of identity and alienation as the intervening mechanisms in their explanation. Even in the more complex versions, people are unaware of what it is that energizes them to act, and their actions are not directed at the underlying conditions that produce the alienation or anxiety.

Mass behavior, Kornhauser argues (1959) is characterized by a focus of attention on objects that are "remote from personal experience and daily life. . . . Concern for remote objects tends to lack the definiteness, independence, sense of reality, and responsibility to be found in concern for proximate objects." Furthermore, the mode of response to these remote objects is direct and unmediated by social relationships. "People act directly when they do not engage in discussion on the matter at hand, and when they do not act through groups in which they are capable of persuading and being persuaded by their fellows." Mass behavior also "tends to be highly unstable, readily shifting the focus of attention and intensity of response."

The most sophisticated statement of the collective behavior perspective is Smelser's *Theory of Collective Behavior* (1963). Although his complex argument appears very different from the crudities of a Hoffer, it is nevertheless kin. In this version, it is assumed that all political actors will sometimes search for solutions to intractable problems by raising the level of generality. This, in itself, is normal and rational. What distinguishes collective behavior is the phenomenon of "short-circuiting." Intervening steps are jumped as the actor moves from a highly generalized and abstract component of action directly to a source of strain. The short-circuit is made for members of a movement by means of what Smelser calls a "generalized belief." Generalized beliefs are distinguished from other kinds of political beliefs by their failure to specify how we get from the abstract norm or value being questioned to the concrete situations that are producing a problem.

A generalized belief is a myth by which to mobilize people. It contains elements of magical thinking and omnipotence. "The proposed reform will render opponents helpless, and will be effective immediately. . . . Because of this exaggerated potency, adherents often see unlimited bliss in the future if only the reforms are adopted. For if they are adopted, they argue, the basis for threat, frustration, and discomfort will disappear" (Smelser, p. 117). For all his sophistication, then, Smelser retains a sharp distinction between the essentially rational action of routine politics and the oversimplified "generalized beliefs" by which participants in mass movements are moved to act.

The collective behavior paradigm, then, rests on a distinction between the politics of social movements and the politics of conventional groups and organizations — mainstream political parties, lobbies, and interest groups. The actors who engage in these two types of behavior are seen as different species. Conventional groups act to achieve goals rather than reacting to express distress. For such creatures, it is perfectly appropriate to ask about the means of influence they employ to achieve their goals, their coalitions, where they get resources and how they manage them, their skill in negotiation and the like.

Pluralist theory is closely linked to this collective behavior tradition; it is the other side of the coin. Its actors are groups that engage in bargaining to achieve goals. The central process of pluralist politics is exchange. You scratch my back and I'll scratch yours, and, in the end, we'll all get some of what we want. Besides this kind of essentially rational, interest-oriented politics there is the other kind—an irrational, extremist politics, operating on a symbolic level with distant and highly abstract objects. The analysis of this kind of politics is left for the social psychologists whose intellectual tools prepare them to understand the irrational.

Part of the appeal of the collective behavior paradigm is its serviceability as an intellectual weapon to discredit mass movements of which one is critical. It has great versatility. It can, for example, be used by conservative critics of revolutionary movements such as Gustave LeBon (1896).

> By the mere fact that he forms part of an organized crowd, a man descends several rungs in the ladder of civilization. Isolated, he may be a cultivated individual; in a crowd, he is a barbarian—that is, a creature acting by instinct. He possesses the spontaneity, the violence, the ferocity, and also the enthusiasm and heroism of primitive beings, whom he further tends to resemble by the facility with which he allows himself to be impressed by words and images—which would be entirely without action on each of the isolated individuals composing the crowd—and to be induced to commit acts contrary to his most obvious interests and his best known habits. . . . Taken separately, the men of the French Revolutionary Convention were enlightened citizens of peaceful habits. United in a crowd, they did not hesitate to give their adhesion to the most savage proposals, to guillotine individuals most clearly innocent, and, contrary to their interests, to renounce their inviolability and to decimate themselves" (LeBon, pp. 32–33).

It can be used equally well to discredit the frightening fascist movements of the 1920s and 1930s. Who could quarrel with an explanation that depicted the followers of a Hitler or Mussolini as irrational victims of a sick society? Books such as *The Authoritarian Personality* (Adorno, et al., 1950) and *Escape from Freedom* (Fromm, 1941) were hailed as benchmarks of social science achievement.

With the advent of the cold war and the shift of concern to the appeal of communism, many were delighted to find such a handy intellectual apparatus, all cranked and ready to be applied. Authoritarianism was reinterpreted to fit the "extreme" left as well as the "radical right." Former communists were seen to convert to new "authoritarian" belief systems, not under a barrage of intense normative pressure and external sanctions, but from an unconscious psychological insecurity that made them seek certainty. The collective behavior tradition has proved itself highly durable.

Then came the Movement of the 1960s. It is undeniably arrogant, of course, to preempt the capital M for the particular movement that one participates in. But it seems equally undeniable that what Ash (1972) calls the "penumbra" of this set of related challenges blanketed the campuses of America. It created an atmosphere, a set of concerns and issues, that defined the political agenda of those who lived and worked in its ambience.

Many of the intellectual workers operating in this ambience became active participants in the challenges. They marched on picket lines to boycott chain stores that discriminated or went to the South to work on voter registration; they organized teach-ins and marched against the war in Vietnam; they organized rent strikes or sit-ins for open enrollment, elimination of ROTC, or many other specific issues. And if they didn't actively participate, they talked to many who did.

This was not a felicitous circumstance for the continuing acceptance of the collective behavior paradigm. Some, of course, found the politicized atmosphere on campus appalling and destructive and were ready to trot out the old intellectual weapons against this latest threat to political civility (cf. Feuer, 1969). But others, more sympathetic to the Movement, were hardly ready to embrace an explanation that would tar themselves and many friends.

Movement sympathizers and participants such as Flacks (1967), Z. Gamson et al. (1967), and Keniston (1968) were quick to produce evidence on student activists that severely undercut any explanation based on malintegration and personal pathology. Paige (1972), Caplan and Paige (1968), and the social scientists of the Kerner Commission (1968) were equally quick to produce evidence discrediting such explanations of urban rioters. The "riffraff" theory, characteristic of the McCone Commission report on the Watts riot, was dispatched in short order.

If the collective behavior paradigm seemed so inadequate to deal with the challenges that one experienced at first hand, perhaps it was equally questionable for other movement phenomena normally viewed at a distance with hostility—for example, McCarthyism. I have full sympathy and admiration for those who lived through the trauma and the viciousness of the McCarthy era and were not too cowed to fight back. The threat was real, and I can understand how beleaguered social scientists turned quite naturally to an intellectual apparatus that had apparently made sense of the rise of fascism and used it to discredit Joe McCarthy's followers under the guise of social science explanation. However, work by Rogin (1967), Polsby (1960), and others suggests that this classical approach does not explain the phenomenon very well at all.

This view would have it that McCarthy drew his basic support, not from established, traditionally conservative groups, but from the alienated. McCarthy was seen as a prototypical demagogue appealing to the mass of people for direct support over the heads of their established leaders. He mobilized those individuals who were psychologically vulnerable, splitting apart existing coalitions and upsetting conventional group alignments.

Plausible as it may sound, this view of the McCarthy phenomenon is apparently false. Rogin's work strongly suggests that there was less to McCarthyism than met the eye. Without searching below the surface for hidden frustrations, the bulk of McCarthy's support can be accounted for by taking the issues at face value. On the basis of county voting records, poll data, and other evidence, Rogin concludes that "McCarthy capitalized on popular concern over foreign policy, communism and the Korean War, but the animus of McCarthyism had little to do with any less political or more developed *popular* anxieties. . . . McCarthy did not split apart an elite, the parts of which had been equally conservative before him. He rather capitalized on an existing liberal/conservative split within the existing Republican elite" (1967, pp. 216, and 220). Polsby's (1960) analysis of poll data points in the same general direction. Party affiliation is the single best predictor of support for McCarthy—Democrats opposed him and Republicans supported him. Rogin concludes from his own review, "In these polls, as in the data reported by Polsby, no other single division of the population (by religion, class, eduation, and so forth) even approached the party split" (p. 234). Rogin rejects the notion that McCarthy was sustained primarily by the vague discontents of frustrated groups. "McCarthy had powerful group and elite support. He did not mobilize the masses at the polls or break through existing group cleavages. . . . Communism and the Korean War played crucial roles" (p. 268). The issues on which McCarthy mobilized support were apparently real ones for his followers, not merely symbolic of private anxieties.

The collective behavior apparatus also proved a convenient one for liberals in explaining the support for Senator Barry Goldwater in 1964. It was frequently assumed that the early supporters of Goldwater were anomic, institutionally detached "cranks," neofascists, or "infiltrators" into the Republican Party. "Little old ladies in tennis shoes" became the popular phrase to capture the lunatic fringe imagery.

McEvoy (1971) has demonstrated that the evidence sharply contradicts this image of the Goldwater phenomenon. Pre-convention supporters of Goldwater were compared on a number of variables with those who ultimately voted for him even though they had preferred another nominee prior to the convention. The early Goldwater supporters were significantly higher on such variables as church attendance, income level, and education. They were more likely to be married. Furthermore, they were much higher in past participation in Republican party politics. Finally, they exhibited average-to-low levels of objective status discrepancy. None of this evidence suggests lack of attachment; on the contrary, early Goldwater supporters seem to be strong conservatives with social support and respect from their friends and neighbors.

RESOURCE MOBILIZATION: THE NEW LOOK AT SOCIAL PROTEST

There are now an increasing number of scholars who have begun reexamining social protest without the incubus of the collective behavior paradigm. The assumptions of the new look have begun to emerge more and more explicitly in their work as they attempt to test its explanatory power on a wide range of collective actions. This book draws sustenance from and hopefully contributes to this growing literature.

Oberschall (1973) has made the most comprehensive effort to state that alternative to the collective behavior approach. He begins with the concept of resources.

In ordinary everyday activity, at work, in family life, and in politics, people manage their resources in complex ways: they exchange some resources for other resources; they make up resource deficits by borrowing resources; they recall their earlier investments. Resources are constantly being created, consumed, transferred, assembled and reallocated, exchanged, and even lost. At any given time, some resources are earmarked for group ends and group use, not just individual use. All of these processes can be referred to as "resource management."

Group conflict in its dynamic aspects can be conceptualized from the point of view of resource management. Mobilization refers to the processes by which a discontented group assembles and invests resources for the pursuit of group goals. Social control refers to the same processes, but from the point of view of the incumbents or the group that is being challenged. Groups locked in conflict are in competition for some of the same resources as each seeks to squeeze more resources from initially uncommitted third parties (p. 28).

The discontented are no more nor less rational than other political actors.

The individuals who are faced with resource management decisions make rational choices based on the pursuit of their selfish interests in an enlightened manner. They weigh the rewards and sanctions, costs and benefits, that alternative courses of action represent for them. In conflict situations, as in all other choice situations, their own prior preferences and history, their predispositions, as well as the group structures and influence processes they are caught up in, determine their choices. Indeed, many are bullied and coerced into choices that are contrary to their predispositions. The resource management approach can account for these processes in a routine way (p. 29).

Charles Tilly and his collaborators have been major developers of this approach and have made especially fertile use of it in explaining specific collective actions. The Tilly strategy has been to spawn a number of different studies using historical data on various European countries. The studies are united by a common theoretical framework, set of guiding questions, and great care in the systematic coding and analysis of the basic historical data used to test their propositions.

Groups are viewed as "forming and dissolving, mobilizing and demobilizing, formulating and making claims, acting collectively and ceasing to act, gaining and losing power, in response to changes in five sets of variables: (1) articulated group interests, (2) prevailing standards of justice, (3) resources controlled by groups and their members, (4) resources controlled by other groups (especially governments) and (5) costs of mobilization and collective action" (Tilly, 1973, pp. 6–7; also cf. Tilly "Revolutions and Collective Violence," 1974). Collective actions are "conceptualized as organizational phenomena which occur, not merely because of widespread discontent with war, unemployment, or whatever, but because organizations exist which make possible the channeling and expression of that discontent into concerted social action" (Aminzade, 1973, p. 6).

In place of the old duality of extremist politics and pluralist politics, there is simply politics. The American Medical Association and Students for a Democratic Society are not different species but members of the same species faced with different political environments. All political groups are assumed to have certain collective goals. These goals are not necessarily the same as the goals of the individuals who join them. A person may become active in the Republican Party because he seeks camaraderie and fellowship and is pulled in by friendship networks; because he is motivated by ideological concerns; because he finds in his allegiance to the party a meaningful way of dealing with a confusing world; because he seeks material rewards, status and contacts; or because he seeks an opportunity to exercise power over his fellow men. Most of these reasons would apply as well to joining the Peace and Freedom Party.

The collective goals of political actors rather than the personal goals of members are assumed to be the relevant part of an explanation of political behavior. Whatever the personal motivation of members, the Republican Party has certain goals of its own. These can be recognized by their status as internal justifications in the group. Should the party take action A or B? One answers by reference to certain end-states — for example, gaining political power — which are recognized by other members as justifications, regardless of their personal goals. Collective goals set the criteria for deciding on collective actions.

Similar reasoning applies to social movement actors. They have certain collective goals, and one can make sense of their actions partly by reference to these end-states. They are seen as essentially instrumental in their behavior. This does not mean that they always act in their best interest. They may make mistakes because of poor diagnosis of their political environment, unwise use of resources, and poor organization. They are no different in this respect from the Republican Party, although they may make more or fewer mistakes because of the different political environment and strategic imperatives they face.

Rebellion, in this view, is simply politics by other means. It is not some kind of irrational expression but is as instrumental in its nature as a lobbyist trying to get special favors for his group or a major political party conducting a presidential campaign. As Aminzade puts it, "The resource mobilization model views revolutionary violence as an extension or continuation, in a particular form, of everyday, nonviolent political activity. An event of collective violence is conceptualized, not as a sudden and unpredictable outburst or eruption of heretofore latent tensions or frustrations which take their manifest form in an organizational vacuum, but rather as the outcome of a continuous process of organizational activity" (p. 5).

The absence of rebellion is in need of explanation as much as its presence. Tilly observes that "collective violence is one of the commonest forms of political participation. Why *begin* an inquiry into [the subject] . . . with the presumption that violent politics appear only as a disruption, a deviation, or a last resort? Rather than treating collective violence as an unwholesome deviation from normality, we might do better to ask under what conditions (if any) violence disappears from ordinary political life." He goes on to suggest several reasons why one should hesitate "to assume that collective violence is a sort of witless release of tension divorced from workaday politics: its frequent success as a tactic, its effectiveness in establishing or maintaining a group's political identity, its normative order, its frequent recruitment of ordinary people, and its tendency to evolve in cadence with peaceful political action" (Tilly, 1973b).

Large scale structural changes such as urbanization and industrialization are important not because they create disorganization but because they "strongly affect the number, identity, and organizations of the contenders which in turn determine the predominant forms and loci of conflict. In the short run, the magnitude of conflict depends on an interaction of the tactics of contenders and the coercive practices of the government. In the longer run, the magnitude of conflict depends on the established means by which contenders can enter and leave the polity, and the frequency with which entries and exits actually occur" (Tilly, 1970, p. 4).

The form that protest takes is viewed as the result of an interaction. Confusion on this issue "has led most analysts to jump far too quickly from the fact that a riot occurred to the investigation of why such individuals turned to violence." In fact, the standard sequences for violence occurring are (a) "A group representing a contender for power offers a public show of strength or performs a symbolic act which implicitly lays claim to disputed power and another rival group challenges, which leads to fighting of some sort between the groups and finally to the intervention of repressive force," or (b) "A group representing a contender for power (especially a non-member of the polity) performs an act which lays claim to disputed power, and repressive forces intervene directly to counter that claim" (Tilly, 1970, pp. 26–27). "Whether violence occurs or not [in collective action] depends largely on whether members of one group decide to resist the claims being made by members of another group" (Tilly, 1973a, p. 6).

There are, in this paradigm, some important distinctions to be made among different kinds of political actors. What I have called here "challenging groups" are special kinds of actors with a set of problems that are peculiar to the class. Established groups must maintain the loyalty and commitment of those from whom they draw their resources; challenging groups must create this loyalty. Both attempt influence but established actors have resources routinely available for use and have different relationships to other important political actors.

Powerless groups have special kinds of strategic problems. They cannot call on existing resources but must create their own on the basis of mass support. Or, if the supporting population is not sufficient, they must find ways of bringing allies to their cause. As Lipsky (1968) writes, "The 'problem of the powerless' in protest activity is to activate 'third parties' to enter the implicit or explicit bargaining arena in ways favorable to the protestors. This is one of the few ways in which they can 'create' bargaining resources."

The central difference among political actors is captured by the idea of being inside or outside of the polity. Those who are inside are *members* whose interest is vested—that is, recognized as valid by other members. Those who are outside are challengers. They lack the basic prerogative of members—routine access to decisions that affect them. They may lack this because it is denied them in

spite of their best efforts or because their efforts are clumsy and ineffectual. Precisely how entry into the polity operates is a matter
for empirical study as in this book.

IMPLICATIONS FOR PLURALIST THEORY

Pluralist theory is a portrait of the inside of the political arena.
There one sees a more or less orderly contest, carried out by the
classic pluralist rules of bargaining, lobbying, logrolling, coalition
formation, negotiation, and compromise. The issue of how one gets
into the pressure system is not treated as a central problem. Crenson (1971, p. 179) writes:

> Where there is pluralism, it is argued, there is likely to be competi-
> tion among political leaders, and where leaders must compete with
> one another, they will actively seek the support of constituents. A
> leader who fails to cultivate public support runs the risk of being
> thrust aside by his rivals when the time comes to submit himself and
> his policies to the judgement of the electorate. . . . The pluralistic or-
> ganization of the political elite, therefore, helps to assure that the
> great bulk of the population will enjoy a substantial amount of indi-
> rect influence in the making of almost all public decisions, even
> though it seldom participates directly in the making of any public
> decision.

Since no fundamental distinction is made between insiders and
outsiders, there is little sensitivity to the differences in their political imperatives. Differences in political situation are treated as differences in character, between rational actors pursuing interests
and irrational actors expressing frustration with social conditions.

The results presented in earlier chapters contradict pluralist imagery at a number of crucial points. First of all, when we examine
the behavior of challengers rather than members, we do not find
any connection between success and the means of influence pre-
scribed for members. On the contrary, those who are unruly have
the most notable success. A willingness to use constraints, including violence in some cases, is associated with gaining membership
and benefits, not with its opposite. This is only true for groups with
certain kinds of goals, but it cannot be said that, in general, violation of the rules of pluralist politics is self-defeating for challengers.

The same point can be made with respect to the use of social
control strategies by members against challengers. The restraint
which pluralist theory claims for political actors does not cross the

boundaries of the polity. One uses only limited means against members, but challengers are fair game for a whole gamut of social control techniques. The rules are regarded as just; hence, their violation gives license for repression. Righteous indignation is available to fuel the faint-hearted and to ease the overly scrupulous conscience.

In fact, the set of activities symbolized by Watergate can best be understood in these terms. The Nixon administration introduced an innovation of a special and limited sort: means of political combat that were normally reserved for challengers were applied to members. Nixon was able to claim, with justification, that wire-tapping, burglary, the use of agents provocateur, and the use of the Justice Department and the FBI as a weapon to harass were all practices employed by previous administrations. The special genius of the Nixon administration was to bring these techniques inside the political arena and to direct them at members, thereby causing great indignation among many who had tolerated their use against political pariahs.

The results here also challenge the pluralist assumption that those with a collective interest to pursue will organize to pursue it. The theory of public goods shows that there is nothing natural about the ability to organize successfully. Its achievement is an accomplishment that can and frequently does elude a group that is poor in resources and can offer its members few if any selective incentives.

A member of the polity may need to wheel and deal, but a challenger should be prepared to stand and fight. If the group threatens strong interests of members and is not ready for combat, it is likely to find itself extremely vulnerable to attack and defeat. Members bargain with other members; with persistent challengers, they are prepared to fight and to destroy or ultimately to yield if the fight proves more costly than the stakes warrant.

The pluralist image, then, is a half-truth. It misleads us when applied to the relations between political challengers and members of the polity. The appropriate image for this political interaction is more a fight with few holds barred than it is a contest under well-defined rules. Lowi (1971, p. 53) says it very well. "The history of the United States is not merely one of mutual accommodation among competing groups under a broad umbrella of consensus. The proper image of our society has never been a melting pot. In bad times, it is a boiling pot; in good times, it is a tossed salad. For those who are *in*, this is all very well. But the price has always been paid by those who are *out*, and when they do get in they do not always get in through a process of mutual accommodation under a broad umbrella of consensus."

Some of these unruly and scrappy challengers do eventually become members. One might be tempted to conclude from this that the flaw in the pluralist heaven is, after all, rather exaggerated. Entry is not prohibited for those with the gumption, the persistence, and the skill to pursue it long enough. But this is, at best, cold comfort. Beyond the unsuccessful challengers studied here there may lie others unable to generate enough effort to mount even a visible protest. If it costs so much to succeed, how can we be confident that there are not countless would-be challengers who are deterred by the mere prospect?

REFERENCES

Adorno, Theodore W.; Frenkel-Brunswik, Else; Levinson, Daniel J.; and Sanford, R. Nevitt. *The Authoritarian Personality*. New York: Harper & Row, 1950.

Aminzade, Ronald. "Revolution and Collective Political Violence: The Case of the Working Class of Marseille, France, 1830–1871." Working Paper #86, Center for Research on Social Organization. Ann Arbor: University of Michigan, October 1973.

Ash, Roberta. *Social Movements in America*. Chicago: Markham, 1972.

Caplan, Nathan S., and Paige, Jeffery M. "A Study of Ghetto Rioters." *Scientific American*, August 1968, 219:15–21.

Crenson, Matthew A. *The Unpolitics of Air Pollution*. Baltimore: Johns Hopkins Press, 1971.

Feuer, Lewis. *The Conflict of Generations*. New York: Basic Books, 1969.

Flacks, Richard W. "The Liberated Generation: An Exploration of the Roots of Student Protest." *Journal of Social Issues*, July 1967, 23:52–75.

Fromm, Erich. *Escape from Freedom*. New York: Rinehart, 1941.

Gamson, Zelda F.; Goodman, Jeffery; and Gurin, Gerald. "Radicals, Moderates, and Bystanders during a University Protest." Paper presented at American Sociological Association meeting, San Francisco, August 1967.

Hoffer, Eric. *The True Believer*. New York: Harper & Row, 1951.

144   The Strategy of Social Protest

Keniston, Kenneth. *Young Radicals*. New York: Harcourt, Brace, and World, 1968.

Kerner Commission. *National Advisory Commission on Civil Disorders: Final Report*. New York: Bantam, 1968.

Kornhauser, William. *The Politics of Mass Society*. New York: The Free Press, 1959.

LeBon, Gustave. *The Crowd*. London: Ernest Benn, 1896.

Lipsky, Michael. "Protest as a Political Resource." *American Political Science Review*, December 1968, 62:1144–58.

Lowi, Theodore J. *The Politics of Disorder*. New York: Basic Books, 1971.

McEvoy, James III. *Radicals or Conservatives: The Contemporary American Right*. Chicago: Rand-McNally, 1971.

Oberschall, Anthony. *Social Conflict and Social Movements*. Englewood Cliffs, N.J.: Prentice-Hall, 1973.

Paige, Jeffery M. "Political Orientation and Riot Participation." *American Sociological Review*, October 1971, 36:810–20.

Polsby, Nelson W. "Toward an Explanation of McCarthyism." *Political Studies*, October 1960, 8:250–71.

Rogin, Michael Paul. *The Intellectuals and McCarthy: The Radical Specter*. Cambridge, Mass.: M.I.T. Press, 1967.

Smelser, Neil J. *Theory of Collective Behavior*. New York: The Free Press, 1963.

Tilly, Charles. "From Mobilization to Political Conflict." Center for Research on Social Organization. Ann Arbor: University of Michigan, March 1970.

———. "Collective Action and Conflict in Large-Scale Social Change: Research Plans, 1974–78." Center for Research on Social Organization. Ann Arbor: University of Michigan, October 1973a.

———. "The Chaos of the Living City." In Herbert Hirsch and David C. Perry, eds. *Violence as Politics*. New York: Harper & Row, 1973b.

———. "Revolutions and Collective Violence." In Fred I. Greenstein and Nelson W. Polsby, eds. *Handbook of Political Science*. Vol. 3. Reading, Mass.: Addison-Wesley, 1974.

chapter ten

Challenging Groups Since 1945

Would the results be the same for a sample of challenging groups since the end of World War II? Much has changed and the answer is not simple or obvious. This chapter reexamines the major arguments of *Strategy*,[1] treating as an open question whether they still hold or need revision to explain the experiences of more recent challengers.

CHANGES IN AMERICAN SOCIETY

Since 1945 two profound changes in American society have created a radically different environment for challengers. I will continually return to these changes in different sections of this chapter. The first centers on the rise of the national security state and particularly the sophisticated covert action capability that is a part

This chapter has been added to the original 1975 edition of this book. I am grateful to David Croteau, Paulo Donati, William Hoynes, Sharon Kurtz, Charlotte Ryan, Ted Sasson, and David Stuart for their comments and suggestions on an earlier draft.

[1] Since much of this chapter is a dialogue with the earlier edition of this book, I will shorten the title to "*Strategy*" for ease of reference when I wish to criticize, revise, or put some gloss on a point made in the 1975 edition.

of it. The second centers on the rise of television and, with it, the much more central role for the mass media, affecting the strategies of both challengers and authorities.

Neither, of course, is completely new. Pre-1945 challengers experienced company spies and agents provocateur but compared to the use of overt repression to disrupt and demobilize a challenger, covert action was rarely of any significance. Since 1945 the expansion of the intelligence apparatus has added to the social control repertoire of authorities' sophisticated new ways of attacking challengers. As Donner (1980) notes, "None of the manifold excesses of the past can compare in scope and intensity with the secret war waged continuously for over 50 years against all shades of dissenting political groups by the domestic intelligence community."

The term "national security" might seem to have been with us forever but as Yergin (1977) observes, it was not common in American political discourse until the middle 1940s. Along with its cognates "internal security" and "subversion," it serves to weave external and domestic threats into a seamless whole. Domestic intelligence protects us against threats to internal security while foreign intelligence provides the same protection against external threats. "The distinction between the two concepts and their cognate intelligence programs is filmy at best," Donner notes. These terms provide "the rhetorical path by which intelligence entered the political process and became institutionalized."

The net result has been a greatly increased capacity for covert action aimed at disrupting and demobilizing challengers. The expanded domestic intelligence community is a coordinated network of federal and local agencies with minimum accountability to outsiders, including public officials. The network even includes private components, providing an additional layer of insulation from the media spotlight and offering authorities enough plausible deniability to keep journalists at bay for want of a smoking gun.

The repertoire of specific techniques for promoting disruption of challengers represents a great leap forward in sophistication and subtlety over anything that pre-1945 challengers experienced. Without settling which is morally preferable, the problems of defending against physical attack versus defending against a fabricated story planted with a journalist are quite different. It is clearly an open question whether a tactic or organizational form that helps to protect against one form of social control is equally effective against another.

It is not as if there weren't mass media before 1945. Even in the 1830s, challengers had to deal with the penny press, and in the 1930s radio had already become politically significant. Father Coughlin, "the radio priest," demonstrated the potential of electronic media by mobilizing a following for the National Union for Social Justice. Ultimately this challenge collapsed, but not before Coughlin had foreshadowed a use of television that Jerry Falwell and others would exploit by mobilizing the Moral Majority 40 years later. Although photojournalism was already an established part of news reporting before 1945, there is no evidence that it played a significant role in the careers of any of the challenging groups studied in *Strategy*, as it was to do with later groups.

Is it possible to write a book about the experiences of modern challengers without discussing how the mass media enter into the process? The word "television" never appears in *Strategy*, nor is there any systematic discussion of the role of the media.[2] But today, virtually every aspect of a challenger's experience—recruitment efforts, organization, strategy, and tactics—is affected by a potential or actual media presence.

Similarly, the media presence affects how authorities respond, especially in relation to the effectiveness of overt versus covert repression. It dramatically changes the scope of a conflict, enlarging the role of the audience and the intervention of potential third parties, who may act as allies, opponents, or brokers.

The central role of television and the mass media more generally forces us to pay much more attention to the symbolic contest waged by challengers and their opponents. Challengers are engaged in battles over meaning. The images, catchphrases, and metaphors used by the media to define the challenge and the challenger are central in determining their fate. In postwar America, the media have become the central battleground, which challengers ignore at their peril.

These two enormous changes require a piece-by-piece reassessment of the arguments in *Strategy*. Given the rise of the national security state and the enlarged role of the media, does it still help to think small? How is the free-rider problem affected? Are vio-

---

[2] Section five of the questionnaire dealt with the communication system (see Appendix D, pp. 298–99), including the mass media; but no codes from this material were used, in part because of the difficulty of getting reliable, comparable information on most of the groups.

lence and other constraints still associated with success? Are the organizational functions that were once met by bureaucracy and centralization now met in other ways?

CHANGES IN SOCIAL MOVEMENT THEORY

If challengers now operate in a changed environment, so do the students of social movements who write about them. When the first edition of *Strategy* appeared in 1975, the resource mobilization approach to social movements was just emerging and had barely been articulated. Paradigmatic statements such as McCarthy and Zald's "Resource Mobilization and Social Movements" (1977) and Tilly's *From Mobilization to Revolution* (1978) had yet to appear. Indeed, *Strategy* itself was an early attempt at developing this nascent perspective.

The field of social movements has flourished in the past 15 years and I have become sensitized to issues that were not on my intellectual agenda in the early 1970s. In *Strategy* I didn't address the innovation and portent of a radio priest mobilizing millions for political causes with this then-new medium. Or that during the 1930s a popular president was using radio "fireside chats" to gain support for his policies on a number of issues.

Nor is there discussion of the symbolic contests that went on long before radio had entered the scene. For example, every strike or demonstration involved a struggle to define the issues and characterize the contending parties. The outcome of these contests had consequences for which strategies of influence and social control appeared legitimate in the eyes of a broader public and therefore affected what means were used.

Nor was there much attention in *Strategy* to the way in which collective identity is created and transformed, or to shifts in consciousness and emergent norms. To be sure, some of this neglect was methodological in origin, reflecting the difficulty of getting reliable and detailed information on such elusive processes from secondary sources. But some of the neglect was theoretical as well, reflecting a too-sweeping rejection of traditional collective behavior theory and an isolation from European work on "new social movements" that emphasized such concerns.

The field has moved on and my own thinking with it. The complicated ways in which challenging groups and media interact has become an important subtopic (see Molotch, 1979; Gitlin, 1980; and Ryan, 1990). Resource mobilization theorists have taken up the questions of how issues are framed and how challengers can reframe them (see Snow et al., 1986; Gamson, 1988; Snow and Benford, 1988; and Ryan, 1990). New social movement theory has brought the creation and transformation of collective identity back to center stage (see Melucci, 1980, 1985; and Klandermans, Kriesi, and Tarrow, 1988) and has been combined with resource mobilization theory in creative syntheses (see Klandermans, 1984, 1986; and Klandermans, Kriesi, and Tarrow, 1988).

In addition, there have been dozens of studies of particular social movements with theoretical insights and detail rich enough to illuminate these processes. The discussion below attempts to reflect these theoretical developments in applying the results of *Strategy* to the experience of modern challengers.

THE STRATEGY OF THINKING SMALL (Chapter Four)

Nothing that has happened since 1945 suggests any change in the basic conclusion of Chapter Four. Groups that strive to displace their antagonist seem no more likely to be successful today than the earlier groups. Neither our pre-1945 sample nor the experience of groups since then call this into question. This unsurprising finding in no way challenges the basic pluralist assumption that only those groups whose objectives leave pluralist social structure and values intact will be successful. Demanding entree to the political arena is one thing; demanding that others be tossed out is another.

But the advent of television and the enhanced role of the media do have some implications for goal articulation. Modesty of goals conveys no special advantage and, to the extent that it reduces drama and newsworthiness, might even convey a disadvantage. A union striving for a narrow material benefit, for example, is less likely to attract sympathetic media treatment than one able to present itself as seeking social justice and dignity for its members.

Ryan shows how Boston's Local 26 (Hotel, Restaurant, Institutional Employees, and Bartenders Union, AFL-CIO) dramatically improved its media coverage over a seven-year period. After Domenic Bozzotto won the presidency of Local 26 in 1981, he led an organizing campaign among Boston's multilingual, multiracial hotel workers around the themes of justice and dignity. "You can't organize people over money," he told an interviewer from the *Boston Globe Magazine*. "You have to organize people over ideas . . . We talk about non-negotiable issues, like dignity, respect on the job, social justice."

Local 26's goal articulation strategy dealt with a basic media problem faced by unions. As the Glasgow University Media group points out (1976), union actions other than contract battles are not seen as newsworthy and thus go uncovered. Then, having failed to cover the process that brought a union to the point of striking, mainstream media coverage implicitly places blame on unions for disrupting orderly life. Add to this a common framing of unions as special interest groups, grubbing for financial gain, and one has an uphill struggle in gaining public sympathy and support.

Ryan's account shows how Local 26 gained excellent media coverage that presented its framing of the issues quite successfully in a sustained fashion over several years. The articulation of goals is only one small piece of this success, but it illustrates some of the advantages of universalizing the appeal of a challenger's goals. "The hotels have a long history of discrimination, racism and sexism," Bozzotto was quoted in the *Boston Ledger*. In organizing food service workers at Harvard, Local 26 used the slogan, "Our dignity and rights are non-negotiable" and made much of the admission by Harvard's chief negotiator that "I could not raise a family on what [food service workers] are making." As Ryan points out, in its contract demands the union "chose to highlight issues of racial and language discrimination, unfair job practices, harrassment of women workers. Economic issues were presented from a justice perspective, the right of workers to a living wage and health benefits, the right to support their families in dignity."

By articulating their goals in this fashion, Local 26 was attempting to activate larger collective identities that members shared with others in their communities—identities of gender, class, race, and ethnicity. The impact of such a strategy is to broaden the constituency from which one can draw resources and support; but to do this the social justice message used to frame the issues must be successfully conveyed in the mass media. Without the media, it would have been difficult if not impossible for Local 26 to enlarge its constituency beyond those most directly affected—the immediate pool of workers and their families.

Local 26 succeeded not because it used some clever public relations strategy but because it skillfully integrated the media into its

overall strategy. It used media coverage to articulate genuine grievances deeply felt by its constituents and to enhance the union's
day-to-day organizing.

If there is a lesson to be drawn about goals, it is to put greater
emphasis on how they are framed and articulated in the media.
Even if long-range goals involve the displacement of antagonists, it
serves a group well to present more limited, intermediate goals.
But it is also possible to think too small. If a challenger's goals can
easily be framed as benefits for a special interest group, media
coverage is unlikely to help the group enlarge its constituency. A
challenger is better off framing its goals in ways that engage larger
shared identities and solidarities. If "thinking small" means
"thinking narrow," it offers no path to success.

THE LIMITS OF SOLIDARITY (Chapter Five)

Today I would call this chapter "The Limits of Self-Interest."
Strategy raises some questions about the validity and completeness of Olson's (1965) argument in *The Logic of Collective Action*.
However, his central hypothesis—that selective incentives are the
most significant way of overcoming the free-rider problem—receives sympathetic treatment and some mild support from the
data. This hypothesis deserves more critical treatment than it received in *Strategy*, since its usefulness for understanding modern
challengers seems highly limited.

Fireman and Gamson (1979) remind us to "beware of economists
bearing gifts."[3] Olson's utilitarian model had an appeal to students
of social movements who were moving away from collective behavior theories that emphasized irrationality and expressive behavior.
It was easy to recognize examples of the free-rider problem in its
varied social movement manifestations and plausible enough that
challengers would be affected, especially when the personal cost
of participation can be extremely high.

But the argument is flawed and the evidence for it is thin, both
in *Strategy* and elsewhere.[4] To begin with, the free-rider phenom-

---

[3] Much of the argument in this section draws on this earlier article.

[4] There is overwhelming evidence against what Dawes and Thaler (1988) call the
"strong free-rider hypothesis"—that is, that no one will contribute to the collective
good. For example, Marwell and Ames (1981) ran a series of experiments that showed
that, depending on the experimental condition, subjects contributed 40 to 60 percent of
their stake for the public good, with one exception: when graduate students in economics
were the subjects, the rate fell to 20 percent.

enon is not necessarily a serious problem. It is important mainly when it threatens commitment, undermining the solidarity and morale of the challenger and raising questions for active participants about the personal costs they are bearing. But this effect of free riders depends on a number of specific variables.

1. *Nature of the collective action.* Some types of action are severely undermined by free riders while others are barely affected. Consider demonstrations. In June, 1982, an estimated 750,000 people gathered in Central Park in New York City to urge a bilateral freeze on the production, testing, and deployment of nuclear weapons. Public opinion polls at the time showed that a majority of Americans supported this demand. In effect, there were more than a hundred million free riders who never made it to Central Park. No one paid the least attention to the fact that these free riders outnumbered participants by better than 100 to 1. The organizers and the media emphasized the absolute size, not the free-rider ratio, and judged the numbers as impressive.

Contrast this with the free-rider problem for strikers. Workers who cross the picket line are a threat to the success of the strike. If there are enough free riders to keep the company operating profitably, it will be under no pressure to negotiate and the more marginally committed workers will begin trickling back to work. One can tolerate 10 or 20 percent free riders—as long as the percentage is below the threshold of profitable operation—but at some point, too many nonstrikers will destroy the strike.

The free-rider problem is even more extreme for a producer boycott group, such as the Tobacco Night Riders, who attempted to force up prices by selling their product collectively. If the action succeeds, prices go up and increase the temptation for tobacco farmers to pursue their personal interest (that is, to sell their tobacco individually). Every free rider here works directly against the attempt to limit the supply of tobacco in the market and increases the tendency for the marginally committed to defect.

2. *Scarcity of supply.* Olson makes little of an important variable concerning the nature of the collective good being supplied. Some public goods are undiminished by the number of people who enjoy them—for example, safe streets, a pollution-free environment, or a world free of nuclear devastation. But other public goods *are* diminished by use—for example, a wilderness area for hiking or a commons on which to graze sheep.

The free-rider problem is less serious for unlimited goods. Peace movement activists, for example, can readily tolerate billions of people reaping the benefits of a peaceful world, knowing full well that few of the beneficiaries have ever contributed to achieving it. In contrast, activists who spent long hours demonstrating and lobbying to keep a local park from being developed may be bitter toward those who, having refused to join the effort, now monopolize the facilities.

3. *Degree of participant sacrifice.* If participants are asked to support a campaign by making a $10-a-year donation, free riders are quite tolerable. For example, if some people listen to my favorite public radio station without contributing to the annual fund drive, it has little effect on my tendency to contribute in the future. However, when major sacrifices are involved—for example, risking one's life—those who proclaim the importance of the goal but do not share the risks will be resented. Note that "free riding" here is a matter of interpretation. The Vietnam hawk who rode out the war writing press releases for the National Guard is resented as a free rider. However, an opponent of the war who served in the same fashion is not. If people reject the "good" being supplied, one doesn't expect them to contribute—even if they end up receiving it in spite of themselves. Hence, they are discounted and don't undermine the commitment of those who sacrificed to achieve it.

4. *Relationship to past commitments.* Free riders who back out of commitments already made are more damaging than those who never promised to contribute. Expectations about a collective action's success are part of the calculations that participants use in deciding whether to join. When actors indicate their commitments in advance, they provide the basis for each other's expectations. When free riders renege on past commitments, they are guilty of misleading other participants in a way that uncommitted free riders avoid.

In sum, the free-rider phenomenon is not a universal problem for challenging groups, but one that occurs only under special circumstances. Olson's argument (and to some degree, the first edition of *Strategy*) exaggerates its importance for challengers.

If the free-rider problem is exaggerated, so are selective incentives as a basis for participation. Consider first the narrow meaning of positive material incentives—some tangible good or service that an organization provides its members as an inducement to participate. Social movement organizations are actually at a competitive disadvantage in providing selective incentives, compared to businesses and social clubs, for example. The latter are not saddled with the burden of diverting resources for the provision of collective goods; they can offer better deals in the selective incentives market.

A challenger can offer unique selective incentives, but these take their value from the meaning with which the individual participant invests them. The poster, bumper sticker, T-shirt, or other challenger insignia is valuable only because of the movement's worth in the eyes of the beholder. To display them is an expression of shared identity. They appeal to participants as symbols of commitment and loyalty, not as a quid pro quo for participation.

One attempt to rescue the concept of selective incentives is to broaden it beyond tangible goods and services to include a variety of "soft" incentives. If people experience satisfaction, guilt, or shame depending on whether they join a worthwhile collective action or ride free, then it is simple enough to designate satisfaction, guilt, and shame as potent selective incentives. Why not allow moral satisfaction and money to count simply as different types of selective incentives?

To follow this route is to destroy the raison d'être of the selective incentive argument by reducing it to a useless tautology. One begins by assuming that people do not participate in collective action unless they get something of value for participation, but when one finds no specific good or service offered, one postulates some "soft" incentive such as moral satisfaction, alleviation of guilt, or feeling of pride. This redefinition removes the cutting edge from the selective incentive argument. By blurring together diverse incentives (such as a specific material inducement and the satisfaction from participating in a worthwhile cause), the idea that people participate because of selective incentives loses its potency. Immediately, one must ask whether material incentives or some other kind of incentives are involved. Any apparent parsimony in explanation is lost, and the idea of selective incentives becomes so much excess baggage, as the weight of explanation is carried by the subsequent necessary distinctions among types of incentives.

For the concept to be useful at all, it should be limited to the specific goods or services that an organization provides as inducements. If people participate because they feel that some solidarity group with which they identify is threatened or because they feel responsible for contributing their share to achieving some collective good, no useful purpose is served by forcing these motivations into a selective incentive concept with the utilitarian calculation it implies.

What of the evidence in Chapter Five that shows a higher success rate for groups that employed selective incentives? There were nine groups in the sample that made use of selective material inducements, seven of them unions. Some of these unions began as benevolent societies, offering members the promise of a decent burial, and no doubt this was important to many workers. But it is implausible that workers were ready to risk loss of livelihood, severe beatings, and perhaps even death to support the union in bitter strikes, mainly because they wanted that cemetery plot.

With modern challengers, it is equally difficult to find one in which selective incentives were central in explaining why people supported the challengers. In fact, participation in the civil rights or anti-Vietnam war movement involved many material hardships and sacrifices. To be sure, the participants found personal gratification and fulfillment through their activity. But this occurred through their greater sense of self and its investment in a collective identity or through the satisfaction generated by acting on deeply held beliefs and participating in a successful collective effort reflecting them.

It is clear that selective incentives—referring only to material inducements—play a very secondary role if they are relevant at all. They may even be counterproductive: if the constituents adopt a utilitarian attitude toward the challenger, the effects of a mobilizing frame may be lost. A mobilizing frame, as Ryan argues, has three central elements: (a) it defines the root of the problem and its solution collectively rather than individually; (b) it defines the antagonists—"us" and "them"; and (c) it defines an injustice that can be corrected through the challenger's action. In this logic, selective incentives are pretty much beside the point.

This does not deny that self-interests frequently are asserted in complicated and inconvenient ways that social movement theorists have yet to adequately formulate. But the key lies in understanding how people blend the personal and the collective in their own identities. When people bind their fate to the fate of a group, they feel personally threatened when the group is threatened. Solidarity and shared identities blur the distinction between the individual and the collective good. When such processes operate, the logic of collective action is unlikely to be utilitarian.

THE SUCCESS OF THE UNRULY (Chapter Six)

The arguments of this chapter most directly confront pluralist arguments on the permeability of the American political system. Is it true that only those who use the institutionally provided means will be successful while those who resort to the tactics of the streets will be unsuccessful? Is it true that authorities respect the rules of the game and find that when they use illegal and violent means to keep challengers out it backfires? The results of Chapter Six seem to suggest otherwise. Groups that were active and disruptive have fared better than those that were passive when attacked and never used constraints as a means of influence. When authorities used extralegal and violent means to control the challenger, it didn't backfire on them.

The results are subject to easy misinterpretation. The most common oversimplification is that they show that violence works. *Strategy* argues that violence is more a symptom of success than a cause, that it arises out of impatience and hubris rather than desperation. Further, it should be thought of as a property of an interaction, not as a conscious strategy of a challenger. Only one group, the Tobacco Night Riders, employed it in a proactive way; for other active participants in violent interactions, it represented a choice about how to respond to the violence or potential violence of their antagonists.

It is more accurate to interpret the results as "feistiness works" rather than "violence works." Feistiness includes the willingness to break rules and use noninstitutionalized means—to use disruption as a strategy of influence. However, it can't be simply verbal feistiness, that is, the strategy of "speaking loudly and carrying a small stick." This combines provocativeness with vulnerability, allowing antagonists to get away with repressive means of social control such as arrest and violence.

Most of this argument holds for challengers since 1945 but major changes have complicated repressive means of social control and reduced the vulnerability of some types of unruly challengers. The media spotlight—especially television footage and news photos— makes any public encounter between challengers and their antagonists a potentially critical event, which can have enormous consequences if the whole world is watching.

To get a better sense of how unruly protest strategies interact with media coverage and symbolic processes, I will briefly reexamine the civil rights, anti-Vietnam war, and antinuclear power movements. Each of these produced feisty challengers willing to break rules and disrupt their antagonists.

Civil rights challengers, while self-consciously nonviolent, employed a variety of disruptive tactics—economic boycotts, for example.[5] Injunctions against demonstrations were sometimes violated and laws enforcing segregation were repeatedly violated, all in a highly public way. By the criteria used in *Strategy*, challengers such as the Congress on Racial Equality (CORE), the Southern Christian Leadership Conference (SCLC), and the Student Nonviolent Coordinating Committee (SNCC) were active and unruly, however dignified and nonviolent their public demeanor.

Furthermore, the collective action repertoire of the civil rights movement provided great television. The prize-winning PBS documentary *Eyes on the Prize* recalls the dramatic images that helped to define the movement for an audience of millions: black children walking into newly integrated schools through a gauntlet of jeering, name-calling adults; well-dressed marchers walking in dignified procession set upon by police dogs and their club-wielding masters. When the whole world is watching, that which could normally demoralize a movement's supporters might instead mobilize them further. Far from being cowed when Martin Luther King was arrested in Birmingham, civil rights activists were cheered by a phone call from a sympathetic president.

Social control strategies that might work in the dark backfire when the media spotlight shines on them. When civil rights activists were kidnapped and murdered by local law enforcement officials or shot with the tacit support of local authorities, a flood of nosy journalists descended on the heels of the inevitable investigations and legal proceedings. However well overt repression may have worked before 1945, the interaction of challenger strategy and media coverage made it ineffective against the civil rights movement, where it frequently backfired.

The anti-Vietnam war movement, drawing heavily on the civil rights repertoire of collective action, followed a similar strategy.[6]

---

[5] There is a large body of work on the civil rights movement but the books that provide the most insight on the issues addressed in *Strategy* are Schmeidler (1980), McAdam (1982), and Morris (1984).

[6] Again there is a voluminous literature and I will cite only those works that are especially relevant for the issues addressed here: Sale (1973), Gitlin (1980, 1987), Breines (1982), Miller (1987), and Flacks (1988).

Until the last stage of the movement, when the student wing (associated with Students for a Democratic Society—SDS) split into irreconcilable factions, movement tactics rarely went beyond nonviolent, direct action. However, from the beginning the strategy clearly included various disruptive and unruly tactics—occupations of buildings, draft resistance, and violation of march permits, for example.

Building occupations and demonstrations sometimes led to confrontations with the police, but antiwar activists—like civil rights demonstrators—were typically passive recipients rather than perpetrators. The police riot at the Chicago Democratic National Convention in 1968 is the prototype here: demonstrators used verbal taunts and fled from police attacks but did not fight back physically.

From 1969 on, the movement's repudiation of violence began to change when one significant faction began to justify the "trashing" of property, "days of rage," and even bombings against selected targets. In our analysis, the Weathermen faction would be treated as a new challenger, with a more active relationship to violence than earlier anti-Vietnam war groups. But during the major mobilization phase of the movement from 1965 to 1969, antiwar challengers qualify as passive recipients rather than active users in accordance with the violence code used in *Strategy*.

Again, the combination of nonviolence and unruliness interacted with media coverage to limit the effectiveness of overt repression as a means of social control. When Chicago police chased and beat unarmed demonstrators in front of television cameras, many delegates in the convention hall were shocked and outraged—even though the demonstrators were outside the boundaries of the polity. The subsequent conspiracy trial of some of the organizers of the demonstration proved a further social control error. By supplying a continuing media story, it failed to cow the challengers and provided a forum for continued mobilization.[7]

Finally, we turn to the antinuclear power movement for additional insight on unruly challengers who use nonviolent disruption as a tactic. A number of antinuclear challengers occupied the sites of nuclear power plants and, taking their cues from the civil rights movement, were scrupulously nonviolent. For example, the Clamshell Alliance, famous for its actions against the nuclear reactor at

---

[7] The trial did force the diversion of challenger resources and energy to defense which might have been used instead to initiate and enhance further antiwar activity.

Seabrook, New Hampshire, required participants in its site occupation to attend training sessions in nonviolent, direct action, conducted by specialists from the War Resisters League and the American Friends Service Committee.

These training sessions, as described by Barkan (1979), included role-playing of tense confrontations with the police, the press, and nuclear workers. Nonviolent discipline included guidelines banning weapons, alcohol, and drugs, plus prohibitions against destroying property. Through such disciplined nonviolence, the Clam hoped to achieve several immediate tactical objectives. Barkan lists five:

1.   To present a favorable image to the public and elected officials through the news media

2.   To reduce the potential for outbreaks of violence, which could not only lead to physical injury but also discredit the movement and divert attention from the nuclear power issue

3.   To present a contrast to the "violent technology" that the protesters claim nuclear power represents

4.   To deflect actions by possible agents provocateur of the kind that helped undermine the Vietnam peace movement (see discussion of covert action below)

5.   To maintain good relations and develop lines of communication with the police and National Guard

In its most significant action ever at Seabrook in 1977, the Clamshell Alliance largely succeeded in achieving all the above. In the process, over 1,400 protestors occupying the site were arrested and held for over two weeks. "Governor Meldrim Thomson," as Gamson puts it, "blessed the Clam with a major social control error." The demonstrators were not released on their own recognizance, as expected, but were instead charged with criminal trespass and asked to post bail, ranging from $100 to $500. When they refused to do this, they were then held in five national guard armories for twelve days, creating a continuing national story. Each of the three national television networks ran stories on five different days (albeit sometimes merely a brief update).

The coverage barely touched upon the reasons for protesting, but it succeeded in solidifying the emerging status of nuclear power as a "controversial" issue. This is no small achievement since it triggers different media behavior. Once an issue is designated as controversial, journalistic practice calls for balance. Journalists typically meet this vague norm by providing two sides (even though an issue may be many sided). Typically the media offer the official side; then to achieve balance, Tuchman (1974) suggests, reporters search for an "establishment critic [or for a] 'responsible spokesman' whom they have themselves created or promoted to a position of prominence."

Balance is rarely interpreted to include challengers as spokespersons, even when no other alternative is available. Challenger actions can have an important indirect impact but one would need to depart from the methodology used in *Strategy* to be able to see it. By using the social movement organization as the unit of analysis, *Strategy* fails to illuminate the dynamics among a set of challengers in the same broad movement. Challengers sometimes complement and sometimes undercut each other's strategies but one can understand this process only at a more aggregate level of analysis.

This is well illustrated in the nuclear power movement, where the collective action of challengers helped to create conditions for more established critics to gain media prominence. The Clamshell Alliance did not succeed through its action in becoming the media-designated "other side" called for by the balance norm. This honor fell to the Union of Concerned Scientists which presented all the proper cues for media credibility. The actions of the Clam plus other antinuclear demonstrations and site occupations across the country helped to create the conditions for media-initiated contacts. When demonstrators were arrested at Seabrook, phones rang at the Union of Concerned Scientists.

Gamson and Modigliani (1989) describe the ways in which the Seabrook demonstrators were depicted on television and other news media (images of people wearing backpacks and playing frisbee). "Visually, one sees beards and long hair, bandanas, 'no nuke' buttons, people playing guitars and doing needlepoint. Outside the courthouse after the demonstrators were released, we see happy family reunions with many children." The most favored adjective to describe the protesters in newsmagazines and television was "scruffy."

These visual images do not have a fixed meaning, of course. An unsympathetic viewer may see frivolous flower children and environmental extremists who look as if they won't be happy until they turn the White House into a bird sanctuary; a sympathetic one may see loving, caring, earthy people who are socially integrated and concerned about our shared environment. (But it's difficult to make these images accord with the interpretation suggested by the late publisher of the *Manchester Union Leader*, William Loeb, who likened the Clam to "Nazi storm troopers under Hitler.")

In addition to its use as a partial defense against some repressive forms of social control, the media spotlight can be used proactively. The anti-Vietnam war movement pioneered new, media-oriented strategies to ridicule and embarrass its antagonists. Treating politics as a form of theater, Jerry Rubin wore a Revolutionary War uniform to testify before the House Un-American Activities Committee and refused to take the proceedings seriously. The circus atmosphere he helped to create proved the final nail in the committee's coffin. (Shortly after the hearing, the House of Representatives voted it out of existence.) Abbie Hoffman created marvelous visual images of capitalist greed by showering dollar bills from the balcony of the New York Stock Exchange. Guerilla theatre dramatized the tiger cages in which the government of South Vietnam kept its political opponents. These tactics would have had much less meaning or impact in the absence of mass media geared to visual symbolism.

Gitlin (1980) points to the drawbacks and vulnerabilities in such media-oriented strategies. The media, he argues, did much to determine who became leaders by certifying some individuals and ignoring others. Those who were media certified may not have been major leaders, but with their media-created celebrity, they soon found followers where none had existed before.

Journalists follow their own principles in singling out certain individuals for attention. They don't search for those who have the largest group of supporters or have been building the organization in working groups, but instead look for human interest—people who will symbolize the preferred news frame and make good copy. As Gitlin (1980) puts it, "The all-permeating spectacular culture insisted that the movement be identified through its celebrities; naturally, it attracted personalities who enjoyed performance, who knew how to flaunt some symbolic attribute, who spoke quotably."

Covert Action and the Media

Although the media spotlight to a degree protects nonviolent, unruly challengers from overt attack, covert means of repression are a different story. In late March, 1947, President Truman issued Executive Order No. 9835, which established a federal loyalty program and authorized committee investigations into the political beliefs and associations of all federal employees, regardless of the nature of their jobs. In the same year, the attorney general's list of "subversive organizations" was established. These two products of the early Cold War years helped to legitimize the internal security issue in American politics and paved the way for the broader institutionalization of domestic intelligence and covert action that followed (see Yergin).

Mass media coverage of domestic intelligence has tended to focus on a few celebrated cases, so that a reader would have difficulty recognizing the extensive scope of the operations. In one year, 1972, the FBI opened some 65,000 domestic files with an internal or national security classification; a General Accounting Office report for that year estimated 1,265 Bureau agents assigned to political intelligence work.

The CIA was also in on the act. In the National Security Act of 1947, its charter had barred it from "internal security functions" and for 20 years this was generally observed. But dramatic change came in 1967, when under prodding from President Johnson "to uncover foreign influence behind domestic unrest," the CIA launched a full-fledged domestic intelligence mission under the code name Operation CHAOS (Donner). In the next six years, Operation CHAOS compiled some 10,000 files on individuals and over 100 files on domestic challengers. By the fall of 1968, more than 25 CIA agents were assigned to monitor antiwar activity in New York City alone.

Monitoring, of course, is not the same as disruptive covert action, but there has been plenty of the latter. In data presented to the U.S. Senate Committee (the Church Committee) investigating domestic intelligence abuses, the FBI acknowledged 715 approved actions "designed to cause disruption within a group or between two groups" (Donner). But, as Donner points out, this excludes many disruptive actions that were undertaken without requests for approval from the central office.

Targets of domestic intelligence included a broad range of challengers from different movements. Civil rights groups and black leaders were an early and frequent target. As early as 1941, the FBI began its surveillance of the NAACP. By 1963, Martin Luther King and the SCLC had become targets. After the civil rights March on Washington, Bureau intelligence chief William Sullivan wrote a memo to Director J. Edgar Hoover about King, noting that "we must mark him now, if we have not done so before, as the most dangerous Negro of the future in this Nation from the stand-point of Communism, the Negro, and national security" (Donner). Not long after, virtually every major civil rights group and black leader became a target including Ralph Abernathy, Jesse Jackson, Andrew Young, Floyd McKissick, Roy Wilkins, and Bayard Rustin.

The anti-Vietnam war movement and New Left groups became a frequent target, and the intelligence operation spilled over to include a broad penumbra of related groups. At one point, in the late sixties, the FBI decided to open an investigative file on every individual who lived in a commune. When a coalition of environ-mental groups launched Earth Day in 1970, the FBI was there in force to monitor, among other things, the keynote speech by Sen-ator Edmund Muskie. The women's movement became the target of a surveillance program from 1969 to 1973. The FBI justified the targeting of these nonviolent groups on the grounds that they lent aid and comfort to disruptive allies (Donner).

The most sophisticated use of covert action against challengers involves the exploitation of naturally occurring internal cleavages and power struggles. The FBI's COINTELPROs (short for coun-terintelligence programs) were especially resourceful and imagi-native. As Donner summarizes them, they included:

> anonymous or fictitious letters attacking an ally, a membership sec-tor, or a leader through false, defamatory, or threatening informa-tion; forging signatures, letterheads, membership cards, press credentials, or other items of identification for the purpose of disrup-tion; instructing informers to spread false rumors, or promote fac-tionalism or mistrust, and creating bogus organizations ("notionals") to attack or disrupt a bona fide group. Another script, "putting a snitch jacket" on an individual (raising the charge of in-former), was designed to eliminate or discredit a subject and to disrupt his [or her] organization.

Exacerbating racial tensions and the disruption of white-black coalitions was a major priority of these efforts. Donner relates one successful effort, described to him by former FBI agent Robert Wall. To disrupt a 1969 antiwar rally, the FBI "forged a letter in the name of the Black United Front, demanding that the planners of the rally pay a $20,000 'security bond' to the group. The letter was approved by the Bureau's counterintelligence desk and signed with the forged signature of a leader of the group."

Many of the FBI tactics used in COINTELPRO campaigns were explicitly media oriented. In March, 1965, FBI offices were requested to compile lists of reliable reporters who could be called on for COINTELPRO work. In one instance, the Miami FBI boasted about an FBI-instigated television program run by a local station, saying that "each and every film segment produced by the station was submitted for our scrutiny to insure that we were satisfied and that nothing was included which could in any way be contrary to our interests" (Donner).

Repeatedly, COINTELPROs made use of sympathetic media contacts to leak information, some of it fabricated, to disrupt and discredit civil rights and antiwar challengers. These covert means of control drew no media attention at the time and most of them didn't become public until after the end of the challenge—too late to backfire.

In addition to the media's occasional direct cooperation, media practices dovetailed nicely with the purposes of covert action. In covering social movement organizations, internal splits and the personalizing of conflicts are common themes. However, personalizing the conflicts of an organization makes them more difficult to resolve. In this case, the media are a natural ally of disruptive action, without necessarily being aware of it or consciously attempting to support it. An embarrassing and discrediting piece of information on a major movement leader is good copy; so is a walkout or a rancorous fight between two factions.

Covert action included the widespread use of agents provocateur, as documented by Marx (1974): activists whose "allegiance lies not with the movement, but whose role instead is to create internal dissension, gain information, and/or provoke a group to illegal activity that would then justify official action and possibly turn public sentiment against them." He reviewed 34 cases from the 1960s and early 1970s, drawing upon interviews, media sources, police literature, court records, and congressional investigations.

In antiwar demonstrations at the University of Alabama, for example, a police agent reportedly urged violence, set fire to at least one campus building, and threw firebombs and other objects at police. The most famous of these agents, "Tommy the Traveler," posed as an SDS organizer and offered bombs and guns to students at various New York campuses. A police agent at Northeastern Illinois State College led a sit-in and threw the school's president off the stage. He was the only member of the Weatherman faction represented on his campus and later acknowledged, as a prosecution witness during the Chicago conspiracy trial, that he proposed plans for sabotaging public facilities and military vehicles.

It is not easy to evaluate the effectiveness of these disruption programs, but Chomsky (in Blackstock, 1976) concludes that "surely, it was not slight." They certainly stimulated widespread paranoia in the groups that were subjected to them. Media publicity about fabricated or real internal problems made life even more perilous for challengers.

In sum, the civil rights, anti-Vietnam war, and antinuclear power movements all generated major challenging groups who used nonviolent but unruly means of collective action to achieve their goals. All experienced arrests; civil rights and anti-Vietnam war challengers experienced extralegal violence as well and were also subjected to illegal covert action by authorities, aimed at disrupting and demobilizing their challenge.[8]

Chapter Six in *Strategy* seems to argue for the success of both sides in such conflicts—for unruly challengers and repressive authorities. A full analysis of how successful different challengers were in the three complex movements discussed here is well beyond the scope of this chapter. But leaving this question unresolved, these three broad examples suggest some tentative lessons or hypotheses regarding unruly challengers and repressive authorities.

1. *The spotlight effect.* A media presence complicates authorities' efforts to control challengers, greatly increasing the risks of using overt repression. The absence of challenger violence alone is not an overwhelming obstacle, since it's not very difficult to frame any disruptive or illegal action as a provocation. Furthermore, the more feisty the challenger—the more its participants taunt authorities and resist their efforts at control—the easier it is to frame

---

[8] To the best of current knowledge, the antinuclear movement has never been the target of covert action by authorities. However, my study of a broad range of challengers does not make me confident that this won't change in the future. Lest covert action against domestic challenge be regarded as a vestige of the past, it is worth noting that as of January, 1988, there had been approximately 85 break-ins at offices of challengers opposed to administration policies in Central America. Computers and other valuables were typically left untouched but numerous information files were taken or copied. The culprits are unknown at this point but it would require an unshakable pluralist faith to believe that no government intelligence agency is directly or indirectly involved.

challengers as "asking for it." With the help of cooperating journalists, the most provocative participants among the challengers draw the media spotlight, which helps to frame the whole group for the general audience—regardless of whether these participants are typical or isolated.

Movement activists make a distinction between the absence of violence and nonviolence as an active tradition with a philosophy and practice of collective action.[9] Challengers who link their actions to the nonviolent tradition get an extra measure of protection from the media spotlight. If a group publicly identifies itself with this tradition—and its demeanor and words reflect such central principles as respect for one's adversaries—any overt attack will seem unprovoked to many in the media audience. Attacks on the group will draw the spotlight, thereby promoting divisions among authorities between the more and less fastidious. Under such conditions, overt repression of such challengers becomes an especially risky tactic.

Covert action against challengers is, of course, a different story. In the absence of a media spotlight, authorities can safely undertake actions that would cause a public scandal if acknowledged and publicized. The fear that such actions may eventually become public can act as some deterrent, but delayed exposure may be too late to do the challenger any good.

2. *The twin pitfalls of novelty and ritual.* The media's desire for good action footage tempts challengers to provide it. The unpredictable and spontaneous make better television especially when the tension of confrontation and possible violence is present. To keep media attention, challengers are tempted to ever-more extravagant and dramatic actions—regardless of their contribution to the challenger's goals.

The nonviolent tradition offers some protection from this pitfall but can easily run afoul of the other horn—the ritualization of collective action. Feistiness and disruption may disappear altogether in actions that court arrest but could hardly be called unruly. For example, some forms of civil disobedience become scripted events in which demonstrators, police, and journalists play well-rehearsed and thoroughly predictable roles. Far from disrupting the system, the challenger-authority interaction

---

[9] I am indebted to David Croteau for pointing out the usefulness and implications of this distinction for the issues discussed in this section.

is absorbed into its routine operation. Lacking the criteria of newsworthiness, the action is back-page, local news at best, essentially invisible to any larger audience whom the challengers hoped to move by example.

The most successful challengers seemed to have found the narrow path between these two pitfalls. They remained newsworthy not because of the novelty of their action but because they successfully mobilized a constituency and thereby became a "player" in the eyes of journalists. And they refused to follow a script that absorbed them into the routine functioning of the social control system. They kept their eyes on the prize, not on the camera.

3. *The reframing effect.* The unruliness of modern challengers works less by directly inconveniencing or disrupting authorities and more through its effect on reframing media discourse. The effects are typically indirect and dependent on the challenger's role in a broader movement. Unruliness in collective action can help to reorient media practice in ways that broaden the scope of conflict and alter the issue discourse. By increasing the opportunity for some challengers to reframe the issue, nonviolent, unruly tactics can increase the mobilization potential for others in the same movement.

COMBAT READINESS (Chapter Seven)

Strategy argues that challenging groups, inevitably engaged in conflict with an organized antagonist, are more successful when they organize themselves for political combat. Certain predictable problems—such as internal division and the tendency for members to drift away to other pursuits—must be dealt with in some fashion. But which precise organizational forms best solve these problems remains an open and complex question.

Note that within such broad challenges as the civil rights and antiwar movements, there were many different social movement organizations (SMOs). The kind of organizational variables considered in *Strategy*—bureaucracy, centralization, and factionalism, for example—cannot be measured at the movement level. The civil rights movement, for example, spanned a range of SMOs from well-established prior organizations (NAACP and Urban League) through challengers as different as SCLC, CORE, SNCC, the Black Panthers, and various black nationalist groups.

Challengers such as SCLC and SNCC were dramatically different from each other on a variety of organizational characteristics.
For instance, SCLC was centralized through the personal leadership of Martin Luther King, Jr., whereas SNCC and CORE were
highly decentralized and segmented, with a great deal of local
autonomy. Hence, it is no simple matter, short of a detailed and
systematic study of postwar challengers, to say whether the experience of these groups confirms or disproves any specific
hypothesis.

It is possible, however, to analyze theoretically how the rise of
television and the national security state are likely to interact with
these organizational variables. It turns out, I will argue, that the
media and covert action systems reinforce each other to make
organizational life more difficult and complicated for challengers.

Centralization

Centralization, *Strategy* argues, facilitates the ability of an organization to respond quickly and collectively in a turbulent and
frequently hostile environment. The theoretical argument would
have been sharper if it had contrasted the familiar bureaucratic
and centralized structure with another type that Gerlach and Hine
(1970) argue is typical of social movement organizations. They
characterize the alternative as a "segmented, usually polycephalous, cellular organization composed of units reticulated by various
personal, structural, and ideological ties."

There is a lot of jargon here but it is worth wading through for
the insight. By segmented, they mean localized groups or cells
that have a large degree of independence and are not subordinated
to a power center. By polycephalous, they mean having many
heads or centers of leadership rather than a single one. By reticulated, they mean "weblike, resembling a network—with crossing
and intercrossing lines" (Gerlach and Hine). The cells are linked
not through their relationship to a common central point but
through intersecting sets of personal relationships and other group
linkages. They argue that this organizational form is characteristic
of social movement organizations but there is, in fact, great variation. The question remains whether, as they argue, it is more
adaptive than centralized organizations in certain ways.

The problem of being able to respond collectively and rapidly
still must be faced by modern challengers although it has taken on

a new form. With the enlarged media role, the issue is frequently more one of timely comment, than of timely action. Challengers on any issue are likely to encounter what Chilton (1988) calls "critical discourse moments." Typically, these are events that create some perturbation and bring heightened media attention. From the standpoint of challengers and their antagonists, these moments provide dangers and opportunities in a framing contest—a battle over whose interpretation will prevail.

These opportunities may sometimes grow out of collective actions initiated by a challenger, as in the Clamshell Alliance's occupation of the Seabrook nuclear plant site. Or they may be created by unplanned events, beyond the control of the combatants, as in the nuclear accidents at Three Mile Island and Chernobyl. In either case, if a challenger is going to have an impact on interpreting the meaning of the event, it must be able to provide spokespersons who can respond in a timely way.

Furthermore, skill is required if a challenger is going to comment in ways that both reflect the organization's frame and are likely to be picked up and quoted by journalists. Ryan discusses the special problems that challengers face in this contest: collective action may be necessary simply to create the opportunity to comment. But once the opportunity has been forged, Ryan shows how an understanding of media conventions such as pegs, leads, and sound bites can increase the chances of conveying the message one wants. The perils involved are well illustrated by the story she tells of a delegation of dignitaries and celebrities, sympathetic to the nonintervention movement, who returned from a trip to Nicaragua at a critical discourse moment in the early 1980s. The press met them at the airport:

> The first two delegates approached by the press were established academic authorities on Central America. Each gave a complex answer: multiple determinants, historical perspectives from the 16th century onward. The cameras shut off. A stockbroker active in politics descended and reeled off a 15-second, one-line reaction to the tour. The stockbroker—not the experts—was invited to be on radio and TV talk shows for the next two weeks (Ryan).

Clearly one can learn to be a good spokesperson but it takes time and experience to acquire proficiency. There are definite advantages for a challenger to have experienced professionals in this role.

The need to respond both rapidly and skillfully pushes a challenger toward centralization. Consider the problems faced by the kind of decentralized and segmented organization described by Gerlach and Hine. In the fall of 1965, Students for a Democratic Society (SDS) was in the media spotlight and under attack. Evans and Novak, widely syndicated columnists, were accusing SDS of organizing a national "draft dodging" campaign to "sabotage the war effort."[10] The U.S. attorney general announced a national investigation of groups behind the antidraft movement; the Illinois attorney general claimed that SDS was guilty of "treasonous activity" and announced that his staff had already begun a full investigation.

The SDS national office, although organizationally weak, was led by able and sophisticated movement veterans who felt that something needed to be done "to take the heat off" (as National Secretary Paul Booth told Sale, 1973). Booth and SDS president Carl Oglesby flew to Washington and rented the grand ballroom of the National Press Club to hold a press conference. With the help of a number of other experienced movement veterans, Booth crafted a statement that he read to reporters. Gitlin (1980) quotes the crucial passage:

> Let us see what happens if service to democracy is made grounds for exemption from the military draft. I predict that almost every member of my generation would choose to build, not to burn; to teach, not to torture; to help, not to kill.

Booth's statement received widespread coverage and apparently achieved its immediate tactical purpose in reframing the discourse to center on the immorality of the war rather than on draft resistance. Widely distributed, it proved helpful in recruiting on a number of campuses. In addition, it temporarily reduced the pressure on SDS while bolstering its allies and supporters.

However, Booth's apparent success produced mostly harsh internal criticism from SDS chapters around the country. It was not only the content that dismayed many locals but, as Gitlin (1980)

---

[10] The columnists must have had an informer in SDS, since they culled some speculative proposals from an internal newsletter. All these proposals had been explicitly rejected at the SDS National Council meeting, well before the columns appeared, but Evans and Novak presented them as having been adopted.

puts it, "There was much feeling that Booth had usurped the right to make any policy statement at all." The national secretary was not entitled to set policy in SDS. One strong supporter of decentralization suggested that reporters "should have simply been referred to local chapters which would tell them what was going on in any particular area" (Sale).

However, failing to provide its own spokespersons, a challenger allows the media to designate them. By granting celebrity, the media create a new class of leaders who are attached to participants *only* through their media image and are unaccountable to rank-and-file activists. Gitlin argues that these media-designated leaders are precisely the ones who are likely to advocate extravagant and dramatic actions that generate good media copy. Strategies carefully worked out in planning meetings of movement activists may be overridden by actions of such unaccountable, media-generated leaders.

If centralization is an asset in dealing with the media, its value is much less clear in dealing with covert action. When centralization is based on personal leadership, the leader becomes a logical target of harassment; the media will be especially receptive to leaks and disinformation. If the harassment campaign works as intended, the challenger will be seriously disrupted by the neutralization and distraction of its leader. Centralization based on a strong national committee or office seems less vulnerable in this regard but far from immune to the exploitation of factional differences.

Decentralized, segmented challengers may even have an advantage here, as Gerlach and Hine suggest. If one infiltrates a local chapter and succeeds in disrupting it, the organization as a whole is not devastated. Even disruption of a central office matters less when collective action depends largely on local initiative rather than a national center. Furthermore, organizations that foster a climate of openness and trust may make it harder for agents provocateur to succeed. False allegations are more readily believed and spread when internal decision making is centralized and secretive, with little accountability to the rank and file. Organizations without secrets provide poor hiding places for secret agents.

In sum, the demands of (1) dealing effectively with the media to influence political discourse and (2) withstanding the greatly increased covert action potential of the state have different implications for centralization. For dealing with the media, centralization offers definite advantages but it is no particular help and possibly a hindrance in surviving covert disruption efforts.

Bureaucracy

Bureaucracy, *Strategy* argues, is helpful in maintaining member commitments that can be quickly activated when the challenger wishes to engage in collective action—that is, it helps to solve the problem of pattern maintenance. However, the evidence for groups before 1945 suggests that bureaucracy is mainly related to gaining acceptance and adds little or nothing to gaining new advantages. More specifically, if we look only at groups with nondisplacement goals, then nonbureaucratic, centralized groups do as well as or better than those that are both bureaucratic and centralized (see Appendix A, p. 260). One might conclude from this that, while pattern maintenance may be theoretically important, it is not clear that bureaucracy is really the best or only way to achieve it.

In discussing these issues, *Strategy* fails to give sufficient attention to the importance of recruitment networks and interpersonal ties to activate and maintain commitment. Explanations of movement participation that emphasize individual motivation alone are now recognized as inadequate and incomplete. As Snow, Zurcher, and Eckland-Olson (1980) put it, "However reasonable the underlying assumption that some people are more (psychologically) susceptible than others to movement participation, that view deflects attention from the fact that recruitment cannot occur without prior contact with a recruitment agent."

Successful mobilization depends on recruitment networks in which friends and acquaintances from other organizations and social contexts are drawn into collective action by those already involved.[11] These ties are important not only in drawing people in but in keeping them from drifting off as well. Hence, pattern maintenance depends much more on having a close link to other members than on having a clearly designed organizational task and role (a bureaucracy).

---

[11] For evidence and elaboration of this point in a variety of movement settings, see Gerlach and Hine (1970), Bolton (1972), Orum (1974), Wilson and Orum (1976), Snow, Zurcher, and Eckland-Olson (1980), Klandermans (1986), McAdam (1986), and Klandermans and Oegma (1987).

Exactly what types of social linkages among participants are most useful for different organizational purposes remains an open question. A reasonable hypothesis is that, as Granovetter's (1973) work suggests, a wide circle of "weak ties" is especially important for allowing a challenger to broaden its constituency in significant ways. But for the maintenance of commitment, especially for what McAdam (1986) calls "high-risk activism," strong, primary group ties are critical.

McAdam analyzed project applications from northern college students who volunteered for the 1964 Mississippi Freedom Summer campaign. The campaign brought hundreds of people to Mississippi for all or part of the summer to help staff freedom schools, register black voters, and dramatize the continued denial of civil rights throughout the region. Participants knew they were volunteering for an emotionally harrowing and dangerous experience.

The first contingent arrived in early June and within the first week, three project members—James Chaney, Andrew Goodman, and Mickey Schwerner—were kidnapped and killed by a group that included several Mississippi law enforcement officials. This set the tone for a summer in which the remaining volunteers were subjected to beatings, bombings, arrests, and other forms of harassment.

Of the approximately 1,000 applicants approved for participation in the project, one-quarter did not follow through. McAdam compared the participants and the drop-outs on a variety of measures. Although the two groups showed no significant differences on various attitudinal and ideological measures of support for the project, "participants consistently score higher than withdrawals on both organizational and interpersonal items measuring integration into activist networks" (McAdam, 1986). Furthermore, strong ties rather than weak ones make the most difference. "Having a close friend apply," McAdam concludes, "mitigates against the individual's later withdrawal from the project."

A number of contemporary challengers have experimented with alternative organizational forms that meet the pattern maintenance problem in a nonbureaucratic way. The movements against the Vietnam war, nuclear power, and intervention in Central America all spawned challengers that made use of "affinity groups." This organizational device, in effect, recognizes and formalizes the Gerlach and Hine insight that "one of the most important facts about recruitment to a movement is that individuals are not recruited to a *movement* but to a cell within the reticulate structure of the movement."

Ideally, an affinity group, which is small (perhaps ten to twenty people), takes responsibility for activating its own members and participates as a unit in collective action. In addition to providing members with emotional support, these groups are typically expected to provide for many of their members' personal needs for transportation, food, and shelter.

Affinity groups may, in some cases, employ an internal division of labor. The Pledge of Resistance, a challenger in the Central American antiintervention movement, sometimes used site occupations as a tactic. Members of its affinity groups would decide in advance which ones would risk arrest and jail and which ones would act as partners for those detained, helping them to meet family and work obligations disrupted by their arrest. When affinity groups are employed in training sessions in nonviolence, as in the case of the Clamshell Alliance described above, they can be better prepared for what follows by honing their teamwork in lifelike rehearsals.

Whatever their virtues for integrating members and maintaining commitment, affinity groups create major organizational problems when they also serve as centers for decision making. Barkan describes some of the problems that the Clam experienced with such groups. For example, when the Seabrook occupiers were unexpectedly allowed into the plant's parking lot, the affinity groups' decision-making processes broke down. Not surprisingly, different groups came to different decisions about what to do next. An informal norm for deciding by consensus rather than majority vote further complicated their ability to make rapid decisions.

Nor was the Clam's coordinating committee, consisting of affinity-group representatives, given the ability to act for the challenger. A decentralized decision-making structure required returning to the affinity groups for consent. When decisions were made by the coordinating committee under pressure of time, members questioned their legitimacy and charged that the Clam was "controlled by a few 'heavyweights' " (Barkan).

The affinity-group structure also complicated the Clam's ability to control its media image. Affinity groups draw as much as possible on prior social networks and shared identities among members. Not surprisingly, some of these groups actively assert their outside identities while participating in an action. Barkan describes how a lesbian, feminist affinity group at Seabrook dressed themselves in lavender and publicly proclaimed their identity, prompting local organizers to complain that this behavior impeded the Clam's ability to enlist the participation of local New Hampshire residents. Whether or not this complaint was justified, the affinity-group structure necessarily surrenders a degree of control over the challenger's public image.

Affinity groups, then, help with some organizational problems but exacerbate others. There are good theoretical grounds for arguing that this structure will be more effective than bureaucracy in achieving pattern maintenance since it uses naturally occurring social relationships and meets a variety of organizational and individual needs for emotional support, integration, sharing of sacrifice, and expression of shared identities. However, unless it is combined with some degree of centralization, it can create severe problems for facility in collective action. Affinity groups in a challenger that has at the same time a strong center for action initiatives and rapid response seems a rare or nonexistent phenomenon. Such a combination offers challengers the best of both worlds.

THE HISTORICAL CONTEXT OF CHALLENGES
(Chapter Eight)

A societal crisis will benefit a challenger, *Strategy* argues, when the challenge has been well established prior to the crisis. The mechanism is third-party pressure on the challenger and antagonists to negotiate, compromise their differences, and normalize their relationship. For the antagonist, at the minimum this implies the acceptance of the challenger.

To apply this argument to groups since 1945, the mushy concept of "crisis" needs further specification. *Strategy* used World War I and II and the Great Depression of the 1930s to define crisis situations—events that neither challengers nor their antagonists controlled. Since 1945 the United States has not been involved in major wars or depressions, although it fought long wars in Korea and Vietnam and has experienced a number of economic recessions. For political reasons, authorities did not treat either the Korean or Vietnam war as system-wide crises requiring emergency war measures. However, the United States has suffered innumerable crises (to use the term loosely) since World War II—an energy crisis, an urban crisis, an education crisis, a fiscal crisis, a moral crisis, a missile crisis, a drug crisis, and so on. By one reckoning, we live in an age of perpetual and continual crises.

To be useful as an explanation, the term crisis requires a tight definition. I will limit it here to system-wide events beyond the control of both challenger and antagonist that require the reserve capacity of the polity to deal with them on a temporary, emergency basis. In these terms, a crisis is an externally generated condition that leaves insufficient slack resources readily available for social control purposes. Urban riots and the unruly actions of anti-Vietnam war resisters that threaten stability do not qualify as crises under this definition because they are not externally generated. To argue that such "crises" contribute to challenger success is circular if the challenger has contributed significantly to the crisis condition.

By this tight definition of crisis, challengers since 1945 have yet to experience a period in which the mechanism by which crises enhance success is brought fully into play. While there have been no high-level crises during these years, it can be argued that the United States has experienced low-level crises. The Cold War (rather than a hot one), for instance, is a low-level crisis. But rather than creating less slack for social control, low-level crises seem to create more. Therefore, they are ideal incubators for the growth of covert action against challengers.

However, if a major crisis should occur—for example, a system-wide natural disaster—the enlarged media role since 1945 should enhance the effect observed for earlier challengers. The media spotlight increases the probability that third parties will intervene and pressure antagonists to make peace with their challenger during the state of emergency—as well as pressure potential new challengers to hold their peace for the duration.[12]

CONCLUSION

What do the changes in American society and the experience of challengers since 1945 tell us about the permeability of the political system and the pluralist interpretation of American politics?

---

[12] For additional discussion of the role of crises, see the exchange between Goldstone and Gamson in Appendix A, especially pp. 242–46 and 263–64.

Issues of goal articulation, the role of self-interest in motivating participation, and the most effective form of challenger organization have little direct bearing on this question. They may help us to understand the careers of challengers but they do not address the central issues between pluralists and their critics.

The heart of the permeability issue concerns the means of influence that are used successfully by challengers and the means of social control that are used successfully by their antagonists. The pluralist interpretation seems inadequate on both these questions. There have been a number of nonviolent but unruly challengers since 1945—the kind that refused to move to the back of the bus or from the segregated lunch counter, that boycotted businesses, marched without permits or in defiance of court injunctions, burned draft cards, and occupied buildings or other sites. We don't know if these unruly challengers really had a higher success rate than those who stuck to election campaigns, law suits, and lobbying, but the spread of such unruly tactics from one movement to another suggests that challengers, at least, were convinced of their usefulness.

In any event, it is clear that television adds to the effectiveness of such tactics. Visually they are much more interesting than their quieter alternatives. Furthermore, the media provide an opportunity for the use of a new constraint—the disruption and discrediting of antagonists through embarrassing media publicity. In sum, an enlarged media role appears to enhance high-profile, nonviolent forms of collective action.

As for the social control strategies of authorities, the frequent use of sophisticated covert action against a variety of nonviolent and even law-abiding challengers is itself an argument against pluralism. Authorities who *overtly* violate the pluralist rules of social control by using illegal and violent means to keep out challengers sometimes find that such strategies backfire, as pluralist theory suggests. But covert repression has been widely used against modern, nonviolent challengers, remaining covert during the period of challenge; there is no evidence that it backfired while the challenge was still active.

If authorities succeed in disrupting challengers by means that if revealed would create a public scandal, this is no well-functioning pluralist democracy. Rather, it is a members-only system with formidable ways of keeping the door shut. That some challengers have the pluck and perseverence to gain entry in spite of such obstacles is sorry evidence for permeability. Hence, pluralist arguments on the openness and permeability of the American political system continue to seem overly sanguine and misleading.

At this basic level, the experiences of challenging groups since 1945 do not seem greatly different from their historical predecessors. The moral for challengers remains the same: be ready to use disruptive, extrainstitutional means of influence since you may well need them to succeed, but don't be surprised if you become the target of parallel means of social control.

REFERENCES

Barkan, Steven E. "Strategic, Tactical, and Organizational Dilemmas of the Protest Movement against Nuclear Power." *Social Problems*, 1979, 27: 19–37.

Blackstock, Nelson. *COINTELPRO: The FBI's Secret War on Political Freedom*. New York: Vintage Books, 1976.

Bolton, Charles D. "Alienation and Action: A Study of Peace Group Members." *American Journal of Sociology*, 1972, 78: 537–61.

Breines, Wini. *Community and Organization in the New Left*. New York: Praeger, 1982.

Chilton, Paul. "Critical Discourse Moments and Critical Discourse Analysis." Working Paper #7, Institute on Global Conflict and Cooperation. San Diego: University of California, 1988.

Dawes, Robyn M., and Thaler, Richard H. "Anomalies: Cooperation." *Journal of Economic Perspectives*, 1988, 2: 187–97.

Donner, Frank J. *The Age of Surveillance*. New York: Knopf, 1980.

Fireman, Bruce, and Gamson, William A. "Utilitarian Logic in the Resource Mobilization Perspective." In Mayer N. Zald and John D. McCarthy, eds. *The Dynamics of Social Movements*. Cambridge, Mass.: Winthrop, 1979.

Flacks, Richard W. *Making History*. New York: Columbia University Press, 1988.

Gamson, William A. "Political Discourse and Collective Action." In Bert Klandermans, Hanspeter Kriesi, and Sidney Tarrow, eds. *From Structure to Action*. Greenwich, Conn.: JAI Press, 1988.

Gamson, William A., and Modigliani, Andre. "Media Discourse and Public Opinion on Nuclear Power: A Constructionist Approach." *American Journal of Sociology*, 1989, 95: 1–37.

Gerlach, Luther P., and Hine, Virginia H. *People, Power, and Change*. Indianapolis: Bobbs-Merrill, 1970.

Gitlin, Todd. *The Whole World Is Watching*. Berkeley: University of California Press, 1980.

_____. *The Sixties*. New York: Bantam, 1987.

Glasgow University Media Group. *Bad News*. London: Routledge and Kegan Paul, 1976.

Granovetter, Mark. "The Strength of Weak Ties." *American Journal of Sociology*, 1973, 78: 1360–80.

Klandermans, Bert. "Social Psychological Expansions of Resource Mobilization Theory." *American Sociological Review*, October 1984, 49: 583–600.

_____. "New Social Movements and Resource Mobilization: The European and the American Approach." *Journal of Mass Emergencies and Disasters: Special Issue on Collective Behavior and Social Movements in Comparative Perspective*, 1986.

Klandermans, Bert; Kriesi, Hanspeter; and Tarrow, Sidney, eds. *From Structure to Action*. Greenwich, Conn.: JAI Press, 1988.

Klandermans, Bert, and Oegema, Dirk. "Potentials, Networks, Motivations and Barriers: Steps towards Participation in Social Movements." *American Sociological Review*, 1987, 52: 519–31.

Marwell, Gerald, and Ames, Ruth. "Economists Ride Free, Does Anyone Else?" *Journal of Public Economics*, 1981, 15: 295–310.

Marx, Gary T. "Thoughts on a Neglected Category of Social Movement Participant: The Agent Provocateur and the Informant." *American Journal of Sociology*, 1974, 80: 402–42.

_____. *Undercover: Police Surveillance in America*. Berkeley: University of California Press, 1988.

McAdam, Doug. *Political Process and the Development of Black Insurgency*. Chicago: University of Chicago Press, 1982.

_____. "Recruitment to High-Risk Activism: The Case of Freedom Summer." *American Journal of Sociology*, July 1986, 92: 64–90.

McCarthy, John D., and Zald, Mayer N. "Resource Mobilization and Social Movements." *American Journal of Sociology*, May 1977, 82: 1212–41.

Melucci, Alberto. "The New Social Movements: A Theoretical Approach." *Social Science Information*, 1980, 19: 199–226.

_____. "The Symbolic Challenge of Contemporary Movements." *Social Research*, 1985, 52: 789–816.

Miller, James. *"Democracy Is in the Streets": From Port Huron to the Siege of Chicago.* New York: Simon & Schuster, 1987.

Molotch, Harvey. "Media and Movements." In Mayer N. Zald and John D. McCarthy, eds. *The Dynamics of Social Movements.* Cambridge, Mass.: Winthrop, 1979.

Morris, Aldon D. *The Origins of the Civil Rights Movement.* New York: The Free Press, 1984.

Oliver, Pamela. "If You Don't Do It, Nobody Else Will: Active and Token Contributions to Local Collective Action." *American Sociological Review,* 1984, 49: 601–10.

Olson, Mancur, Jr. *The Logic of Collective Action.* Cambridge, Mass.: Harvard University Press, 1965.

Orum, Anthony M. "On Participation in Political Protest Movements." *Journal of Applied Behavioral Science,* 1974, 10: 181–207.

Ryan, Charlotte. *Media Strategies for Organizers.* Boston: The South End Press, 1990.

Sale, Kirkpatrick. *SDS.* New York: Random House, 1973.

Schmeidler, Emilie. "Shaping Ideas and Actions: CORE, SCLC, and SNCC in the Struggle for Equality, 1960–66." Ann Arbor, Mich.: University Microfilms International, 1980.

Snow, David A., and Benford, Robert D. "Ideology, Frame Resonance, and Participant Mobilization." In Bert Klandermans, Hanspeter Kriesi, and Sidney Tarrow, eds. *From Structure to Action.* Greenwich, Conn.: JAI Press, 1988.

Snow, David A.; Rochford, E. Burke, Jr.; Worden, Steven K.; and Benford, Robert D. "Frame Alignment and Mobilization." *American Sociological Review,* 1986, 51: 464–81.

Snow, David A; Zurcher, Louis A., Jr.; and Eckland-Olson, Sheldon. "Social Networks and Social Movements: A Microstructural Approach to Differential Recruitment." *American Sociological Review,* 1980, 45: 787–801.

Tilly, Charles. *From Mobilization to Revolution.* Reading, Mass.: Addison-Wesley, 1978.

Tuchman, Gaye. *The TV Establishment.* Englewood Cliffs, N. J.: Prentice-Hall, 1974.

Wilson, K., and Orum, Anthony M. "Mobilizing People for Collective Political Action." *Journal of Political and Military Sociology,* 1976, 4: 187–202.

Yergin, Daniel. *Shattered Peace: The Origins of the Cold War and the National Security State.* Boston: Houghton Mifflin, 1977.

appendix a

Further Analysis and Disputation

The original edition of *Strategy* included the complete data set on 53 challenging groups (see Appendix E in this book). In effect, this extended an invitation to other scholars to have a go at analyzing these cases in other ways to see whether they would arrive at the same conclusions. Enough people accepted the invitation to spawn what Steedly and Foley (1980) refer to as a "growth industry." This appendix gathers together these additional analyses and the scholarly exchanges around them.

Two of the articles (Steedly and Foley, 1979; Mirowsky and Ross, 1981) reanalyze the variables in *Strategy* using a variety of multivariate techniques including cluster analysis, multiple regression, and discriminant function analysis. Goldstone (1980) substantially recoded the measures used in *Strategy* and his analysis disputes many of the arguments and conclusions. My response to Goldstone's critique is included, as well as further commentary by Goldstone and Steedly and Foley. These exchanges go beyond the substantive arguments in *Strategy* to show contrasting approaches to general issues of sociological theory, methods, and practice.

The Success of Protest Groups: Multivariate Analyses

HOMER R. STEEDLY AND JOHN W. FOLEY

University of South Carolina

This paper reviews earlier research and presents new analytical findings regarding the outcomes of social movements. Using the resource mobilization/ management approach, empirical propositions that seek to explain protest group success or failure are tested. Based upon data gathered from a sample of 53 US protest groups, the causal models explained the majority of the variance in degree of success between these groups. Our findings indicate that protest groups which threaten to replace or destroy established groups are usually unsuccessful, and those having many strong alliances tend to be more successful than groups fighting alone. The use of violence does not greatly aid the prediction of group outcome because of the unpredictable, ambivalent reaction to violence by established groups.

Both scholars of collective behavior[1] and leaders of social movements have had widely differing views concerning the determinants of success or failure. Some of these views have been converging recently into what has been labeled the resource mobilization approach (McCarthy and Zald, 1977). This approach emphasizes political sociological and economic theories rather than social psychological propositions to explain collective behavior. Rather than discussing levels of relative deprivation and structural strain, the resource mobilization approach "examines the variety of resources that must be mobilized, the linkages of social movements to other groups, the dependence of movements upon external support for success, and the tactics used by authorities to control or incorporate movements" (McCarthy and Zald, 1977, p. 1213). For example, some (Ash, 1972, p. 231; Turner and Killian, 1972; Oberschall, 1973, pp. 206–207) suggest that reform movements are more likely to succeed when they gain the support of political and economic elites. Gerlach (1971, p. 834) argues that less formally organized, radical, or conspiratorial protest groups are more likely to survive. Ash (1972, p. 12) proposes that the less a movement challenges basic political values and interests the more likely that it will succeed.

The authors wish to express their thanks to William A. Gamson for making his data readily available for further analysis. Requests for reprints should be sent to John W. Foley, Department of Sociology, University of South Carolina, Columbia, SC 29208.
[1]See Marx and Wood (1975) for an excellent review of the collective behavior literature.

Reprinted, with permission, from *Social Science Research*, 1979.

Garner (1977, p. 11) indicates that: "Reform movements aimed at altering institutions that do not directly transform class structure are most likely to be successful on their own terms. They have a more limited goal than class conscious movements and hence call forth less intense social control." Finally, Turner and Killian (1972, p. 420) state that a reform movement will only have a long term impact if it develops an ideology, involves vested interest groups in the changes, and offers society something to bargain with or negotiate.

One long-standing debate among leaders of social movements concerns the use of violence. In the US civil rights movement of the 1960's, differing opinions developed concerning the utility of violence. Dr. Martin Luther King, Jr. advocated nonviolence to bring about desired social and political change. Opposing his approach were the more militant black leaders, seeking to use all available resources, including violence, to insure the success of civil rights movement. Furthermore, a popular belief states that, to be successful, a group must concentrate its leadership to allow for quick decisions and decisive action. Another question concerns the optimum size for a protest movement. Some opt for larger numbers, while others argue for smaller selected membership. These and many more questions about the attributes of a successful protest group have not been, as of yet, fully resolved.

In 1975, William A. Gamson made a significant contribution to the task of answering these questions. Eschewing mere verbal theorizing, he subjected these and other hypotheses to empirical tests. In *The Strategy of Social Protest* (1975), he examined "the experiences of a representative collection of American voluntary groups that, between 1800 and 1945, have challenged some aspect of the status quo." (1975, p. ix). Using this perspective of resource management,[2] Gamson studied 53 collective movements in the United States.[3] Under chapter headings of "The Strategy of Thinking Small," "The Limits of Solidarity," "The Success of the Un-

---

[2]See Oberschall (1973) and Tilly (1973a,b) for more discussion of resource management as a perspective from which to view protest groups.

[3]The 53 challenging groups studied included the American Association of University Professors, Brotherhood of the Kingdom, National Union for Social Justice, Revolutionary Workers League, Brotherhood of the Cooperative Commonwealth, Order of Railway Conductors, American Federation of Teachers, Tobacco Night Riders, Christian Front Against Communism, Independence League, and the Union Trade Society of Journeyman Tailors.

ruly," "Combat Readiness," and "The Historical Context of
Challenges," Gamson discussed those forces which he found to be
important in determining the success of a protest group.

"The Strategy of Thinking Small" studied the effect of the magnitude of group goals on the success or failure of that group. Ac-
knowledging the multidimensional nature of this variable, he
employed three aspects suggested by Roberta Ash (1972). According to Ash, "All movements must make a series of choices:

Between single issue demands and multiple demands.
Between radical demands and demands that do not attack the
    legitimacy of present distributions of wealth and power.
Between influencing elites (or even incorporating movement
    members into the elite) and attempting to replace elites."
(Ash, 1972: 230)

Gamson found that groups with single issue demands were more
successful than those having multiple issue demands. He also
found that groups which had the displacement of an established
member of the polity usually failed. In measuring the effect of
radicalism on group success, Gamson found that, once the effect
of target displacement was controlled for, the difference between
groups with radical demands and moderate demands was indistinguishable.

"The Limits of Solidarity" examined the role of public goods
and selective incentives in group success or failure. Drawing on
the work of Mancur Olson (1966), Gamson noted that when benefits are gained regardless of group membership, the group is not
very often successful in obtaining its goals. The problem with a
group offering benefits to members and non-members alike, is that
an individual is often reluctant to join and work for a goal which
will provide public goods. To overcome this "free-rider" problem,
Olson suggests the use of selective incentives. Selective incentives
are the by-products of organizing to provide a collective good.
These added incentives were found by Gamson to be the usual
tactic of successful groups.

The core of the research is its analysis of group tactics. The
chapter entitled "The Success of the Unruly" examined the role of
violence in determining the outcome of a group's challenge. Users
of violence were found to be more successful than violence recipients. As might be expected, groups using violence tended to be
large, while those on the receiving end were small. The same rela-

tionship was found among those groups which used/received some form of nonviolent constraint (i.e. arrests, boycotts).

"Combat Readiness" dealt with the degree of bureaucratization, centralization of power, and factionalism in the groups. Gamson says:

> Each of these variables makes a contribution to success, and there is a substantial interaction between centralization and factionalism. A centralized, bureaucratic group that escapes factional splits is highly likely to be successful; so, in fact, is a decentralized bureaucratic group that escapes factionalism, but it is less likely than its centralized counterpart. A decentralized, nonbureaucratic group that experiences factionalism is doomed to failure; but if it somehow manages to escape factionalism, it still has a modest possibility of success. Its chances of escaping a split are considerably enhanced if it has a centralized power structure. There are, then, definite advantages for a challenging group, inevitably engaged in conflict with an organized antagonist, to organize itself for facility in political combat.
>
> (Gamson, 1975, p. 108)

In "Historical Context of Challenges," time was carefully considered as a variable. Although the effect of time did not produce major changes in the earlier relationships, this variable did point out the effect of a crisis on the success of a challenge. A crisis such as war or economic collapse does not appear to aid groups established before the crisis occurred. Also, in more recent times, one type of group is often more unsuccessful. "This group seeks to displace its antagonists and relies on ideological appeals without selective incentives, it lacks bureaucratic organization, and, although not a user of constraints as a means of influence, it experiences attack by hostile authorities." (Gamson, 1975, pp. 128–129)

STATEMENT OF THE PROBLEM

In presenting his findings, Gamson gives the number of cases, a goodness of fit statistical test (the Chi square), and the percentage of successful groups for each condition of the particular independent variable under study using a histogram. This relatively straight-forward manner of presentation has the advantage of facilitating reader interpretation. But by restricting himself to these tools, Gamson unnecessarily limited the confidence one may place in his conclusion. For example, his tabular analysis does not control more than one conditional or confounding variable at a time. Gamson does not make causal relationships explicit in a formal manner and no clear predictive statements are articulated concerning the kind of groups that are expected to be successful. These omissions prevent the reader from gaining a clear insight into the relationships between the independent or predictor variables and the dependent or outcome variable (i.e., the success or failure of a challenge). The development of an explanatory, predictive model would both clearly identify relevant variables and demonstrate their relative importance in determining the likelihood of a group's success. Additionally, the research is hampered by the usually dichotomous level of measurement. More recently developed techniques to deal with this problem such as nonmetric multidimensional scaling were not then available to Gamson.

It is the purpose of this paper to re-examine and extend Gamson's argument using the original data but employing multivariate statistical techniques. In addition to re-examining his original findings, the use of these techniques will permit an examination of the inter-relationships between the attributes of successful protest groups and a more specific statement of the determinants of the outcome of protest groups. While Gamson stated the attributes of successful protest groups, the present study will attempt to extend the work of Gamson by developing predictive equations demonstrating the unique, relative importance of each attribute to the eventual success or failure of the movement. In this manner a contribution to the social movement literature may be made, the resource mobilization model assessed, and social theory advanced.

Initially, we formed a correlation matrix to permit an inspection of the bivariate relationships among these variables. These relationships are presented below in Table 1. (Only 30 of the original 39 variables are presented because nine variables were redundant, summary, or composite measures. Accordingly, they were deleted). As might be expected, the highest correlation is between the variables Faction and Faction Timing. The rest of the coefficients are below .77 and present no potential problems of multicollinearity. To reduce this data matrix to a set of dimensions that represent the underlying analytic structure in a parsimonious and visually appealing manner, some paring is necessary. Two data reduction techniques were considered: factor analysis and non-metric multidimensional scaling. Multidimensional scaling was chosen because of the ordinal level of measurement of the variables.[4] Inputting a similarities matrix[5] developed from the correlation matrix of logical independent variables, five basic dimensions were derived.[6] These dimensions and the variables that loaded on them are presented below in Table 2. From the above, it is clear that three of the dimensions: D1, D3, and D4 (Thinking Small, Success of the Unruly, and Combat Readiness) contain variable clusters similar to the corresponding chapters in *The Strategy of Social Protest*. The dimension labeled Limits of Solidarity (D2) appears to measure the same kind of group attributes as Gamson discusses in his chapter "The Limits of Solidarity." The fifth dimension (D5) has no direct parallel in Gamson's findings but is apparently a measure of the scope of the perceived threat of the challenge. This variable cluster appears to measure the reliability and availability of information about the other dimensions. Clearly a secret, exclusive group with a violent ideology with the entire system as their target of change is not going to be easy to penetrate and the reliability, as well as the amount, of information on such groups will be less than that for more open groups. The addition of dominant leadership makes the information even less reliable, since such leadership is capable of quickly changing positions on an issue.

After identifying these five dimensions, a causal model was estimated using regression techniques that would predict success or failure of a group using its values on each of the five main dimensions. The parameter estimates are presented below in Table 3.[7] Because the dependent variable was not measured at the interval level of measurement, it is thought more appropriate to estimate

---

[4]See Young (1970), Jones (1974), Rabinowitz (1975), and Kruskal and Wish (1978) for an introduction to multidimensional scaling.

[5]A similarities matrix, formed by transforming the correlation coefficients to range from zero (in the case of perfect negative correlation) to plus one (in the case of perfect positive correlation), served as input to the multidimensional scaling program. See Young and Torgerson (1958) for a description of the program.

[6]The number of dimensions presented was determined by using those needed to arrive at an acceptable goodness of fit as measured by Stress (Type I).

[7]Each dimension variable is a composite variable composed of the sum of each variable on a dimension that loaded .35 or greater, multiplied by its loading. Because these groups do not constitute a probability sample, statistical tests of significance are not reported.

TABLE 1
Intercorrelation Matrix for Variables Used to Predict Group Outcome*

	X_1	X_2	X_3	X_4	X_5	X_6	X_7	X_8	X_9	X_{10}	X_{11}	X
Variables**												
Type group X_1	I											
Violence present X_2	.05	I										
Violence used X_3	−.24	.62	I									
Violence used on X_4	−.13	.77	.60	I								
Nonviolent constraints X_5	.22	.60	.54	.45	I							
Violent ideology X_6	.23	.38	.12	.15	.47	I						
Target displacement X_7	−.75	−.14	.09	.03	−.33	−.36	I					
Goods X_8	.58	−.20	−.23	−.19	−.07	.11	−.32	I				
Benefits X_9	−.32	−.16	.01	−.03	−.01	−.16	.47	−.15	I			
Systemic vs local X_{10}	−.41	−.19	.11	.07	−.33	.37	−.31	−.03	−.03	I		
Dominant leader X_{11}	.07	.03	−.06	.06	−.04	−.04	−.02	.17	−.26	−.11	I	
Secrecy X_{12}	.15	−.14	−.06	−.08	−.12	−.27	.02	.07	.01	.14	.06	
Factions X_{13}	.20	−.00	−.13	−.03	.13	−.18	−.14	.08	−.02	−.01	.17	.2
Factional timing X_{14}	.23	.04	−.08	.03	.12	−.20	−.21	.13	−.09	.05	.23	.1
Constitution X_{15}	.16	−.01	.10	−.12	−.09	.09	−.19	.17	−.11	−.02	−.28	−.0
Membership list X_{16}	.28	.03	.04	−.08	−.04	−.13	.23	.29	−.01	−.20	−.03	.1
Full time employee X_{17}	.37	.07	.03	.03	.08	.07	−.40	.28	−.08	−.13	.02	.0
Levels of hierarchy X_{18}	.34	−.21	−.15	−.28	.02	.15	−.31	.28	−.07	−.32	−.06	.0
Group size X_{19}	−.22	.12	.22	.12	.09	−.14	.05	−.27	−.03	.17	−.18	−.
Electoral salience X_{20}	−.27	.16	−.02	.17	.05	.12	.33	−.14	.30	−.01	.07	−.0
Means of influence X_{21}	.34	−.39	−.49	−.36	−.39	−.20	.01	.53	−.03	.02	.20	.3
(??(Σμ)X_{22}	.15	.15	−.21	.14	.07	.03	−.07	.04	.17	−.10	−.16	.0
Class origins X_{23}	.27	.12	.10	.08	.16	.14	−.42	−.22	−.11	.01	−.13	−.1
Initial resources X_{24}	.04	−.02	−.03	−.16	−.21	.04	.02	.10	−.16	.11	−.03	.1
Competition X_{25}	.10	−.05	.12	.01	−.13	−.12	.18	.21	.10	.17	.13	−.0
Antagonists X_{26}	.38	.09	.02	.11	.11	−.08	−.50	.07	−.31	−.02	.11	.1
Incentives X_{27}	.45	.10	.07	.02	.03	.18	−.30	.27	−.31	−.23	.06	.3
Inclusive vs exclusive X_{28}	.10	.26	.02	−.06	.28	.64	−.19	.05	−.10	−.31	−.02	−.3
Internal authority X_{29}	.21	−.12	−.18	−.10	−.02	−.02	−.23	.10	−.14	−.05	.64	.0
Date began X_{30}	.16	.11	.09	−.13	.25	.25	−.29	−.23	−.27	−.30	−.11	−.0

*Spearman rank-order coefficients used.
**For a fuller description of these variables, see footnote.

the parameters using discriminant function analysis.[8] Using the five composite dimension variables, this technique correctly predicted group outcome of 55% of the 53 cases when all four categories of success/failure were included in the classification. Using only two polar classes of total success and total failure, 88% of the 42 cases in these groups were correctly classified by the discriminant function. By contrast, the multiple regression equation developed earlier correctly classified only 28% of the 53 cases when all four categories were used and 88% of the 42 cases when two cate-

---

[8]For an overview of this technique see Aldrich and Cnudde (1975) who compare discriminant function analysis to the more familiar regression analysis.

| X_{13} | X_{14} | X_{15} | X_{16} | X_{17} | X_{18} | X_{19} | X_{20} | X_{21} | X_{22} | X_{23} | X_{24} | X_{25} | X_{26} | X_{27} | X_{28} | X_{29} | X_{30} |

```
 I
96    I
25 -.21    I
27 -.24  .56    I
02  .10  .38  .55    I
15 -.14  .49  .47  .61    I
12  .11 -.30 -.36 -.60 -.56    I
09  .03 -.20 -.24 -.10 -.05 -.18    I
20  .19  .14  .15  .09  .19 -.34 -.15    I
24  .27 -.12 -.22  .06 -.05 -.13  .23  .12    I
06 -.02  .16  .05  .12 -.06  .17 -.21 -.35  .04    I
18 -.17  .29  .28 -.09 -.01  .07 -.20  .16 -.17  .13    I
19  .21  .21  .12 -.07 -.23 -.23  .09  .13 -.10  .05  .04    I
32  .40 -.08  .02  .01 -.24  .28 -.41 -.05 -.06  .37  .03 -.10    I
04  .09  .34  .28  .40  .38 -.42 -.10  .35  .08  .11  .27  .09  .07    I
10 -.12  .21  .08 -.01  .01 -.04  .15 -.16 -.08  .11 -.03 -.15 -.10 -.03    I
31  .36  .02  .04  .25  .18 -.31  .04  .23  .07 -.01 -.19  .09  .02 -.02  .10    I
07 -.09  .10 -.02 -.11  .01  .22 -.05 -.20 -.13  .25  .25 -.12  .20  .21  .23 -.15    I
```

gories were used. The discriminant functions and their coefficients are presented in Table 4.

For comparison, another set of multiple regression and discriminant function equations were calculated using the variables identified by Gamson as important to group outcome. These discrete variables were placed in a stepwise multiple regression equation and those changing the coefficient of determination more than .015 were used to produce the multiple regression equations shown in Table 5.

These nine variables were further used to develop the discriminant function equation presented in Table 6.

Additionally, the predictive ability of the discrete and composite variables was compared in both the discriminant function and

TABLE 2
Multidimensional Scaling Dimensions

"Thinking small" (D1)		"The limits of solidarity" (D2)		"Success of the unruly" (D3)	
Benefits	.619	Factions	.461	Means of influence	.523
Target displacement	.554	Constitution	−.436	Violence used on	−.498
Electoral salience	.479	Alliances	.418	Violence used by	−.491
Antagonists	−.428	Faction timing	.416	Violence present	−.446
Class origins	−.394	Competition	−.390	Goods	.389
		Initial resources	−.367	Nonviolent constraint	−.371
		Membership list	−.365		

"Combat readiness" (D4)		Threat potential (D5)	
Group size	.588	Inclusive vs exclusive	−.535
Levels of hierarchy	−.527	Secrecy	.472
Full-time employees	−.450	Violent ideology	−.462
Systemic vs local	.366	Systemic vs local	.429
		Date began	−.376
		Dominant leader	.348

regression equation models. In both the multiple regression and the discriminant function equations, the selected individual variables classified more cases correctly than equations based on the composite dimension variable.

This somewhat unexpected result may be a function of the cancelling effect of the variables within a dimension. In any specific case, only a few of the variables on a dimension may be actually relevant. The other variables may sum to a value which counters the effect of these key variables.

Finally, the explanatory power of the type of linear model used was compared. The predictive power was the same for the multiple regression and discriminant function equations when the dependent variable was strictly a dichotomy, success or failure. When the dependent variable was a four-value measure of outcome the explanatory power of the regression model decreased significantly. Table 7 presents the combined comparisons of the predictive power of the discrete and composite variables in both regression and discriminant function format for both the dichotomous and four-fold measures of protest group success.

When we restrict our efforts to prediction of the outcome for only the 42 groups that were completely successful or complete failures, our analysis shows that either multiple regression or discrimination function analysis will predict correctly 98% of the cases in these two categories. Since the level of measurement for most of the data is ordinal, the discriminant function equation shown in the lower half of Table 6 will be used as our prediction equation.[9] The standardized discriminant function coefficients may be interpreted in a manner similar to beta weights in multiple regression. The magnitude of the coefficients shows the relative importance of the variable to the discriminate function. The sign indicates whether that variable is making a positive or negative contribution to the function and is dependent upon the manner of coding the raw data. In the predictive equation developed during this analysis, the most important predictor of group success was target displacement. This variable measures the extent to which the protest group's goal specifies the replacement or destruction of the agency responsible for implementing their desired policy change. Those groups which attempt to replace or destroy their target groups are doomed to failure. It appears that talk of change is acceptable, even change itself is tolerable, but if that change endangers a member of the polity, then the establishment reacts quickly and with overwhelming strength to end the protest as soon as possible.

The second most important variable for predicting group success is the number of a group's alliances. This variable measures the effect of groups other than the target group or competing groups on the success of a protest group's effort. Generally those groups that were not hindered, especially those who were actually helped by outside groups, were more successful in achieving their goals. This variable measures the protest group's support from

---

[9]The discriminant function classification coefficients given below were used to make the actual predictions.

	Predictions	
	Success	Failure
Target displacement	2.67	1.17
Alliances	−.38	.94
Full time employees	2.07	3.89
Faction timing	−.48	.85
Systemic vs local	11.14	7.85
Means of influence	.99	1.53
Constant =	−19.34	−17.05

TABLE 3
Multiple Regression Coefficients and Coefficients of Determination for
Composite Dimension Variables on Group Outcome

	Outcome I* (n = 53)		Outcome II* (n = 42)	
	b	Beta	b	Beta
"Thinking small"	−.11	−.07	−.12	−.45
"Limits of solidarity"	−.33	−.43	.13	.45
"Unruliness"	.35	.45	.01	.04
"Combat readiness"	.04	.06	−.14	−.41
"Threat"	−.36	−.37	−.02	−.03
Constant	3.37		5.81	
(R^2) =	.50	(R^2) =	.56	

*Outcome I is for the dependent variable using four measures of outcome: full-response, re-emption, co-optation, and collapse. Outcome II used the two polar categories of full-response and collapse to measure outcome as either success or failure.

nonrival groups. Another measure of the power of a challenging group is the number of full-time employees working for the movement. The number of full-time employees is apparently a measure of the organizational strength of the movement. As a movement grows in strength, the number of full-time employees usually increases. This measure of group strength also helps predict the eventual outcome of a protest. A third measure of group power is the existence and timing of any factional disputes. The energy expended by the group on factional disputes results in a weakening of the effort directed toward goal attainment.

Another variable that helps predict group success is the scope of the changes it seeks. If the group attempts to bring about a change of the entire system, such as a movement to fight capitalism, they are unlikely to be successful. In the groups studied, those with specific goals were more successful than those which attacked the entire system.

The final variable in our predictive equation regards the means of influence used by the challenging group. It appears that groups using some form of sanctions or constraints (i.e., boycotts, *ad hominum* attacks, or injury to persons or property) are usually more successful than those groups who do not. This variable should be carefully evaluated, however, since violence may work

TABLE 4
Standardized Discriminant Function Coefficients and Classification Results and Composite Variables

	Outcome I* (n = 53)			Outcome II* (n = 42)
	Function 1	Function 2	Function 3	Function 1
"Thinking small"	.60	.29	.75	.61
"Limits of solidarity"	-.63	-.48	.63	-.60
"Combat readiness"	.59	-.78	-.27	.56

Outcome I* (n = 53)

Actual group	No. of cases	Predicted group			
		GP1	GP2	GP3	GP4
1. Full response	20	8	5	6	1
2. Preemption	6	1	4	0	1
3. Co-optation	5	2	0	3	0
4. Collapse	22	0	4	4	14

Outcome II* (n = 42)

Actual group	No. of cases	Predicted group	
		GP1	GP4
1. Full response	20	18	2
4. Failure	22	3	19

	Outcome I*	Outcome II*
Percent of cases correctly classified:	53.7%	88.1%

*Outcome I is for the dependent variable using four measures of outcome: full-response, pre-emption, co-optation, and collapse. Outcome II used the two polar categories of full-response and collapse to measure outcome as either success or failure.

TABLE 5
Multiple Regression Coefficients and Coefficients of Determination
for Selected Variables on Group Outcome

	Outcome* (n = 53)		Outcome II* (n = 42)	
	b	Beta	b	Beta
"Target displacement"	−.39	−.42	−.13	−.38
"Alliances"	.24	.27	.09	.27
"Full time employees"	.23	.16	.11	.21
"Faction timing"	.38	.29	.12	.26
"Systemic vs local"	−.72	−.22	−.26	−.22
"Competition"	.57	.21	.19	.12
"Nonviolent constraints"	−.43	−.21	−.10	−.14
"Violence present"	.50	.20	.12	.14
"Means of influence"	.11	.11	.04	.11
Constant	2.80		5.59	
(R^2) =	.71	(R^2) =	.74	

*Outcome I is for the dependent variable using four measures of outcome: full-response, pre-emption, co-optation, and collapse. Outcome II used the two polar categories of full-response and collapse to measure outcome as either success or failure.

to bring about either success or failure, depending on certain other group traits. Violence, like a two-edged sword, can strike in either direction. When a group is large and powerful, it may ignore the adverse affects of violent tactics, but small groups are quick to learn that in violent encounters they are usually losers. The confounding factor is the sympathetic support that the use of violence may bring to either the protest movement or to the establishment, depending on the sway of public opinion. The difference between violent and nonviolent constraints is subtle and those who use constraints must be careful not to confuse the two unless they are sufficiently powerful to withstand the possible adverse affects of violence.

CONCLUSIONS

From the resource mobilization and management approach this paper uses a variety of multivariate techniques including multidimensional scaling, regression analysis, and discriminant function analysis to explore the determinants of US protest group success.

TABLE 6
Standardized Discriminant Function Coefficients and Classification Results for Selected Variables

	Outcome I* (n = 53)			Outcome II* (n = 42)
	Function 1	Function 2	Function 3	Function 1
Target displacement	-.48	.42	.22	-.41
Alliances	.32	-.12	.27	.37
Faction timing	.25	.80	.31	.31 (Full-time employees)
Systemic vs local	-.28	-.15	-.33	.25 (Faction timing)
Competition	.21	-.44	.50	-.25 (Systemic vs local)
Nonviolent constraints	-.20	.65	-.47	.13 (Means of influence)
Violence present	.19	-.21	-.04	

Note — Outcome II variables (right column) are: Target displacement (-.41), Alliances (.37), Full-time employees (.31), Faction timing (.25), Systemic vs local (-.25), Means of influence (.13).

Outcome I classification

Actual group	No. of cases	Predicted group			
		GP1	GP2	GP3	GP4
1. Full response	20	12	5	2	1
2. Preemption	6	0	6	2	1
3. Co-optation	5	0	0	5	5
4. Collapse	22	1	2	2	17

Percent of cases correctly classified: 75.5%

Outcome II classification

Actual group	No. of cases	Predicted group	
		GP1	GP4
1. Full response	20	19	1
4. Collapse	22	0	22

Percent of cases correctly classified: 97.6%

*Outcome I is for the dependent variable using four measures of outcome: full-response, pre-emption, co-optation, and collapse. Outcome II used the two polar categories of full-response and collapse to measure outcome as either success or failure.

TABLE 7
Comparison of Predictive Equations

Multiple regression equations			
Composite dimension variables		*Selected individual variables*	
Outcome I*	*Outcome II**	*Outcome I**	*Outcome II**
N = 53	N = 42	N = 42	N = 42
28%	88%	55%	98%
Discriminant function equations			
Composite dimension variables		*Selected individual variables*	
Outcome I*	*Outcome II**	*Outcome I**	*Outcome II**
N = 53	N = 42	N = 42	
55%	88%	76%	98%

*Outcome I is for the dependent variable using four measures of outcome: full-response, pre-emption, co-optation, and collapse. Outcome II used the two polar categories of full-response and collapse to measure outcome as either success or failure.

Our predictive methodologies accomplished several objectives. First, we illustrated the potential of the resource mobilization model in studying protest group outcomes. Secondly, through multivariate analysis we confirmed the propositions of Ash, Turner and Killian, Garner, Gamson, and others. We found that the forces that lead to protest group success are, in order of relative importance, a desire on the part of the protest group not to replace an established member of the polity, the number of alliances a group has with other groups, the absence of factional disputes, quite specific and limited goals, and a willingness to use sanctions against other groups. In testing these hypotheses we built predictive equations to assess the cumulative impact of these components on eventual group success or failure. In doing so, we were able with our model to correctly classify as winners or losers the vast majority of these protest groups. In analyzing the prediction equations, the importance of a given independent variable shifted somewhat from case to case according to the salience to a specific group. But, overall, regardless of the mode of causal analysis used or the format of the variables, the findings were remarkably consistent. This enhances the confidence we may place in these findings and should encourage additional multivariate model building *appendix a / further analysis and disputation*   197

in the social movement field from the resource mobilization perspective.

Further research into this topic should include an examination of the protest groups for which our models incorrectly predicted success or failure.[10] Deviant case analysis, often on a case by case basis, can be as fruitful as the original analysis in illuminating social phenomena. Additionally, the nonlinear interaction effects between the independent variables should be assessed. Do groups that are willing to both use violence and engage in supportive alliances increase exponentially their chance of success? Finally, research into this topic should include a test of the predictive power of one discriminant function equation on data for additional, possibly nonUS, protest groups.

REFERENCES

Aldrich, J., and Cnudde, C. F. (1975). "Probing the bounds of conventional wisdom: A comparison of regression, probit and discriminant analysis," *American Journal of Political Science* (August): 571–600.

Ash, R. (1972). *Social Movements in America*. Markham, Chicago.

Dahl, R. (1951). *Who Governs?* Yale University Press, New Haven.

Gamson, W. A. (1975). *The Strategy of Social Protest*. Dorsey, Homewood, IL.

Garner, R. A. (1977). *Social Movements in America* (2nd Ed.). Rand-McNally, Chicago.

Gerlach, L. P. (1971). "Movements of revolutionary change: Some structural characteristics," *American Behavioral Scientist* 14 (July-August): 812–836.

---

[10]Of the 42 groups that were either completely successful or unsuccessful, only one was incorrectly classified using the discriminant classification functions. That group was the League of Deliverance, a nativist workers group seeking to prevent employment of Chinese labor on the West Coast around 1882. They had displacement of their antagonists as their goal and because this is the best predictor of eventual failure the discriminant function analysis incorrectly classified this successful group. We feel there are reasons to believe that this was not their true goal. Clearly qualitative research is now needed to determine the context of this group's success when our quantitative methods predicted failure. More generally, qualitative research is now needed to interpret the disproportionate number of labor movements that succeeded after the Civil War. The work force discipline and resulting productivity provided by stable unions was a necessary condition to postCivil War economic development. Recognition of this potential may explain a great deal of the success the American labor movement had after the Civil War.

Hunter, F. (1953). *Community Power Structure*. University of North Carolina Press, Chapel Hill.

Jones, B. D. (1974). "Some considerations in the use of non-metric multidimensional scaling," *Political Methodology* (Fall): 1–30.

Kruskal, J. B., and Wish, M. (1978). *Multidimensional Scaling*. Sage, Beverly Hills.

Lowi, T. J. (1971). *The Politics of Disorder*. Basic Books, New York.

McCarthy, J. D., and Zald, M. N. (1977). "Resource mobilization and social movements: A partial theory," *American Journal of Sociology* (May): 1213–1241.

Marx, G. T., and Wood, J. L. (1975). "Strands of theory and research in collective behavior," *Annual Review of Sociology* 1:363–428.

Mills, C. W. (1956). *The Power Elite*. Oxford University Press, New York.

Nie, N. H.; Hull, C. H.; Jenkins, J. C.; Strenbrennen, K.; and Bent, D. H. (1975). *Statistical Packages for the Social Sciences* (2nd Ed.). McGraw-Hill, New York, 320–360 and 434–462.

Oberschall, A. (1973). *Social Conflict and Social Movements*. Prentice-Hall, Englewood Cliffs..

Olson, M. (1966). *The Logic of Collective Action*. Harvard University Press, Cambridge.

Rabinowitz, G. (1975). "An introduction to non-metric multidimensional scaling," *American Journal of Political Science* (May): 343–390.

Tilly, C. (1973a). "Collective action and conflict in large-scale social change: Research plans, 1974-78." Center for Research on Social Organization, University of Michigan, Ann Arbor (October).

Tilly, C. (1973b). "The chaos of the living city," in *Violence as Politics* (H. Hirsh and D. C. Perry, Eds.), Harper & Row, New York.

Turner, F. W. (1970). "Non-metric multidimensional scaling: Recovery of metric information," *Psychometrika*, 35:455–473.

Turner, R. N., and Killian, L. (1972). *Collective Behavior* (2nd Ed.) Prentice-Hall, Englewood Cliffs.

Young, F. W., and Torgerson, W. S. (1968). "TORSCA, a Fortran IV program for non-metric multidimensional scaling," *Behavioral Science* (July): 343–344.

Protest Group Success: The Impact of Group Characteristics, Social Control, and Context*

JOHN MIROWSKY AND CATHERINE E. ROSS

University of Illinois at Urbana-Champaign

In this study we test eight hypotheses about the relative control of protesters, third parties, and elements of the situation (movement context and confrontation) over two types of protest group success: goal achievement and recognition. A path analysis indicates that two sets of protester-controlled factors decisively affect protest group success: organization and beliefs and goals. Of the two, beliefs and goals is the more significant, although bureaucracy is very important for recognition. For the most part, the impact of protester-controlled factors is not due to the reaction of third parties; however, revolutionary activism, one factor in the realm of beliefs and goals, is a notable exception. Revolutionary activism's negative association with success is largely due to suppression by third parties.

In the process of mobilization for collective action only some protest groups are successful. The question of what characterizes these successful protest groups has recently received increased attention both generally (Brill, 1971; Fainstein and Fainstein, 1974; Gamson, 1975; Jenkins and Perrow, 1977; Lipsky, 1970; Schumaker, 1975, 1978; Shorter and Tilly, 1974; Snyder and Kelly, 1976) and specifically in the reanalysis of Gamson's data (Goldstone, 1980; Gamson, 1980; Steedly and Foley, 1979). In this study, a protest group or social movement organization (McCarthy and Zald, 1977; Zald and Ash, 1966) is defined as an organization with beliefs and goals directed at changing some part of the social structure (from more benefits for dairy farmers to world communism). In accord with Gamson's definition (1975), a protest group must meet two criteria: (1) it must be trying to mobilize an unmobilized constituency, and (2) it must either influence or gain the offices and authority of non-members in order to achieve its goals. Thus we are interested in groups which are in the process of organizing, attracting a constituency, and attempting to gain the support of third parties in order to achieve their goals. In short, they are in the process of resource mobilization.

*We wish to thank Paul Burstein, Mary Curran, D'arcy Myjer, Barry Seltser, Blair Wheaton, and Bonnie Wilhite for their help.

Reprinted, with permission, from *Sociological Focus*, August 1981, 14:177–92.

There are two types of success which a protest group may achieve. First, the group may realize the goal it set out to achieve. We call this goal achievement. Second, its antagonist or target group may come to recognize the protest group as a legitimate spokesman for a particular interest. We call this recognition. Although recognition is sometimes a protest group's main goal, usually it is not. Therefore we treat goal achievement and recognition separately.

In this study we attempt to find the locus of control over protest group success. Can a protest group engineer its own success, or is success due to factors beyond the group's control? If a group can affect its own success, is it because the characteristics of the group and its style of protest directly influence the target's response, or is the protest group's impact primarily indirect, via its influence on agents or agencies not directly targets of the protest?

To answer these questions we analyze success as flowing from three sources: (1) the protest group, which can shape its own beliefs and goals and organization; (2) third parties, such as agencies or influentials which are not directly targets of the protest but may be a source of aid (social support) or hindrance (social control); and (3) the situation, which is important both as context and as dynamic interaction, especially active confrontation.

The first area controlled by the protest group is its beliefs and goals. Theorists from diverse camps agree that protest groups that intend to change the system are less likely to be successful than those that do not. Garner (1977:11) states: "Reform movements aimed at altering institutions that do not directly transform class structure are most likely to be successful on their own terms. They have a more limited goal than class conscious movements and hence call forth less intense social control." This is empirically supported by Gamson (1975), Schumaker (1975), and Snyder and Kelly (1976).

In a study of American challenging groups in action between 1800 and 1945, Gamson (1975) finds that groups that attempt to alter the personnel of their antagonists and/or attempt to destroy or replace their antagonists have a low probability of success. Thus, displacement goals are associated with failure. In his analysis of protest incidents in U.S. cities, Schumaker (1975) finds that two dimensions of radical demand—the demand for equal rights and zero-sum demands—are associated with a decreased chance

of success. In addition, he finds that some of the effect of radical
demands is indirect, due to the response of third parties. However,
it is difficult to determine what portion is indirect, due to the
negative reaction of third parties, and what portion is direct, due
to increased resistance on the part of target officials and groups.
Snyder and Kelly (1976), in a study of labor disputes in Italy between 1878 and 1903, find that groups concerned with material
rather than ideological issues have a greater chance of success.
This underscores the similar finding by Schumaker under vastly
different circumstances.

In addition to its beliefs and goals, the group may also shape its
organizational structure. Thus, our second question is, what are
the direct and indirect effects of organization? Schumaker measures both organizational stability and the number of active participants. He finds these have small and inconsistent effects. Gamson
finds that both bureaucracy and centralization lead to success,
although centralization is important only for goal achievement, not
recognition. Overall, there is some evidence that organization
leads to success, although the mechanisms are not clear.

Beliefs and goals and organization are the two realms which are
largely controlled by the protest group itself. The second source of
success or failure is third parties. Social support (aid) and social
control (hindrance) are essentially controlled by third parties, although the protest group may influence the actions of the third
parties. Lipsky (1970) hypothesizes that protest groups need to
gain the support of third parties in order to create bargaining resources for a successful movement. Schumaker confirms this hypothesis, finding that the "environment of social support" is
important in protest group success: support from agency officials,
elected officials, the media, active community groups, and the
community in general, is positively associated with success. He
also finds that these forms of social support together are much
more important in determining the outcome of a protest than the
combined protester-controlled variables. In addition, a portion of
the effects of protester-controlled variables is indirect, due to their
associations with social support variables. Jenkins and Perrow
(1977: 253), in a study of farm workers, find that "the success of a
'powerless' challenge depended upon sustained and widespread
outside support coupled with neutrality and/or tolerance from the
national political elite." On the other hand, Gamson (1975) finds

that privileged groups (which enjoy the patronage of some individual or group with significant power or wealth) do not have an
appreciable advantage over other groups. While privilege is not
related to success, hindrance *is* related to failure. Groups whose
members are exposed to violence but do not use violence, or whose
members are subject to arrest, are less likely to succeed.

Concerning violence, Gamson finds that, although passive recipients of violence are more likely to fail, groups which *use* violence
neither damage nor improve their chance of success. In contradiction, Snyder and Kelly find that the use of violence decreases the
probability of a successful strike by about .10. Also, Gamson finds
that groups which use constraints such as strikes and boycotts are
more likely to succeed than those that do not, although, according
to Schumaker (1978), the effectiveness of those tactics varies, depending on the degree and direction of third party involvement.
Overall, the findings concerning the effects of confrontation on
success are equivocal. (For a discussion of the equivocal findings
on the effectiveness of constraints see Schumaker, 1978.) The issue of violence and other forms of confrontation also leads to
potential ambiguity concerning the locus of control. We treat active confrontation as a situationally-determined interaction, controlled by both sides. We assume that neither side can create
confrontation by itself: a hostile action on one side will become
confrontation only if the other side responds with a hostile action.

Movement context is another situationally-controlled variable.
Our definition of movement context corresponds to McCarthy and
Zald's (1977) definition of a Social Movement Industry. The movement context consists of the prevalence of protest groups in a
certain period appealing to roughly the same constituency concerning roughly the same issues. The movement context is different from confrontation because context is not determined by the
interaction of the protest group with its target and third parties. It
exists outside of any one protest group. It is the environment of
protest groups.

There are two perspectives on the effect of movement context.
The first argues that within the social movement sector, movement
organizations must compete for scarce resources (community aid,
constituents, leadership, etc.). When there are many competing
movement organizations, no one of them is able to gather sufficient
strength to mount a successful protest. A similar argument is relevant when the movement's goal is to establish the representation

of some hitherto unrepresented interest. Because it is difficult for authorities to deal with several competing representatives of a single interest, it seems probable that they will recognize only one group. Therefore, if one group succeeds, the rest fail; the more groups, the more failure.

The second view argues that the existence of competing organizations in the same movement makes success more likely. The various groups may specialize in appealing to particular segments of the constituency, thereby putting to use a high percentage of the resources potentially available to the movement (McCarthy and Zald, 1977). The various groups may also specialize in terms of tactics, which may widen the movement's breadth of appeal, while increasing the probability that at least one group will hit on the most effective tactic. In addition, the variety of contributors and the variety of tactics may give the protesters' target the feeling of getting all kinds of pressure from every quarter, something which may encourage cooperation. In addition, since the various groups share a common goal, then (if winning does not involve recognition) every group wins when any of them wins. Thus, the proliferation of groups makes success more likely.

In summary, a number of hypotheses can be put forward based on research and theory concerning protest group success. The hypotheses may be ordered according to whether they refer to factors controlled (1) by the protest group, (2) by those outside the protest group, (3) by the situation, or (4) whether they refer to a comparison of the relative influence of two or more centers. The specific hypotheses, controlling for relevant variables, are:

> *Hypothesis 1a—The more radical a group's beliefs and goals, the less likely it will be successful.*
> *Hypothesis 1b—The more organized a group, the more likely it will be successful.*
> *Hypothesis 2a—Aid from third parties makes success more likely. This refers to general support activities, not only economic aid.*
> *Hypothesis 2b—Hindrance by third parties (most notably acts of suppression by non-target agencies) makes success less likely.*
> *Hypothesis 3a—Active confrontation (marked by the use of unconventional tactics on the part of the protest group and acts of aggression by the target or third parties*

*against the group) has an equivocal effect on success.
Thus there is no significant relationship between confrontation and success.*

*Hypothesis 3b—A flourishing movement context makes suc-
cess more likely, except when success refers to recognition, at which time a flourishing movement context makes
success less likely.*

*Hypothesis 4a—The support or hindrance of third parties
are stronger determinants of protest group success than
are the variables controlled by the protest group itself (organization and beliefs and goals).*

*Hypothesis 4b—Much of the effects of protester-controlled
variables are indirect, due to their influence on variables
controlled by third parties.*

SAMPLE AND METHODS

The data used here were collected by Gamson (1975), based on
a random sample of 53 protest groups active in the U.S. between
1800 and 1945. A protocol was used to "interview" historical
source material on each case. (For an in-depth description of the
sample and sampling procedure, see Gamson (1975), Chapter 2 and
Appendices A, B, and C.)

In order to test our hypotheses we will perform several steps.
(1) Divide a large universe of variables into a small number of
realms that may be causally related to each other. (2) Factor analyze the variables within each realm. We assume that the variables
within a realm are logically but not causally related and that they
may represent more than a single dimension. For instance, the
realm of organization may vary along dimensions of bureaucracy
and openness. (3) Enter the estimated factors of each realm into a
path analysis. (4) Test our hypotheses by interpreting the path analysis in terms of the direct and indirect effects attributable to each
of the three centers of control: the protest group, third parties,
and the situation.

FACTOR ANALYSIS: FINDINGS AND DISCUSSION

We divided the independent variables into five *a priori* categories: (1) movement context, (2) beliefs and goals, (3) organizations,

(4) action and interaction, and (5) length of the challenge. We then factor analyzed the variables in the first four categories, since length of the challenge consists of only one variable. Indices based on factor score coefficients derived from this factor analysis could then be used as variables in a path analysis.[1] We chose to estimate orthogonal factors in order to avoid the indeterminacy of path analysis with correlations for which no direction of cause can be assumed.[2]

Movement context consists of two variables: whether there were competing protest groups appealing to roughly the same constituency about similar issues, and the date the challenge ended. Since there were only two variables in this realm we simply summed the standardized scores on each variable to create the movement context factor.

The factor analysis of *beliefs and goals* shows an underlying structure of three factors[3] which together account for 72 percent of the variance in the eight items (see Table 1). Displacement goals have the highest loading on the first factor. Such goals signify a group's intention to either replace or eliminate its antagonist. The number of concerns has the second highest loading on the factor, followed by the intention to produce pooled, collective benefits; and by a concern with other issues besides boundaries and benefits. The dimension suggests a style of political thought characteristic of the more extreme progressives. Among the groups with

TABLE 1
Beliefs and Goals

	Rotated Factor-Structure Matrix		
	Displacement Reformism	Revolutionary Activism	Union Activism
Number of concerns	.75*	−.26	.08
More than benefits at issue	.49*	.08	.04
Displacement goal	.90*	.43*	.00
Pooled benefits	.52*	.41*	−.48*
Goal: Change the system	.05	.71*	−.15
Belief in legitimacy of violence	.08	.60*	.14
Belief in strikes, boycotts, etc.	−.11	.44*	.73*
Constituents get the benefits	.19	−.13	.57*

*Loading is .40 or greater.

very high scores on the factor are the Progressive Labor Party, Teddy Roosevelt's Bull Moose Party, The American Party, and the Native American Party. These groups seem to span the left-right ideological continuum. Commitment to a third-party challenge, public spirited intentions, and grandiose visionary goals seem to be their shared traits. The label "displacement reformism" seems appropriate.

The highest loading on the second factor in the realm of beliefs and goals is the intention to change the system, not merely one element of the system or one industry or specific institution. The second highest loading is associated with the explicit legitimation of violence, followed by the intention to produce pooled benefits, having displacement goals, and accepting strikes and boycotts as legitimate tactics. The Social Revolutionary Clubs (also known as the Anarcho-Communists), the Revolutionary Workers League, the Communist Labor Party, and the German American Bund all have unusually high scores on the factor. Apparently the factor measures commitment to revolutionary action, whether left or right. The label "revolutionary activism" seems appropriate.

Belief in the legitimate use of strikes and boycotts is the core item in the third factor. Loading with it are two intentions: first, the benefits go to constituents of the group and second, that benefits *not* be pooled, as in a public good. Labor unions consistently have high scores. High scores also go to the National Student League and the American Student Union, both leftist offspring of the Student League for Industrial Democracy, and to William Randolph Hearst's Independence League. Although the factor seems to differentiate mainly on the basis of commitment to labor union-type goals and practices, some high scorers seem to combine unionism with middle-class activism. Overall, "union activism" seems to be an appropriate label.

Thus we find three factors in the realm of beliefs and goals: displacement reformism, revolutionary activism, and union activism. Each factor is an index on which every group has a score. It is therefore appropriate to speak of a group's degree of revolutionary activism, rather than to say the group *is* a revolutionary activist group. Since the factors are uncorrelated, it is just as possible for a group to have high scores on all three as it is to have a high score on one and low scores on the others. Taken together, then, the three factors in the realm of beliefs and goals are a way of describing protest groups by using three points of reference. Taken separately, the factors are variables which may influence organization, activity, and success in distinctive ways.

In the realm of *organization*, three factors account for 63 percent of the variance in the 12 items (see Table 2). The highest loading on the first factor is for bureaucracy, followed by hierarchy, number of employees, maintaining a membership list, having a constitution, providing selective incentives, and group size. We call this factor "bureaucracy."

The second organizational factor is characterized by centralization of authority and domination by a single leader with whom the group is identified. There is a moderate positive loading for group size and small negative loadings for the presence of either a constitution or factions. The substance of the factor appears to be captured by the label "centralized leadership."

The third factor is characterized by inclusiveness and the absence of institutionalized secrecy. There is also a minor negative correlation with the provision of selective incentives and a minor positive correlation with the presence of factions. It seems reasonable to label the factor "openness," since it is characterized primarily by the absence of secret rituals and covert activity, as well

TABLE 2
Organization

	Rotated Factor-Structure Matrix		
	Bureaucracy	Centralization	Openness
Formal bureaucracy	.90*	−.17	.17
Hierarchy	.77*	−.02	.03
Full time employees	.69*	.20	−.02
Formal membership list	.68*	−.08	.02
Written constitution	.66*	−.29	.12
Selective incentives	.56*	.03	−.30
Size at peak	.48*	.40*	.02
Centralized authority	.03	.97*	.11
Single dominant leader	−.06	.65*	−.06
Institutionalized secrecy	.17	.04	−.78*
Anyone can join	.09	.04	.48*
Factions	.23	−.33	.30

*Loading is .40 or greater.

as the absence of a probationary period, investigation, or formal induction for new members.

In the realm of *action and interaction* there are three factors that explain 68 percent of the variance in the eight items (see Table 3). The first factor is characterized by the use of violence, either in self defense or in the pursuit of goals; by the use of strikes, boycotts, or character assassination; by subjection to violence, and the arrest or constraint of members by police. The factor is labeled "confrontation."

Being helped with resources by outside authorities (third parties) has the highest loading on the second factor. An outside authority is defined as an established interest group, political party, or government agency that is not itself the target of change but can, by its actions, help or hinder the efforts of the protest group. The second highest loading is for sponsorship by wealthy backers, prestigious patrons, or patrons in important decision making positions in institutional hierarchies. There is a moderate positive correlation with the protest being made through the electoral system, and a small negative correlation with members being arrested or constrained by police. Generally the label "aid" seems appropriate.

The third factor in the realm of action and interaction is characterized by tangible harassment by powerful outsiders that hinders the group in its efforts to mobilize and influence (excluding

TABLE 3
Action and Interaction

	Rotated Factor-Structure Matrix		
	Confrontation	Aid	Hindrance
Use of violence	.92*	.12	.07
Subject to violence	.68*	−.16	.19
Use of strikes, boycotts, etc.	.60*	−.02	−.09
Arrested or constrained	.60*	−.26	.35
Hindered by outside authorities	.10	.02	.85*
Helped by outside authorities	.07	.76*	.10
Sponsorship	−.13	.51*	.03
Third party, elect members, or referenda	−.04	.39	−.21

*Loading is .40 or greater.

arrests and violence, which are coded as separate variables). Censorship is an example of the type of hindrance measured. There is also a moderate to small correlation with the arrest and constraint of members by police. The factor is labeled "hindrance."

There are three realms that each have three orthogonal factors. In the realm of beliefs and goals, the factors are displacement reformism, revolutionary activism, and union activism. In the organizational realm, groups may be characterized by their degree of bureaucracy, centralization of leadership, and openness. All factors in the realms of organization and beliefs and goals are essentially under the control of the protest group. There are three factors in the realm of action and interaction. Two are essentially controlled by third parties: aid and hindrance. The third, confrontation, is situationally controlled. In addition to the three complex realms there is a fourth realm, movement context, which constitutes a single situational factor.

PATH ANALYSIS: FINDINGS AND DISCUSSION

The factor analysis resulted in the extraction of three factors in each of the three large realms. Factor score coefficients were used to estimate factors, which were then employed as variables in a path analysis. Since these variables are indices based on factor score coefficients they are all coded intervally from low to high. The ultimate dependent variables—the degree of recognition and goal achievement—are coded ordinally from low to high. (See Bohrnstedt and Carter on ordinal measures, 1971.)

In the path analysis, our causal assumptions reflect the fact that protest groups are intentional emerging associations. Within a particular context a group of people develop a set of beliefs and goals. They organize in some way appropriate to their analysis and intentions. The imperative of their intentions forces them into action and interaction, the extent and quality of which may depend on the extent and type of organization. These things may affect the length of time a group sustains its challenge and, ultimately, its probability of success. Here is the assumed causal order of path analysis:

movement context	beliefs and goals	organization	action and interaction	length of challenge	success

It is assumed that there may or may not be an effect in the direction indicated by the arrow, but that there is not an effect in the opposite direction. The assumption is hierarchical, so that a variable may have a direct effect on any of the other variables to its right, and may be affected by any to the left.[4]

We began the path analysis by estimating two unrestricted models: one for recognition and one for goal achievement. We did this by regressing every variable on every higher level variable. Then we estimated a pair of restricted models, eliminating every path that was not significant at the .10 level in the unrestricted models. A decomposition of effects indicated that by eliminating all paths not significant at .10 we had introduced considerable bias into the recognition model. Therefore we estimated the restricted model for recognition, including the variables whose omission had caused the bias. All the paths in both restricted models were significant at .10. Those which were not significant do not appear in the models.

The path analysis (represented in Figures 1 and 2) may be interpreted in terms of the following eight hypotheses posited in the introduction:

Hypothesis 1a: The more radical a group's beliefs and goals, the less likely it will be successful.

The negative effects of displacement reformism and revolutionary activism substantiate this hypothesis. Furthermore, in the realm of beliefs and goals, displacement reformism is the least successful approach a protest group can take. In contrast, union activism, a third dimension of beliefs and goals along which groups may be more or less radical, does not have a negative total impact. Three things distinguish union activism from the other two dimensions: (1) it is positively rather than negatively associated with bureaucracy, (2) the constituents of the group are the prime beneficiaries, and (3) it is not associated with displacement goals. Thus, union activism escapes the fate of displacement reformism and revolutionary activism by being more bureaucratic and less threatening to incumbents in target positions.

Hypothesis 1b: The more organized a group is, the more likely it will be successful.

We find that bureaucracy is the only dimension of organization that has a substantial impact on success, and it is only related to recognition, not to goal achievement. In fact, bureaucracy not only has the largest direct effect on recognition, but its influence is

FIGURE 1
Restricted Path Model for Factors of Recognition

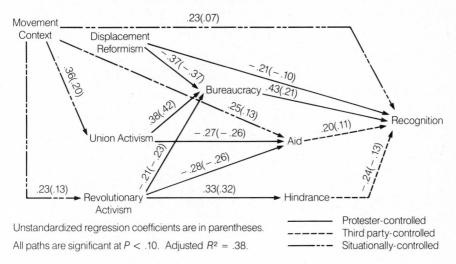

Unstandardized regression coefficients are in parentheses.
All paths are significant at $P < .10$. Adjusted $R^2 = .38$.

———— Protester-controlled
- - - - - - Third party-controlled
———--- Situationally-controlled

greater than the total effect (direct + indirect) of any other variable (see Figure 1). On the other hand, protest groups concerned primarily with goal achievement might do well to put their resources into direct attempts to influence their target and third parties rather than into building a bureaucracy.

The importance of bureaucracy for recognition may be due to the need of established organizations for a stable environment. If they are to recognize a group as the representative of a particular interest they must be assured of the group's continuity. Otherwise they could not be assured that a bargain struck today would not be forgotten tomorrow. Bureaucracy, then, may work not so much to force recognition as to allow it.

Hypotheses 2a and 2b:

As expected, aid from third parties makes success more likely, and hindrance makes it less likely (see Figures 1 and 2).

Hypothesis 3a: Active confrontation has an equivocal effect on success.

This hypothesis is substantiated when success is measured in terms of recognition. However, confrontation does have a significant positive impact on goal achievement (see Figure 2). Thus we may revise the hypothesis: involvement in confrontation does not

FIGURE 2
Restricted Path Model for Factors of Goal Achievement

Unstandardized regression coefficients are in parentheses.

All paths are significant at $P < .10$. Adjusted $R^2 = .50$.

—————— Protester-controlled
- - - - - - Third party-controlled
——·——·—— Situationally-controlled

generally hurt a protest group's chance for recognition and may improve its chance for goal achievement.

Here it is important to reiterate that confrontation is not simply the use of violence. Rather, it is aggressive interaction between the protest group and third parties. The basis for conceptualizing confrontation as an active interaction between the protest group and third parties is found not only in the factor analysis (see Table 4) but in a regression in which confrontation is operationalized as an

TABLE 4
Regression of Goal Achievement on Use of Violence, Subjection to Violence, and Active Confrontation

Variable	Regression Coefficient	Standardized Regression Coefficient
1. Use of violence	.00	.00
2. Subjection to violence	−1.08*	−.60*
3. Active confrontation (interaction of 1 and 2)	1.51*	.72*
	Constant = .59	
	$R^2 = .18$	

*$P < .05$

interaction term. When the use of violence, the subjection to violence, and the interaction between the two are included in a regression, we find that the use of violence has no effect by itself, while active confrontation—the interaction term—increases the probability of goal achievement.

Hypothesis 3b: A flourishing movement context makes success more likely, except when success refers to recognition, at which time a flourishing movement context makes success less likely.

The total effect of movement context on goal achievement is insubstantial. However, movement context is positively related to recognition. Thus the hypothesis is disconfirmed. Perhaps long term growth in a group's Social Movement Industry is associated with generally increasing acceptance of that type of group. This seems to be the case especially in regard to unions. Familiarity with a cause may breed sympathy or at least tolerance.

Hypothesis 4a: The total effects of variables controlled by the protest group are much smaller than the total effects of variables controlled by third parties.

In our analysis, just the opposite is true. By themselves, factors in the realms of organization and beliefs and goals explain 36 percent of the variance in both goal achievement and recognition. Aid and hindrance by themselves account for 18 percent of the variance in goal achievement and only six percent of the variance in recognition.

Factors controlled by the protest group have by far the largest total impact on success. A large part of this is due to the effects of beliefs and goals. Yet, many groups may be unwilling to change their beliefs and goals in order to improve their chance of success. Given such resolve, a group must depend on organization to improve its chance of success.

Bureaucracy, by itself, accounts for 28 percent of the variance in recognition. By comparison, aid and hindrance account for only six percent. Since bureaucracy is not related to aid and hindrance, these percentages may be compared directly. Bureaucracy is the key to recognition. Its impact is great enough to overcome the effects of third party action.

The situation is very different with respect to goal achievement. Bureaucracy and the centralization of leadership account for 16 percent of the variance, compared to 18 percent accounted for by aid and hindrance. Since bureaucracy and centralization are unrelated to aid and hindrance, these percentages may be compared directly. The protest group and third parties are essentially matched in their control over goal achievement. It is important to note that the balance is partly due to centralized leadership's association with confrontation. If, because of this relationship, we treat confrontation as a protester controlled variable, the balance of forces does not change. However, it appears that a protest group must engage in some degree of confrontation in order to offset the influence of third parties.

Although we reject hypothesis 4a, our findings give us reason for proposing several modifications of it. First, protest groups that are willing to modify their beliefs and goals have more control over their chance of success than do third parties. Second, bureaucracy has a decisive effect on recognition. And third, a group that is unwilling to moderate its beliefs and goals has about as much influence in achieving its goal as do third parties. The balance may depend on the group's participation in confrontation.

Hypothesis 4b: Much of the effects of protester-controlled variables are indirect, due to their influence on variables controlled by third parties.

Only a small proportion of the effects of protester-controlled variables is indirect, due to aid and hindrance. This is because none of the organizational variables are related to aid and hindrance, nor is displacement reformism. However, revolutionary activism is overwhelmingly unsuccessful because of the response of third parties. Interestingly, revolutionary activism differs from displacement reformism in that revolutionary activism is suppressed by third parties, while displacement reformism, which has direct negative effects on success, appears to be resisted by the target (see Figures 1 and 2).

CONCLUSIONS

A number of researchers, including Gamson (1975), have found that the more radical a group's goals, the less likely it is to be successful. Our analysis adds two dimensions to this basic finding. First, we conceive of and operationalize radicalness as a multi-dimensional construct rather than a unidimensional one. Thus, we allow for the possibility that some dimensions of radicalness affect success differently from others. Second, we address the question of *why* the more radical groups are less successful by examining indirect effects. We also elaborate on Gamson's findings that bureaucracy increases a group's probability of both goal achievement and recognition. We examine the relative impact of bureaucratic organization and third party intervention, whether bureaucratic organization works directly on the target or indirectly through third parties, and the ways in which these relationships differ for the two types of success.

Specifying three dimensions of radicalness allows us to compare the importance of third party intervention for the different dimensions. We find that groups that score high on revolutionary activism are unsuccessful largely because of suppression by third parties. Displacement reformism, on the other hand, is not mediated by third parties. It is resisted directly by the target. Union activism, although unlikely to be aided by third parties, is not hindered by them. Through its association with bureaucracy, union activism is more successful than the other two factors. These dimensions of beliefs and goals are controlled by the protest group and are decisive in influencing success. However, since it is for the implementation of their beliefs and goals that protest groups form in the first place, the groups may be unwilling to modify them in order to increase the chance of success. If this is the case, protest groups have about as much influence in achieving their goals as do third parties. The balance may require that the protest group participate in confrontation. In terms of recognition, protest groups can control their own success by bureaucratizing. Thus, we find that not all types of groups depend on the intercession of third parties in all situations for both types of success. The fact that we include a number of dimensions of radicalness of beliefs and goals, organization, social support, and success may clarify some differences between our analysis and others. First, Schumaker (1975) finds that third parties are stronger determinants of protest group success than are the groups themselves. We expect that Schumaker's finding is because his measures of radicalness capture the same dimension as our measure of revolutionary activism—the very dimension for which we find that the intercession of third parties is decisive.

Jenkins and Perrow (1977) also find that third party support is necessary for success. The farm workers they studied were a classic example of a powerless group. By powerless we mean that, in addition to having few personal resources to invest in the challenge, the farm workers had few cross-cutting memberships because of their social and cultural isolation. Although we have no measure of powerlessness, Gamson's sample includes groups with a wider range of resources and cross-cutting memberships. We hypothesize that the more powerless a group, the more it depends on the intercession of third parties. We feel that future research, rather than treating all protest groups as powerless, should treat powerlessness as a continuum on which protest groups can be placed.

By placing protest groups and their social environment on various dimensions, and by developing a causal model, we have been able to examine the mechanisms through which protest groups succeed or fail in achieving goals and getting recognized. This is only a first step. We hope that in future research, models will be developed which examine causal mechanisms in more detail, first by examining possible reciprocal effects, and second by specifying interaction effects.

FOOTNOTES

1. It might be argued that the indices which we use (estimated factor scores) are inappropriate, either because the factor score coefficients on which they are based tend to be unreliable (Alwin, 1973) or because factor analysis is not appropriate, since much of the original data is dichotomous or ordinal. In order to determine whether the use of factor score estimates is acceptable, we calculated two other sets of indices. The first are factor *based* scores (Alwin, 1973). They are built on the same factor analysis as the factor score estimates. Any variable with a loading above .40 is included in the index. The rest are excluded. Except for standardization, the variables included in the index are not differentially weighted. The second set of indices are based on a completely different set of non-parametric clustering techniques. They were derived by embedding hierarchical clusters within multidimensional space (Kruskal and Wish, 1978; Everitt, 1974). After calculating indices based on the three different techniques, we correlated conceptually equivalent index scores (e.g., bureaucracy scores based on the three techniques were correlated with each other). The lowest correlation between an estimated factor score and its non-parametric equivalent is .87. The highest is .98, the mean is .92, and the standard deviation is .04. Correlating estimated factor scores with factor *based* scores, the low is .85, the high is .98, the mean is .92, and the standard deviation is .04. Correlating factor based scores with their non-parametric equivalent, the low is .85, the high is 1.00, the mean is .94, and the standard deviation is .07. These high correlations with equivalent indices derived by alternative methods indicate that our factor score estimates are adequate measures of the underlying constructs. (Details of this analysis are available from the authors on request.)

2. If, for instance, two factors in the organization realm—bureaucracy (F_1) and centralization (F_2)—are correlated, it is possible to estimate the direct effect of each on success controlling for the direct effect of the other. However, the total effect of each variable is the sum of both direct and indirect effects. If F_1 causes F_2, then the total effect of F_1 on success is equal to its direct effect plus its indirect effect via F_2. On the other hand, if F_1 is the *result* of F_2, then its total effect on success would simply be its direct effect. Clearly, then, if F_1 and F_2 are correlated but a causal order cannot be assumed, it is not possible to tell what the total effect of either variable is. Such problems can be avoided

by assuming that F_1 and F_2 are uncorrelated (orthogonal). Then the total effect of each is equal to its direct effect. In neither case is there an indirect effect via the other. This assumption of orthogonality makes for a parsimonious model. In addition, we find no significant correlations between any indices that we assume to be uncorrelated. The average absolute value of the correlations is .03. The largest is .13, well below significance at the .10 level.

3. Factors were extracted to the point at which the next factor would explain less variance in the correlation matrix than the average standardized variable in the realm (i.e., the minimum eigen value $= 1$). The resulting factors were then rotated using a varimax rotation.

4. It is possible that other researchers might not agree with our causal order assumptions. In particular, some might argue that organization causes beliefs and goals rather than the other way around. While this is probably true once an organization is established, the protest groups being studied are, by definition, emerging associations. Because of this, we think that the overwhelming effect is that of beliefs and goals on organization. However, it must be recognized that these are assumptions, not findings.

REFERENCES

Alwin, Duane
1973 "The use of factor analysis in the construction of linear composites in social research." *Sociological Methods and Research* 2: 191–214.

Bohrnstedt, George and T. Michael Carter
1971 "Robustness in regression analysis." Pp. 118-46 in Herbert Costner (ed.), *Sociological Methodology*. Washington: Jossey-Bass.

Brill, H.
1971 *Why Organizers Fail: The Story of a Rent Strike*. Berkeley: University of California.

Fainstein, Norman and Susan Fainstein
1974 *Urban Political Movements: The Search for Power by Minority Groups in American Cities*. Englewood Cliffs, N.J.: Prentice-Hall.

Everitt, Brian
1974 *Cluster Analysis*. London: Heinemann.

Gamson, William
1975 *The Strategy of Social Protest*. Homewood, Ill.: Dorsey.
1980 "Understanding the careers of challenging groups: A commentary on Goldstone." *American Journal of Sociology* 85: 1043–60.

Garner, Robert Ash
1977 *Social Movements in America*, 2nd edition. Chicago: Rand-McNally.

Goldstone, J. A.
1980 "The weakness of organization: A new look at Gamson's *The*

Strategy of Social Protest." *American Journal of Sociology* 85: 1017–42.

Jenkins, C. J. and Charles Perrow
1977   "Insurgency of the powerless: Farm worker movements (1946–1972)." *American Sociological Review* 42: 249–68.

Kruskal, Joseph and Myron Wish
1978   *Multidimensional Scaling.* Beverly Hills: Sage.

Lipsky, Michael
1970   *Protest in City Politics.* Chicago: Rand-McNally.

McCarthy, John and Mayer Zald
1977   "Resource mobilization and social movements: A partial theory." *American Journal of Sociology* 82: 1212–41.

Schumaker, Paul
1975   "Policy responsiveness to protest-group demands." *The Journal of Politics* 37: 488–51.
1978   "The scope of political conflict and the effectiveness of constraints in contemporary urban protest." *Sociological Quarterly* 19: 168–84.

Shorter, Edward and Charles Tilly
1974   *Strikes in France: 1830 to 1968.* London: Cambridge University.

Snyder, David and William Kelly
1976   "Industrial violence in Italy, 1878–1903." *American Journal of Sociology* 82: 131–63.

Steedly, H. R. and J. W. Foley
1979   "The success of protest groups: Mutivariate analysis." *Social Science Research* 8: 1–15.

Zald, Mayer and Roberta Ash
1966   "Social movement organizations: Growth, decay and change." *Social Forces* 44: 327–41.

The Weakness of Organization: A New Look at Gamson's *The Strategy of Social Protest*[1]

JACK A. GOLDSTONE

Harvard University

In *The Strategy of Social Protest* William Gamson asserted that the organization and tactics of a social protest group strongly influence the group's chances for success. This assertion was based on an analysis of the rates of success of 53 social protest groups arising in America between 1800 and 1945. This article shows first that Gamson's results are based on a series of very weak assumptions and on frequently spurious zero-order correlations. When data on the rates of protest group success are reanalyzed, no effect of organizational or tactical parameters is evident. Additional data on the timing of social protest group success are then introduced, and a stochastic model is presented which closely fits the data ($r > .95$). With the help of this model, the timing of success is also shown to be substantially independent of the organization and tactics of the protest group. Finally, a new interpretation of the probability of protest group success, based on the incidence of broad national crises, is suggested.

William Gamson's *The Strategy of Social Protest* (1975) attempted to find explanations for the success or failure of social protest groups in achieving their expressed goals. Gamson examined detailed data on 53 groups, ranging from labor unions to Christian peace movements, to see whether there were any consistent relationships between rates of success and the organization, tactics, or goals of the challenging groups. He reported that goals, tactics, and organization factors *did* make a difference in a protest group's chances for success; groups which could not marshal the necessary organizational or tactical strengths were considered likely to fail, in their own terms, to wrest any favors from the economic or political system. Thus Gamson concluded that (p. 143) "entry . . . into the pluralist heaven . . . is not prohibited for those with the gumption, the persistence, and the skill to pursue it long enough. But this is, at best, cold comfort. . . . If it costs so much

[1] Thanks are due to Geoff Fougere, whose trenchant criticisms of Gamson's work prompted this reexamination of Gamson's analysis; to Ron Breiger, Kevin Fong, Theda Skocpol, and Harrison White, who provided many helpful comments; and especially to John Padgett, whose patience and penetrating observations in many discussions greatly improved the paper. Research support under National Science Foundation grants no. SOC76-24394 and JER76-17502 and an NSF graduate fellowship is gratefully acknowledged.

Reprinted, with permission, from *American Journal of Sociology*, March and May 1980, 85:1017–42, 1426–32.

to succeed, how can we be confident that there are not countless would-be challengers who are deterred by the mere prospect?" However, a closer examination of the data shows that they do not support this conclusion.

CRITIQUE OF GAMSON'S ANALYSIS

The Analysis Summarized

Gamson's data base is a random sample of 53 groups drawn from a list of 4,500 groups that participated in acts of social protest in America between 1800 and 1945. The final 53 groups were arrived at by a process including random selection, correction for duplication, and examination to see whether the group fitted Gamson's definition of a social protest group as a group seeking to mobilize an unmobilized constituency against an antagonist lying outside that constituency. In Gamson's words, the final groups represent a "random sample of all valid entries in the gross file [of 4,500 groups]" (p. 155).

The success or failure of each group was then determined from a combination of historical studies and, where possible, interviews. Groups that attained their desired ends in regard to most of their goals were considered to have gained *new advantages*. Groups that attained only some of their desired goals, or only partial satisfaction in regard to their chief goals, were considered to have gained *partial advantages*. Groups that failed to attain their goals to any appreciable degree were considered to have gained *no advantages*. In Gamson's analysis, 26 groups (49%) received new advantages; seven (13%) received partial advantages; 20 (38%) received no advantages. Gamson combined groups receiving partial advantages with those receiving none, giving overall success rates of 49% success (i.e., new advantages) and 51% failure (i.e., partial or no advantages).[2]

---

[2] Gamson also assessed success in terms of the acceptance of the group by its antagonist as a valid spokesman for its constituency. However, I shall discuss only the attainment of new advantages, since, except for a very few cases, the two indicators give the same results. In fact, of Gamson's 53 groups, only two that did not gain at least partial advantages gained acceptance, while only six groups that did attain new advantages did not also gain acceptance. Even these differences, however, may be misleading, in the light of Gamson's observation (pp. 51–53) that "in a few cases, there seemed to be no particular desire for acceptance, once gains had been achieved." Examples include the Night Riders, "a clandestine group that never anticipated or sought acceptance for them-

He then coded 39 organizational, tactical, and goal-oriented parameters for each group. The distribution of these parameters was checked for zero-order correlations with rates of success. Seven parameters were stated to have significant correlations with success rates: bureaucratization, centralization, use of selective incentives,[3] and the use of violence were positively correlated; recipience of violence, displacement-type goals, and factionalism were negatively correlated.

Problems in Gamson's Analysis

Several errors and inconsistencies in Gamson's data analysis lead to questions regarding his results. These involve matters of data counting and coding, the definition of success, the follow-up of the groups studied, and reliance on zero-order correlations without testing for the possible spuriousness of the observed correlations.

Spurious correlations.—Gamson's analysis of his 39 tactical, organizational, and goal-related parameters is based on examination of the zero-order correlations between individual parameters, or occasionally a pair of parameters, and the rate of group success. Unfortunately, with 39 parameters at work, if any one parameter is a particularly strong determinant of success or failure, it will generate spurious results in the zero-order correlations between other parameters unless controlled for.

One particularly strong determinant emerges at the outset—the espousal of displacement or nondisplacement goals. Among the 53 groups, 16 were designated as having displacement-type goals, that is, "goals including the destruction or replacement of antagonists" (p. 48). Nondisplacement groups, on the other hand, were those that sought only "to change the policies or organization of antago-

---

selves," and the Society for the Promotion of Manual Labor in Literary Institutions, whose key activists turned to other issues once success had been achieved. Moreover, insofar as differences in the indicators occur, acceptance seems less affected than new advantages by the organizational and tactical parameters I shall be discussing (see figs. 6-1, 6-2, 7-2, 7-4, and 7-5 in Gamson [1975], pp. 79, 80, 94, 95, 102, respectively). Thus acceptance seems a slightly less sensitive, and, given Gamson's remark on groups that did not seek acceptance, a more problematic indicator of success than new advantages. Nonetheless, given the close association between the two, my comments on Gamson's analysis of new advantages generally apply to his analysis of acceptance as well.

[3] "Selective incentives," a term coined by Olson (1965), denotes special benefits or incentives offered exclusively to members of an organization, usually to maintain their allegiance.

nists" (p. 43). Among the 16 displacement groups, the rate of success, as defined by Gamson, was 1 out of 16, or 6%. Among the 37 nondisplacement groups, the rate of success was 11 times greater: 25 out of 37, or 68% (see table 1). The strength of this factor is sufficient to invalidate almost all the zero-order correlations in which the impact of displacement goals was not factored out.

For example, Gamson reports that bureaucracy is a significant factor promoting protest group success. In his analysis, the 24 groups classified as bureaucratic had a success rate of 62%, compared with a 38% success rate for the 29 groups classified as nonbureaucratic (see table 2). However, as table 2 demonstrates, if the 16 displacement groups are removed from the analysis, the success rate for the bureaucratic groups becomes 65%, while that of the nonbureaucratic groups becomes 71%. Thus the difference between the success rates of bureaucratic and nonbureaucratic groups is small and in the opposite direction when the impact of the displacement groups is removed.

Other spurious correlations, as will be demonstrated below, can be attributed to questionable assumptions in defining success, errors in counting and coding, and inadequate follow-up.

The definition of success.—For reasons that he fails to make explicit, Gamson lumps groups that have attained partial advantages with those that received no advantages to yield a success rate of 49%. However, one could just as well argue that partial advantages are evidence of success, and lump groups receiving partial advantages with those receiving new advantages. This would yield a success rate of 62% (33 successes out of 53). The difference this makes in assessing correlations of organizational and other param-

TABLE 1
Displacement Goals and Outcome—Gamson's Analysis

	Nondisplacement Goals		Displacement Goals	
Outcome	%	n	%	n
Success	68	25	6	1
Failure	32	12	94	15
Total	100	37	100	16

NOTE. $N = 53$; $\tau_c = 52$; $\lambda_{rc} = .50$.

TABLE 2
Bureaucracy and Outcome

Outcome	Bureaucratic Groups		Nonbureaucratic Groups	
	%	n	%	n
Gamson's analysis:*				
Success	62	15	38	11
Failure	38	9	62	18
Total	100	24	100	29
Gamson's analysis with displacement groups removed:†				
Success	65	15	71	10
Failure	35	8	29	4
Total	100	23	100	14

*$N = 53$; $\tau_c = .24$; $\lambda_{rc} = .23$.
†$N = 37$ (16 displacement groups excluded, total sample $= 53$); $\tau_c = -.06$; $\lambda_{rc} = 0.0$.

eters with success rates is evident. Thus the decision of how to count the partially successful cases must be made with care.

The nature of the hypothesis that Gamson claims to be testing—the permeability of the American social system by the demands of protest groups—would seem to militate against classifying the attainment of partial advantages as evidence of failure. If the question being probed is when does a group succeed in gaining advantages from the standing social system, surely groups that have attained some advantages must be differentiated from those that have received none. The latter have simply failed—they apparently lack the organizational or other parameters requisite to securing any gains. The partially successful groups, though not gaining complete satisfaction, are nonetheless gaining both attention and some benefits. Thus they should be considered successful in an important sense. Yet as we shall see, Gamson's results rest heavily on his classification of partial successes as failures.

Counting and coding.—Gamson's definition of success or failure of a challenge depends only on whether a group's goals were achieved. Since in two instances pairs of groups were pursuing the same goal at the same time, the success or failure of these groups was not independent. If one group succeeded, the paired group also succeeded, by definition. Yet such pairs are counted as independent groups.

The two pairs that fit this description are (1) the American Anti-Slavery Society and the National Female Anti-Slavery Society, both seeking support for emancipation from the northern white middle class in the 1830s; and (2) the National Student League and the American Student Union, both seeking support for left-wing political activity on campus in the 1930s. Both members of each pair were pursuing the same goals, with the same or related constituencies and similar tactics, during the same time period. If one corrects this double counting, the number of independent groups is reduced to 51 instead of 53.

There is also an apparent error in coding. As noted previously, one of the most important classifications is whether or not a group adopts displacement goals. Gamson defines a displacement group as one whose goals include "the destruction or replacement of antagonists." Yet he codes as a nondisplacement group the First International, which he describes as "the first real Marxist effort in America . . . looking ultimately toward the building of a socialist state" (p. 153). As the professed goal of the International was the destruction of the power of capitalist employers as a class, or their replacement by worker-based management, it seems that the International fits Gamson's criterion for a group with displacement goals and should be coded accordingly.

The effects of these counting and coding corrections will be discussed after a look at problems in Gamson's follow-up of the groups in his sample.

Follow-up.—In following the progress of a group in its course of protest, Gamson ceased to follow the history of the group if its protest activities ceased for five consecutive years. If such a period of inaction occurred before the group had attained any of its goals, the group's efforts were simply counted as a failure. This treatment of periods of inaction as evidence of failure leads to serious inconsistency in the analysis of similar cases.

As examples, let us take the American Federation of Labor and the National Brotherhood of Baseball Players, two of Gamson's protest groups. The AFL began its challenge in 1881. However, success was only fully achieved 54 years later, with passage of the National Labor Relations Act in 1935. During that time, many of the parameters describing the AFL changed—size, levels of organization, tactics, even specific goals. The level of protest activities varied as well, ranging from periods of large-scale strike activity to periods of relative quiescence. Nonetheless, Gamson considers the entire 54 years of activity to constitute one challenge. His coding is organized to provide consistent values for the test parameters in spite of changes over time—for example, size is scored as the group's peak size; use of violence is scored by whether the group ever used violence; factionalism is scored when factionalism occurred either at the genesis or during any reorganizations of the group; if a group's name changes over time, consistency is achieved by simply coding the longest-used name as the unique name of the group. Gamson—quite correctly—considers that insofar as the AFL, during its entire history of activity, sought to mobilize the same constituency, in support of roughly the same set of goals, against the same antagonist, its activities should constitute one challenge.

Consider now the National Brotherhood of Baseball Players. Major league baseball players were first organized by the Brotherhood in 1885 to seek greater freedom and higher base pay and pension benefits from the major league clubowners. No successes were gained by the players in the 1880s, and the Brotherhood's formal activities temporarily ceased. However, various acts of protest, including threats of strikes, were conducted periodically throughout the early and mid-1900s. In the 1960s, the players' union, then called the Major League Baseball Players' Association, won several major concessions. Success was indisputably achieved in 1972, when the players' union conducted the first successful general strike in major league history, delaying the start of the baseball season for three weeks. The owners came to terms, offering major concessions on all issues—contract freedoms, base pay, and pension benefits—that had been fought over intermittently since 1885. Again we find success after a long drawn-out series of protest activities, in which the same constituency was being mobilized throughout against the same antagonist, seeking the same goals. Thus we would expect the activities of the baseball players' union to constitute one challenge in Gamson's analysis.

Yet this is not the case. Since bursts of protest activity by the players' union were separated by intervals of over five years, Gamson considers each burst a separate challenge by a different challenging group. Thus the failure of the union in the 1880s functions in his analysis as an instance of failure by a protest group; the later bursts of activity, and the successful conclusion of the challenge in

1972, are ignored. Though the overall pattern appears similar, the fact that the activity of the AFL was continuous leads to its inclusion as a success in Gamson's data. The discontinuity of the players' union activities leads to classification as a failure.

To see whether discontinuity of protest activities had affected Gamson's analysis and to assure consistent treatment of all cases, I followed up all the groups that Gamson classified as unsuccessful. I considered a group's activities to form part of a longer, discontinuous, challenge, only if *all* the following criteria were met: (1) The original group's protest activities were resumed by a group having the same constituency, espousing the same goals, and challenging the same antagonist. (2) When the challenge was resumed, both the general ideology and the specific goals were the same as those of the original challengers. (3) The basic organizational, tactical, and goal-related parameters (e.g., bureaucratic/nonbureaucratic, used violence/never used violence) of the renewed challenge were the same as those of the original challengers.[4]

Several challenges were found to meet these criteria.

In one case—the challenge by the Young People's Socialist League—two unsuccessful bursts of activity by the same group, only 10 years apart, are counted in Gamson's analysis as two independent instances of failure by two independent groups. Yet since the same goals, antagonist, constituency, organization, and tactics were retained throughout the YPSL's activities, it would be preferable to treat the YPSL's activities as a single, albeit discontinuous, challenge.[5]

Moreover, in several cases, challenges which Gamson classified as failures were successfully resumed. In addition to the major league baseball players, these include:

---

[4] The precise criterion was that when the challenge was resumed, at least five of the six major tactical and organizational parameters—use of selective incentives, bureaucratization, centralization, factionalism, use of violence, and recipience of violence—must be the same. In fact, only two of the challenges discussed exhibited any changes in organization or tactics. These were Planned Parenthood and the Journeyman Tailors' Union, both becoming more bureaucratic in their later stages. In this paper, Gamson's original coding of these challenges as nonbureaucratic has been maintained, because it is valid for much of their duration. However, recoding these challenges as bureaucratic would have no effect on any of the results discussed in this paper. The critique of Gamson's results on bureaucracy in table 2 is independent of the discussion of follow-up, while the results on the effects of bureaucracy presented below would only be strengthened by recoding these challenges as bureaucratic.

[5] With the two instances of double counting noted earlier, this reduces the number of independent challenges in Gamson's sample to 50.

1. *The American Anti-Slavery Society and the National Female Anti-Slavery Society,* established in 1832 and 1833, respectively. Goals as stated by Gamson: "mobiliz[ation of] a middle-class . . . reform constituency for the abolition of slavery" (p. 153). Goals achieved, under the leadership of the founder of the AAS, William L. Garrison, with passage of the Thirteenth Amendment in 1865.

2. *The American Birth Control League,* established 1921. Goals as stated by Gamson: to "mobilize a middle-class reform constituency of women for the greater acceptance of birth control, and more specifically to influence legislation affecting this goal" (p. 147). Goals achieved in the late 1960s, with the success of Planned Parenthood in gaining support for birth control among middle-class women, and with legislative successes in liberalizing abortion laws in California, New York and other states. (The ABCL had changed its name to Planned Parenthood in 1942.)

3. *The Union Trade Society of Journeyman Tailors,* established 1833. Goals as stated by Gamson: "mobiliz[ation of] journeymen tailors for the achievement of benefits to this group" (p. 152). Goals achieved in 1915. The Journeyman Tailors' National Union had taken up UTSJT's cause. In 1914, JTNU merged with a breakaway faction of the United Garment Workers to become the Amalgamated Clothing Workers. The ACW mobilized journeymen and shop tailors for a successful strike in 1915, winning significant benefits.[6]

4. *The National Student League and the American Student Union,* established in 1931 and 1935, respectively. Goals as stated by Gamson: NSL—"A group, formed by former members of the Student League for Industrial Democracy, that attempted to mobilize university students for the achievement of an anti-war, anti-racist, and anti-fascist political program. It also concerned itself with campus issues such as the achievement of a free student press and the elimination of compulsory ROTC." ASU—"A group, formed by former members of NSL and SLID, that attempted to mobilize university students behind a broad . . . set of leftist political goals" (pp. 148–49). In 1962, the parent organization of NSL and ASU—the Student League for Industrial Democracy (SLID)—

---

[6] The Journeyman Tailors Union left ACW later in 1915, over jurisdictional disputes, and maintained a separate existence as an AFL affiliate until 1938. However, major wage, hours, and closed-shop agreements—the goals of the UTSJT—had been achieved. (From 1915 on, the JTU simply sought to maintain jurisdictional separation from the shop tailors of ACW; strike activity by JTU after 1915 was insignificant.)

228 The Strategy of Social Protest

changed its name to Students for a Democratic Society (SDS). Goals achieved in the late 1960s with successful mobilization of university students for antiwar, antiracist activities. Specific goals achieved included abolition of ROTC on many campuses, liberalization of restrictions on free speech and free press at major universities, and various civil rights successes.[7]

Thus five challenges that Gamson considered to have failed did eventually succeed in mobilizing their target constituencies, and attaining full or partial achievement of their original goals. Since the goals, constituency, antagonists, and basic organizational and tactical parameters remained the same throughout each challenge, it appears that Gamson's attribution of failure in these cases is due to inadequate follow-up. Inasmuch as proper follow-up, when corrected for double counting, changes Gamson's success rate from 49% (26 out of 53 groups) to 62% (31 out of 50 groups), inadequate follow-up is a significant factor in Gamson's analysis.

Conclusion.—The critical nature of Gamson's errors and assumptions in the areas of definition of success, counting and coding, and follow-up can be seen in an analysis of the impact of factionalism on group success. Gamson reports that factionalism is nearly fatal to a group's challenge—groups free of factionalism are reported to have a success rate of 70%, while groups touched by it at some time in their history are reported to have a success rate of only 22% (see table 3). Much of this difference is accounted for simply by cases of double counting, lack of proper follow-up, and Gamson's definition of success. As table 3 shows, if these flaws are remedied, the success rate of groups free of factionalism rises to 87% (26 successes out of 30 groups), while the rate for groups that had experienced factionalism becomes 60% (12 successes out of 20). Even this slight difference, however, is erased when the displacement groups are factored out. As table 3 shows, factionalism then makes no difference—both the 23 groups free of it and the 11 affected by it had success rates of 100%.

The final tally of outcomes, if one were to make all the corrections noted and to control for the impact of displacement groups, is presented in table 4. These results deserve close attention.

---

[7] The histories of the AAS, the baseball players' union, and the American birth control movement can be readily found in any good encyclopedia, such as *Encyclopaedia Britannica* (1974). The history of the tailors' union can be found in Commons et al.'s (1934–35) history of American labor, and in Zaretz's (1934) account of the ACW, while the history of SDS is taken from Sale (1973).

A Reexamination: Displacement Groups and Success

The importance of the displacement/nondisplacement factor to group success is immediately apparent from table 4.

All the nondisplacement groups attained their goals, either wholly or in part. Thus it appears that any group willing to accommodate itself to some degree to its antagonist has an excellent chance of attaining its ends. Moreover, the chances of substantial success for protest groups in general look quite good: of the 38 successful groups, 82% (31 of 38) were considered to have achieved most of their goals, only 18% (7 of 38) having been originally classified by Gamson as achieving partial success.

TABLE 3
Factionalism and Outcome

Outcome	Groups without Factionalism		Groups with Factionalism	
	%	n	%	n
Gamson's analysis (uncorrected):*				
Success	70	21	22	5
Failure	30	9	78	18
Total	100	30	100	23
Gamson's analysis (corrected for double counting, follow-up, and counting partially successful challenges as successes):†				
Success	87	26	60	12
Failure	13	4	40	8
Total	100	30	100	20
Gamson's analysis (corrected for double counting, follow-up, and counting partially successful challenges as successes) with displacement groups removed:‡				
Success	100	23	100	11
Failure	0	0	0	0
Total	100	23	100	11

*$N = 53$; $\tau_c = .47$; $\lambda_{rc} = .46$.
†$N = 50$; $\tau_c = .26$; $\lambda_{rc} = 0.0$.
‡The First International is classified as a displacement group; 16 displacement groups are excluded; $N = 34$ (total sample = 50); $\tau_c = 0.0$; $\lambda_{rc} = 0.0$.

TABLE 4
Outcomes in Gamson's Data after Corrections, Controlling for Displacement Groups

	Nondisplacement Groups		Displacement Groups		
Outcome	%	n	%	n	Total
Success	100	34	25	4	38
Failure	0	0	75	12	12
Total	100	34	100	16	50

NOTE.—Includes corrections for double counting and follow-up, counting partially successful challenges as successes, and classifying the First International as a displacement group; $N = 50$; $\tau_c = .65$; $\lambda_{rc} = .67$.

Among the displacement groups, however, 75% met with total failure. We may thus examine with some interest the four displacement groups that did succeed.

One group, Father Coughlin's National Union for Social Justice, is an ambiguous case. Originally organized in 1934 to mobilize immigrants and the unemployed for the achievement of inflationary monetary policies, Gamson considered the NUSJ to have attained partial success when Roosevelt took up inflationary policies to combat the Depression. Success was only partial, however, because the NUSJ had also begun to espouse anticapitalist goals, seeking to replace free enterprise capitalism by nationalization of all banking and all natural resources. In these essentially displacement goals, the NUSJ was a failure. Thus, while the NUSJ is classified as a displacement group that attained success, on closer inspection it fits the general pattern—in its nondisplacement goals, it was able to attain partial success; in regard to its displacement goals, its challenge was a failure.

The three other displacement groups which succeeded, however, are indeed cases of the successful attainment of displacement-type goals. The National Student League and its successor organizations were eventually successful in eliminating ROTC from many campuses. The League of Deliverance, established in 1882 to oppose the employment of Chinese labor on the West Coast, and the Native American Party, an East Coast effort begun in 1843 to counter the rising political and economic power of Catholic immigrants, had some initial successes in obtaining economic and political sanctions against their targets.

All three of these displacement groups sought to displace an unpopular minority. The 12 displacement groups that failed were all minority groups—extremist political groups, third party movements, etc.—presenting a challenge to well-established interests. Thus we may refine our notions of displacement goals and success. For a protest group representing a minority interest, adoption of goals that include the destruction or replacement of the antagonist is almost certain to lead to failure. For a protest group representing a majority or established interest, however, some success in eliminating or displacing an unpopular minority may be quite possible.

These results have two consequences for Gamson's analysis. First, it appears that the permeability of American society to new interests, and the response of the society to new claims upon it, is far greater than Gamson indicates. Any interest group that is willing to accommodate itself to the rules of compromise, to seek advantages "within the system," has an excellent chance of eventually attaining, to some degree, its desired goals. The "flaw in the pluralist heaven," which Gamson seeks to demonstrate, seems to be not that the system is unresponsive to new interests, but that it is responsive even when those new interests seek to displace unpopular minorities.

The second point goes to the heart of Gamson's analysis. He is primarily concerned with seeking evidence for the effect of various organizational and tactical parameters on rates of success. Yet, as table 4 shows, his data are insufficient to support any such conclusions. The single parameter of displacement or nondisplacement goals is sufficiently strong that it must be factored out if the impact of other parameters on success is to be determined. However, if all the displacement groups are removed, unless one counts partial successes and discontinuous challenges, even if later successful, as "failures," the success rate of the nondisplacement groups is 100%. There is thus no apparent variability on which to base a conclusion on the effects of the remaining parameters, other than to note that, prima facie at least, based on the 100% success rate, they do not seem to make much difference.

Thus Gamson's analysis is seriously flawed. In addition to the spurious correlations produced by a failure to control, his results rest heavily on a scheme of data classification—specifying partial successes and discontinuous challenges, even if later successful, as "failures"—which is, at best, questionable.[8]

There is, however, another variable that can be used to test the effects of organizational and other parameters in Gamson's data— namely, the timing of success. Even among the groups that succeeded, there is a great deal of variability in the time from the initiation of their challenge to the attainment of their goals. Some groups were successful within a year; others worked for many decades before gaining success. Although the timing of success was ignored as a potential variable in Gamson's analysis, examining its distribution may tell us something more about the process of accommodation of the American system to social protest.

A STOCHASTIC MODEL FOR THE TIMING
OF PROTEST GROUP SUCCESS

The Time Distribution of Success

The time distribution of success for those protest groups that attained their goals, both in Gamson's original analysis and when augmented by partially successful and discontinuous successful challenges, is shown in figure 1. As can be seen from the graph, the pattern is the same for both populations: a substantial number of groups attain success in 12 years or less; a substantial, but lesser, number attain success in more than 12 but less than 24

---

[8] This conclusion also applies to a recent attempt to recast Gamson's analysis in multivariate form (Steedly and Foley 1979). The recasting uncritically accepts Gamson's definition of success, lack of follow-up, etc., and thus shares the problems of Gamson's study. However, it does eliminate some of the spurious correlations deriving from Gamson's reliance on zero-order correlations. In particular, the authors find that the most important predictor of success is displacement/nondisplacement goals, and that when this predictor is included in a multiple regression on group success, the parameters of bureaucracy (levels of hierarchy), centralization, and use of selective incentives contribute less than .015 to the coefficient of determination (p. 7 and table 5, p. 12). Curiously, the authors find the exclusion of bureaucracy, centralization, and the use of selective incentives from their predictive model unremarkable. They approach their work simply as a methodological strengthening of Gamson's study, that "confirmed the propositions of . . . Gamson" (p. 12). Yet insofar as the authors—accepting all of Gamson's counting, coding, and so forth—still find that several of his propositions regarding the effects of organizational parameters were spurious, their methodological strengthening, even though they seem unaware of it, displays the weakness of several of Gamson's substantive conclusions.

years; and as we go further out on the X axis, we find successively fewer groups taking a longer time to attain success.

One might suspect that differences in group organization or tactics were responsible for differences in the time required. However, the observed pattern can be generated by a simple stochastic model. As we shall show, the model both fits the data extremely well and is independent of any consideration of the effects of organizational or tactical parameters. Thus the timing of protest group success appears to have no causal relation to the organization or tactics of a protest group; instead, the timing of success seems to depend heavily on the incidence of broad political and/or economic crises in the society at large.

Generating the Model

The simplest way to generate the probability model is as follows. In any given year, a group may either attain its goals or not. Let us say that the probability of success in any given year is p. Then the probability that a group will succeed in its first year is simply p. The probability that it will succeed in its second year is the probability it fails in year 1—$(1 - p)$—times the probability that it will succeed in year 2, which is simply p. Thus the probability of success in exactly two years is $(1 - p)p$. Similarly, the probability of succeeding in the third year is the product of the probability of

FIGURE 1
The Time Distribution of Success

failing in years 1 and 2 times the probability of success in year 3, or p (success in exactly three years) $= (1 - p)(1 - p)p$. Thus in general, the probability of succeeding in exactly n years is given by equation (1):

$$p \text{ (success in exactly } n \text{ years)} = (1 - p)^{n-1}p. \qquad (1)$$

If p is small, the values of p for specific years will not vary greatly. Thus if $p = .05$, the probability of success in exactly 20 years is .02, while the probability of success in exactly 30 years is .01—not a large difference. However, significant differences emerge if instead of looking at the probabilities for specific years, we look at the probabilities of success for intervals of several years.

Say we look at the probability that a group will succeed in 20 years *or less*. This is simply one minus the probability that the group will fail in all 20 years, or $1 - (1 - p)^{20}$. In general, the probability of succeeding in n years or less is given by equation (2):

$$p \text{ (success in } n \text{ years or less)} = p_n = 1 - (1 - p)^n. \qquad (2)$$

Using equation (2), we can calculate the probability of success in 20 years or less, if $p = .05$, to be $p_{20} = .64$. Similarly, we can calculate the probability of success in 30 years or less, again with $p = .05$, to be $p_{30} = .785$.

We can think of p_n not only as the probability that a single group will succeed in a given number of years, but also as the proportion of groups in a sample that is likely to succeed in that number of years. Thus, for $p = .05$, the model would predict that 64% of the groups in a sample would have succeeded in 20 years or less, that an additional 14.5% of the sample would have succeeded in 20–30 years, and that the remaining 21.5% would succeed only after 30 years or more. Thus the model is simply tested—one need only compare the proportion of groups in our sample observed to succeed in a given number of years with the proportion predicted from the model.

Testing the Model

Two tests were made of the goodness of fit of the simple stochastic model described above to the time distribution of success data in Gamson's study: the Kolmogorov-Smirnov (K-S) one-sample test, and computation of the semilog linear regression correlation.

1. *Kolmogorov-Smirnov test.*—Figures 2 and 3 compare the time distribution of success for the stochastic model and the observed data sets. In each figure the smooth curve represents the model's specification of $p_n = 1 - (1 - p)^n$; the step curve represents the observed data (i.e., the proportion of the groups in Gamson's study that attained success in elapsed time x).[9] The parameter p has been estimated from the inverse of the sample mean. Thus, for Gamson's original analysis (fig. 2), p is estimated within .98 confidence limits as $p = 1/E(x) = .048 (+.023/-.018)$. If one uses the larger sample including partially successful and discontinuous successful challenges (fig. 3), p is estimated as just a bit smaller, but in the same range, at .041 $(+.021/-.013)$.

The K-S one-sample test (Conover 1971) analyzes the probability that a given sample was drawn from a population with a specified cumulative distribution on a two-valued dependent variable, for example, success/failure. The test focuses on the maximum difference, labeled D, between the cumulative distribution of the sample data and the specified cumulative distribution. If D exceeds the critical value for the $1 - \alpha$ confidence level, then with probability α, the sample was not drawn from a population with the specified distribution.

As can be seen from the figures, the fit to the model in both cases is excellent. To reject the hypothesis that the samples were drawn from a population represented by the model at the .95 level, observed D's would have to exceed the critical values of .259 and .215 for samples of size 26 and 38, respectively. The observed D's, .13 and .085, are well within these limits. Thus the probability is quite good that both samples were drawn from a population with the distribution of success specified by the given model.[10]

2. *Semilog linear correlation.*—The semilog linear correlation coefficient was calculated in order to determine the power of the model in predicting the observed data sets.

The relation between cumulative success and elapsed time specified by the model, $y = p_n = 1 - (1 - p)^n$, can be rewritten as a

---

[9] The model is actually a step function too, with a small step each year, but it has been smoothed out slightly to ease comparison with the data curve.

[10] Even with these small samples, the K-S test is fairly powerful. For example, an alternative stochastic distribution, the Poisson distribution with $\mu = E(x)$, can be calculated and compared with both data curves. The maximum D's in this case are .420 at nine years for Gamson's original data and .419 at 16 years for the larger sample. Thus the possibility that the time distribution of success is a Poisson distribution can be decisively rejected.

FIGURE 2
The Cumulative Time Distribution of Success for Successful Groups in Gamson's Original Analysis (N = 26).

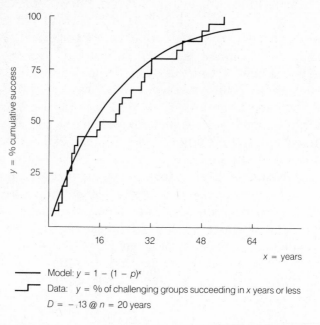

Model: $y = 1 - (1 - p)^x$
Data: y = % of challenging groups succeeding in x years or less
$D = -.13 \; @ \; n = 20$ years

FIGURE 3
The Cumulative Time Distribution of Success for Successful Groups in Gamson's Original Analysis Plus Partially Successful and Discontinuous Successful Challenges (N = 38).

Model: $y = 1 - (1 - p)^x$
Data: y = % of challenging groups succeeding in x years or less
$D = -.085 \; @ \; n = 28$ years

linear relation between a substitute variable, $y^* = \ln(1 - y)$, and n, as follows:

$$y^* = n[\ln(1 - p)]. \tag{3}$$

Thus, if a linear regression is computed for y^* and n, the model predicts that the resulting linear equation will have slope $\ln(1 - p)$ and intercept zero. The computed correlation will be a measure of how well the cumulative success rate y is predicted simply by the elapsed time n and the probability-of-success parameter p.

The results of the linear correlation are given in table 5. As can be seen, the correlations are very high, greater than .95, and the correspondence between the predicted slope and intercept and the observed data is quite good.

In sum, the model gives excellent predictions of the observed distribution of the timing of success; moreover, the accuracy of prediction is robust when partial successes and discontinuous successful challenges are included in the analysis.

Testing for Spurious Correlation

Another way to express the close agreement between the observed time distribution of success and the stochastic model is to

TABLE 5
Regression Analysis Results, Time Distribution of Success

		Data Analysis Results†		
	Estimated ln (1 − p)*	Slope	Intercept	r
Success in Gamson's original analysis (N = 26)	−.049 (+.019/−.024)	−.054 (±.0098)	.11 (±.26)	.97 (+.024/−.080)
Success in Gamson's original analysis plus partially successful and discontinuous successful challenges (N = 38)	−.042 (+.014/−.022)	−.047 (±.0049)	.11 (±.15)	.98 (+.012/−.032)

*Model: $y^* = n[\ln(1 - p)]$; estimates derived using estimates of p from $1/E(X)$, for $N = 26$ and $N = 38$, respectively; .98 confidence limits from Clemans (1959) in parentheses.
†.99 confidence limits on parameters in parentheses.

note that the time distribution of success can be predicted from knowledge of only one parameter—the constant probability of success, p. However, if the entire distribution can be predicted from p, which is assumed to be constant, none of the organizational or tactical parameters of the groups need be known in order to predict the distribution of success. In other words, *the success of the model in predicting the overall time distribution of success implies that organizational and tactical parameters are irrelevant to the timing of protest group success.*

This hypothesis deserves further testing.

If, for example, bureaucratic groups *do* succeed more rapidly than nonbureaucratic ones, but there are more bureaucratic groups in the sample, the overall distribution of success may be skewed in a way resembling the stochastic probability function. Or the overall fit may conceal the effect of individual factors which, in combination, offset each other.

To make sure that the fit of the overall distribution to the model was not in part a result of such effects, the time distribution of success was again examined, focusing on a number of specific organizational and tactical parameters.

Gamson indicated that six tactical and organizational factors had a significant impact on the success of protest groups. The factors were: (1) bureaucratization, (2) centralization, (3) use of selective incentives, (4) use of violence, (5) recipience of violence, and (6) factionalism. The first four factors were held to improve the chances for success, the latter two to make success less likely.

The K-S two-sample test was used to determine whether these factors, examined individually, had any impact on the timing of success. Successful groups were divided first into bureaucratic and nonbureaucratic groups, and the cumulative time distribution of success for the former was checked against that of the latter. If the former had any tendency to succeed more rapidly than the latter, the cumulative success curves would diverge. The maximum divergence, D, could then be compared with the critical value of D that would signify a statistically significant difference in the time distribution of success. Since the test is somewhat weak with samples this small, a .1, rather than the more stringent .05, level of significance was sought.

This analysis was carried out for all six factors, as shown in table 6. Again, the results are essentially the same whether one examines only those groups considered successful by Gamson or includes the partially successful and discontinuous successful groups. Although the impact of most factors is not statistically significant, there are a few surprises.

The difference between Gamson's 15 bureaucratic and 11 non-bureaucratic groups was statistically significant, but in the negative direction (table 6). That is, the bureaucratic groups took significantly *longer* to attain success than the nonbureaucratic ones. The same result occurs for the larger sample. The only other significant factor was the use of selective incentives. Again we find, for both Gamson's and the augmented sample, a negative impact, with groups that used selective incentives taking significantly longer to attain their goals. How can we account for these unexpected results?

These results may in fact imply that bureaucratization and the use of selective incentives tend to cause delays or inefficiencies in

TABLE 6
Kolmogorov-Smirnov Two-Sample Test Results for Impact of Tactical and Organizational Variables on the Time Distribution of Success

Variable	N Groups Having That Characteristic	N Groups Not Having That Characteristic	D	Significance
Success in Gamson's original analysis ($N = 26$):				
Bureaucratization	15	11	$-.618$	*
Centralization	18	8	.486	N.S.
Use of selective incentives	7	19	$-.646$	*
Use of violence	6	20	.350	N.S.
Recipience of violence	3	23	$-.450$	N.S.
Factionalism	5	21	$-.419$	N.S.
Success in Gamson's original analysis plus partially successful and discontinuous successful challenges ($N = 38$):				
Bureaucratization	21	17	$-.423$	*
Centralization	23	15	.365	N.S.
Use of selective incentives	9	29	$-.483$	*
Use of violence	8	30	.270	N.S.
Recipience of violence	6	32	$-.417$	N.S.
Factionalism	12	26	$-.410$	N.S.

NOTE.—Recipience of violence includes both physical abuse and arrest.
*Significant at .1 level.

a group's struggle for success. Or the results may simply suggest that groups that succeed quickly do not need to use bureaucratization or selective incentives to hold together. Conversely, groups that have not succeeded rapidly may adopt these means in order to maintain cohesion and allegiance.[11] In this event, the correlation of bureaucratization and the use of selective incentives with longer challenges may not indicate a causal effect of the mode of organization on the time required for success, but rather the reverse. Without more detailed data on the organizational history of the specific groups in this sample, one cannot confidently point the causal arrow in a specific direction. Suffice it to say that there is definitely no evidence that *any* of the factors Gamson claimed to be significant have a statistically significant effect on the timing of success in the direction that Gamson suggested.

A search was also made for interaction effects by testing various combinations of factors, as shown in table 7. For example, Gamson claims that the combination of centralization and bureaucracy is particularly helpful—but its effect in the two-sample test was not significant. Given that the two strongest positive effects in table 6 were centralization and use of violence, this combination was tested, but again to no effect. Finally, the combination of both of Gamson's negative factors—factionalism and recipience of violence—was examined. Here alone a statistically significant result, in the direction expected from Gamson's study, was found.

Yet there is again a problem of determining the direction of causality. It may be that groups affected by both factionalism and the receipt of violence are particularly likely to take longer in attaining their goals than groups not so afflicted. However, it may also be that groups that both take a long time before attaining success, and are subjected to violence, are more likely to develop factional splits as a result of such stress. There is substantial evidence in Gamson's data for this latter contention.

The overall rate of factionalism in the augmented sample of 38 successful groups is 32% (12 out of 38). However, for the five groups that both were violence recipients and took more than 10 years to attain success, the rate of factionalism is 60% (three out of five). Moreover, Gamson does record whether factionalism was present at the genesis of a group or developed later. Of the three groups that were violence recipients and experienced factionalism,

---

[11] This point is also made by Gamson (1975, p. 122).

TABLE 7
Kolmogorov-Smirnov Two-Sample Test Results for Interaction Effects
(Data Drawn from Larger [N = 38] Data Base)

Variables	N Having Both	N Having Neither	D	Significance
Centralization and bureaucratization	11	5	−.344	N.S.
Centralization and use of violence	6	13	.514	N.S.
Factionalism and recipience of violence	3	23	−.826	*

*Significant at .1 level.

two had no factional disputes at the time of their origin but developed them later. The third experienced factional divisions both at the outset of, and throughout, its challenge. Thus, while it is certainly possible that the interaction of violence recipience and factionalism causes delays in the attainment of success, there is suggestive evidence that the correlation is due instead to delays in the attainment of success, combined with recipience of violence, contributing to factional divisions. Again the time requisite to attaining success may have a causal effect on a group's organization, as well as the reverse.

In sum, no significant advantages in the time distribution of success could be attributed to the presence of any of the "helpful" tactical or organizational parameters, either alone or in combination. Nor could any significant disadvantages be attributed to the "harmful" factors, excepting the combination of violence recipience and factionalism. Such significant effects as were found seem to suggest that the timing of success has more impact on the organization of the challenging group than vice versa. Thus the apparent independence of the time distribution of success from organizational and tactical parameters, implied by the stochastic model, was substantially confirmed.[12]

---

[12] A multiple regression for the timing of success was also run, using Gamson's organizational and tactical parameters as the independent variables. The results were the same as those given above. The tactical and organizational parameters had little explanatory power; such power as they did have was almost entirely due to the correlation of use of selective incentives with longer challenges.

AN INTERPRETATION: CRISES AND THE TIMING
OF SUCCESS

To this point I have provided largely negative results. In regard to rates of success, the overwhelming factor in determining success is the single parameter of displacement/nondisplacement goals. Nondisplacement groups succeed, displacement groups—except those with unpopular minorities as targets—fail; the organization and tactics of the groups appear to have little or no additional impact. Moreover, the timing of protest group success appears to be a simple stochastic process, governed by a constant probability parameter, p. This process can be modeled by equation (2) with excellent predictive results. Thus, tactical and organizational factors appear to be very weak as explanations of either the rate or the timing of success of the protest groups in Gamson's sample.

These results pose several substantial problems of interpretation. First, why should the process of social protest group success be stochastic? What type of model of political processes or social change would generate such stochastic outcomes, and could such a model provide an empirical meaning for the value of p? Second, how can the apparent irrelevance of the organizational and tactical parameters of protest groups to their chances and timing of success be explained? Finally, what does the difference in success rates between displacement and nondisplacement groups imply?

Answers to all of these questions are beyond the scope of the present data analysis. However, I wish to present a few tentative interpretations, based on an apparent connection between the timing of protest group success and the incidence of broad, national, economic and political crises.

A distinction is often made between revolutionary change, which is highly discontinuous, and the normal processes of accommodation and gradual change in ongoing political systems. However, it may be that even the process of accommodation and "routine" change occurs in a rather lumpy, discontinuous manner. For example, we may suggest, following Gamson's results (Gamson 1975, pp. 116–20), that social protest groups, even if seeking nondisplacement goals, will get serious attention only when some external shock occurs, such as a major war or economic or political crisis. Only at such times, when the need for integration and support of the established order is particularly strong, are established interests likely to feel the need to compromise and accommodate to new social protest groups. In this case, the success of protest groups would be tied to the essentially stochastic flow of major shocks to the society.

Empirically, we would then expect, if there were any truth to this hypothesis, that protest group success would tend to be clustered around times of stress or turmoil. In fact, there is substantial evidence in the data of just such a clustering pattern.

In figure 4, the pattern of success over dated time is given for the 38 groups in the sample (including partially successful and discontinuous successful challenges) that attained their ends. There is clearly substantial clustering; moreover, the clustering is significantly in excess of that which would be expected from merely random clumping. (This is true whether or not the partially and discontinuous successful groups are included; see the box in fig. 4.) Most of the dates of success fall into six groups or clusters: one in the early 1830s; another from 1865 to 1873; one from 1905 to 1922; then two close clusters, but with distinguishable peaks, the first running from 1929 to 1937, the second from 1942 to 1948; and finally one from 1968 to 1972. All of these periods are associated with major periods of stress—the Jacksonian Revolution in the 1830s; Civil War and Reconstruction in the late 1860s and early 1870s; the overlapping turmoil of the Progressive Era, World War I, and the postwar recession from 1901 to 1922; and the depression, World War II, and the peak of the Vietnam War corresponding precisely with the last three clusters.

Looked at closely, even the two dates of success that fall outside these periods of national crisis confirm the general rule. The group that succeeded between the first and second clusters was the Native American Party, established in 1843 to oppose the rising power of Catholic immigrants on the East Coast and attaining some success by 1847. If we look at immigration figures for the city of Boston, for example, we find that there was indeed a regional "crisis" by 1847, when the group attained its partial success. In the decade from 1837 to 1846, Irish immigration into Boston totaled roughly 20,000 individuals, as it did in the decade from 1857 to 1866. Yet in the decade from 1847 to 1856, Irish immigrants to Boston totaled 120,000 (Handlin 1959). Thus an immigration "crisis" was occurring at the time and place of the challenging group's success. Exactly the same is true of the group that succeeded between the second and third clusters; this was the League of Deliverance, which succeeded in 1882 in obtaining sanctions

FIGURE 4
The Dated Time Distribution of Success

against Chinese immigrant labor on the West Coast, at a time when Chinese immigration to the coast was reaching "crisis" proportions.

In short, there is a near-perfect match between periods of protest group success and periods of broad crises. This is not to say that groups may not be found that succeeded at other times; yet if Gamson's sample is truly a random sample of groups active in this period, the proportion of groups whose success does not coincide with national or acute regional crises must be small indeed.

We should also note that if one focuses on the date of origination of the challenges in the sample, one does not find the same correspondence with periods of crisis. Instead, only slightly more than half (55%) of the 38 groups began their challenges during one of the periods of crisis listed above. Moreover, as such crises included 42% of the years from 1800 to 1945 (only challenges begun between these dates were in the gross file from which the sample was drawn), the correlation between periods of crises and the start-up of challenges is no more than would be expected from chance (χ^2 test, N.S.). Thus there appears to be little connection between the initiation of challenges and the periods of crisis noted above.

If these periodic crises are indeed the factor that explains the time distribution of success, we should be able to compute the average probability of success parameter p from them as well. This is easily done.

Since there is no connection between the times of start-up and the periods of crisis listed above, the probability of success in any given year, from the perspective of a challenging group, is simply the probability that a year will be a crisis year, times the average probability of success during a crisis year. The probability of a crisis year, or the frequency of crisis years in the time period of Gamson's study, is 42%.[13] The average probability of success during a crisis year can be estimated by observing, for each year of

---

[13] The dates for the full span of the above-named crises, taken from Current, Williams, and Freidel (1975), are: Jacksonian Revolution (through the panic of 1837), 1829–37; Civil War and Reconstruction, 1860–77; Progressive Era and World War I (through the post-war recession), 1901–16 and 1917–22, respectively; the depression, 1929–37; World War II (through postwar economic sanctions), 1942–48; and Vietnam, 1964–72. Different historians differ on precise dates for the beginning and end of these periods, so a year or two may be added or subtracted in various texts. On the basis of the dates above, total years spanned by these crises were 74, or 42% of the years from 1800 to 1975.

the crises listed above, the percentage of active challenging groups that attain success that year. The average success rate for the cited crisis years is .095. Multiplying, we find the estimate of p from the frequency of, and the chances of success during, crisis years to be .040, in close agreement with the range of .041 ($+.021/-.013$) estimated from the simple elapsed-time distribution shown in figure 1, and used in generating the stochastic model. Thus attributing the timing of protest group success to the incidence of crises in the society at large is fully consistent with the stochastic model described above.

CONCLUSION

The irrelevance of group attributes to the chances and timing of group success poses problems for the traditional pluralist model of social structure. Since change is supposed to occur through the resolution of conflicts between competing interest groups, those groups better prepared for the process of competition—that is, those with superior organization or tactics—*should* come out ahead. However, this does not seem to be the case; at least, no one set of organizational or tactical attributes seems to offer significant advantages over others in attaining or hastening success. If there are any conclusions regarding the effects of organization to be drawn from Gamson's data, they seem to be two: First, *any* group capable of expressing its aims in some fashion (enough to get into a gross file sample of protest groups), and adopting nondisplacement goals, has excellent chances of eventually attaining its aims, provided it maintains its challenge until a crisis arises that makes success likely. Second, correlations between longer challenges and the use of selective incentives and bureaucratization suggest that these organizational attributes may be useful to groups that have a long wait prior to attaining success, and find themselves in need of some kind of reinforcement to maintain cohesion.

In regard to the process of accommodation of the American system to social protest and change, we thus find a picture of peculiar flexibility combined with peculiar rigidity, a picture rather different from that drawn by Gamson. Gamson claimed that success was difficult to attain, and painted a picture in which only the best-organized groups, after a long struggle, were likely to attain their ends. Yet if one challenges his definition of partial success as "failure," and follows up discontinuous challenges, a very different picture emerges. As noted, *all* of the nondisplacement groups eventually attain their ends in some degree, regardless of their organization. Moreover, the struggle is as likely to be a short one as a long one—fully 37% of the 38 successful groups attained their ends in less than a dozen years, while only 31% took more than 30 years. And the better organized among those groups, as we have seen, succeed no more rapidly than the rest.

Yet while the American social system thus appears extremely flexible and permeable to new interests, it also exhibits peculiar rigidities. All of the groups with displacement goals, except those with unpopular minorities as targets, fail. Thus there is effective discrimination between groups that accommodate themselves to compromise, and those that do not. While "compromisers" may almost certainly attain success, well-established interests seem to be nearly impervious to attempts to destroy or replace them. In addition, even nondisplacement groups appear extremely limited in their chances for success except during times of broad crises. It thus appears that well-established interests are highly resistant to even compromise or accommodation unless the external pressures of a substantial crisis arise.

To sum up, the American social system appears to be willing to accommodate itself to a tremendous range of social protest, provided that destruction or replacement of well-established interests is not sought. Yet this process of accommodation is a highly intermittent, discontinuous process, in which the incidence of large-scale crises, rather than the organizational or tactical efforts of particular protest groups, determines the timing of protest group success.

REFERENCES

Clemans, K. G. 1959. "Confidence Limits in the Case of the Geometric Distribution." *Biometrika* 46: 260–64.

Commons, John Rogers, David J. Saposs, Helen L. Sumner, E. B. Mittelman, H. E. Hoagland, John B. Andrews, and Selig Perlman. 1934–35. *History of Labour in the United States.* 4 vols. New York: Macmillan.

Conover, W. J. 1971. *Practical Non-parametric Statistics.* New York: Wiley.

Current, Richard N., Harry Williams, and Frank Freidel. 1975. *American History: A Survey.* 4th ed. New York: Knopf.

Encyclopaedia Britannica. 1974. 15th ed. Chicago: Encyclopaedia Britannica.

Gamson, William A. 1975. *The Strategy of Social Protest.* Homewood, Ill.: Dorsey.

Handlin, Oscar. 1959. *Boston's Immigrants: A Study of Acculturation.* Rev. and enlarged ed. Cambridge, Mass.: Harvard University Press.

Olson, Mancur, Jr. 1965. *The Logic of Collective Action.* Cambridge, Mass.: Harvard University Press.

Sale, Kirkpatrick. 1973. *SDS.* New York: Random House.

Steedly, Homer R., Jr., and John Foley. 1979. "The Success of Protest Groups: Multivariate Analyses." *Social Science Research* 8: 1–15.

Zaretz, Charles Elbert. 1935. *The Amalgamated Clothing Workers of America: A Study in Progressive Trade Unionism.* New York: Ancon.

Understanding the Careers of Challenging Groups: A Commentary on Goldstone

WILLIAM A. GAMSON

University of Michigan

The disagreements between Goldstone and myself go beyond the merits or demerits of *The Strategy of Social Protest.* We differ in our approaches to historical materials, in the way we relate argument or theory to data, and in our concern with how theoretical models may be relevant to policy. Furthermore, these differences in approach to understanding the careers of challenging groups lead us to different conclusions on what it takes to gain entry into the American polity. As I shall try to show, Goldstone's criticism is weak, even when taken in its own terms, but our differences must be understood in the context of these wider issues.

THE MEANING OF SUCCESS

There is no more ticklish issue in studying social protest than deciding what constitutes success. The approach in *Strategy* begins with the distinction between the challenge and the challenger.

Reprinted, with permission, from the *American Journal of Sociology* 85 (1980): 1043–60.

"The actor whose political career will concern us is the *carrier* of a challenge to the political system" (p. 28, emphasis added here). This distinction between a social movement and a social movement organization (here, the carrier) is central to the resource mobilization approach to social movements (see Zald and Ash 1966; Oberschall 1973; McCarthy and Zald 1977; Tilly 1978).

Organizational entities that carry a challenge hope or claim that certain people (perhaps everybody) will be affected positively by the changes they seek from their antagonist. Those people for whom benefits are claimed are the challenging group's *beneficiary*. The degree to which the beneficiary gains new advantages must be assessed independently of the success of the challenger qua organization. One group may see its leaders honored or rewarded while their supposed beneficiaries linger in the same cheerless state as before. Another challenger may have leaders who are vilified and imprisoned even as their program is eagerly implemented by their oppressor.

Operationally, there are many specific indicators of success, and *Strategy* divides them into two clusters. One cluster concerns the acceptance of a challenging group by its antagonists as a valid spokesperson for a legitimate set of interests.[1] The second cluster focuses on whether the group's beneficiary gains new advantages during the challenge and its aftermath.

By distinguishing these two meanings of success, *Strategy* describes four outcomes: *full response* (groups that are successful on both clusters); *collapse* (groups that are not successful on either); *cooptation* (groups that gain acceptance without new advantages); and *preemption* (groups that gain new advantages without acceptance).

Of course, the two kinds of success are correlated, and most of the 53 cases fall on the main diagonal, but some 20% do not: 11 groups have either preemption or cooptation as outcomes. Furthermore, virtually all of the theoretical arguments and data analyses in *Strategy* make use of the distinction. Different antecedent variables are related to the two outcomes. The most interesting thing that one can say about how success relates to such variables

---

[1] In the case of groups with displacement goals, it would be more accurate to label this cluster "inclusion" rather than "acceptance."

as factionalism, centralization, bureaucracy, selective incentives, violence, and the like frequently concerns the relative strength of their relationship to these alternative meanings of success.

Goldstone hacks through this artery with a footnote in which he says, "I shall discuss only the attainment of new advantages, since, except for a very few cases, the two indicators give the same results." For him it is a distinction without a difference, not worth making. The elusiveness of the concept of success holds no fascination. There are simply better or worse indicators of a label with unexamined meaning.

Let us accept, for the moment, the meaning of success that Goldstone uses: the spread of new advantages to the challenger's beneficiary. How does one assess it and what rules should one follow to deal with the many troubling problem cases that arise? Our divergences in approaching historical materials are highlighted by our disagreements on such an issue.

The summary measure of success used in *Strategy* was based on a complicated procedure.[2] We are dealing with groups 75% of which had multiple antagonists. Hence, one could gain advantages from some antagonists and not from others. Some groups gave programmatic attention to subgoals in distinct institutional settings, involving quite separate antagonists. The National Student League, for example, focused some of its activity on campus-oriented concerns such as ending compulsory ROTC and compulsory chapel while at the same time it involved itself in the bitter struggle of coal miners in Harlan County, Kentucky. Given separate goal areas, groups may gain new advantages in some but not in others.

The basic measure of success was consensual, relying on perceived agreement by historians, the challenging group itself, and its antagonist. A group received fields of codes reflecting these various assessments, with a separate field for each of its different goal areas and antagonists. Some groups had a dozen or more such fields. Clearly, some summary measure is necessary to reduce this complexity. The one used in *Strategy* distinguished two kinds of borderline cases: those that received peripheral advantages (that

---

[2]The procedures summarized here are described in greater detail on pp. 35–36 of *Strategy*.

is, the positive fields appeared in goal areas that were not central for the group); and those that received equivocal advantages (that is, there was no consensus on whether the particular new advantages actually occurred).

The question arises how one should treat these borderline cases. Goldstone reasons that, inasmuch as I am a critic of pluralist theory and a skeptic about the openness of American society, I ought to bend over backward and take the most liberal possible definition of success. This would be the only fair way of testing my hypothesis that American society is not easily permeable.

I did not approach the issue in this fashion. The intent in *Strategy* is "to make sense of the experience of challenging groups in America" (p. 12) and, in the process, to evaluate parts of the pluralist interpretation of American politics. I do not believe that questions of the magnitude and complexity of the permeability of the American political system can be resolved in some definitive test of a hypothesis—no matter how carefully the sample is selected or the data set prepared. But even if I believed that one could prove or disprove such a hypothesis as Goldstone posits, I certainly would not rely on where the line is drawn between calling a group a success or a failure. *Strategy* never suggests that American society is not open because only half of the groups met the standard of success used. The issue is a red herring.

A better starting point is to ask whether, in summarizing a complex, multidimensional concept like success, one is able to capture the intuitively meaningful differences that exist. If groups as different in their experience and fate as Father Coughlin's National Union for Social Justice and the Steel Workers' Organizing Committee are both considered to have the same "successful" outcome, one is entitled to ask whether this is a discriminating enough standard.

The issue, then, is not one of testing hypotheses but one of data quality. The question to ask is whether subtle enough distinctions are being made to do justice to the historical reality underlying the summary measure of success. By throwing groups with peripheral or equivocal advantages in a bin with more genuine successes, one simply blurs important distinctions and thereby dilutes the quality of the resulting data set. Indeed, this theme of blurring important distinctions is a recurrent one in the discussion below.

THE AFTERMATH ISSUE

The end point of a challenge is marked by any one of the following:[3] (1) the challenging group ceases to exist as a formal entity; (2) the challenging group, while not formally dissolving, ceases mobilization and influence activity for a period of five years; (3) the challenging group's major antagonists accept the group as a valid spokesperson for its constituency and deal with it as such. Since this end point is defined in terms of the acceptance cluster, it is not immediately apparent what the time period should be in assessing new advantages for the beneficiary. Should one look for new advantages only up to the end point of the challenge, or should one continue to look after that? If afterward, for how long a period?

There are two good reasons not to stop at the end of the challenge. First there is the danger that one will miss preemption, mistaking it for failure. A challenger might be crushed or fall apart after setting in motion important changes that reach full fruition only after its demise. Second, there is the danger that one will mistake full response for cooptation. Sometimes groups gain acceptance before any new advantages have appeared. By not looking beyond the end of the challenge, one would ignore the new advantages that followed soon after acceptance.

Strategy elected to assess new advantages for a period of 15 years beyond the end of the challenge.[4] There is obvious arbitrariness in the choice of 15 years, and one might well argue for a shorter period to provide more assurance that there is some causal connection between the activity of the challenger and the advantages to its beneficiary. But Goldstone advocates that an indefinite period be used.

In my view, this advice leads to absurdities, well illustrated by the National Brotherhood of Professional Baseball Players. The Brotherhood began its challenge in 1885 and made quite a bit of headway with professional baseball players in the National League

---

[3]See pp. 30–31 of *Strategy* for a fuller discussion of what is summarized here.
[4]Goldstone apparently thinks that no follow-up period was used, although *Strategy* states (p. 36), "The codes covered changes both during the period of the challenge and in the following 15 years." One might wonder how Goldstone could have missed this since the discussion of how new advantages were measured occupies about a page. It is understandable in view of his muddle on the distinction between challenger and challenge. It is easy to get confused about a five-year period of organizational inactivity and a 15-year period for assessing new advantages when one is not clear on the conceptual distinction.

during the next few years under the leadership of John Montgomery Ward. After initially negotiating with the Brotherhood and agreeing to review the standard player's contract, the owners reneged without warning. Taking advantage of Ward's absence from the country and the geographical dispersion of the players during the off season, the owners sent out contracts ignoring the Brotherhood and unilaterally instituting a new classification system unfavorable to the players. Ward, who was a lawyer as well as a star shortstop, responded by forming a Players' League with outside financial backing. The Players' League competed with the National League during the 1890 season but collapsed after one year, taking the Brotherhood along with it.

Goldstone would have us call this group a success because in the 1970s—80 years later—major league baseball players received significant new benefits! The Brotherhood had certain organizational characteristics such as centralization. But how could one expect to find any meaningful connection between this characteristic of the group and a measure of success that rests on events 80 years after its demise?

THE INDEPENDENCE ISSUE

The unit of analysis in *Strategy* is the challenging group. This might seem a relatively clear unit, but a number of sticky questions arise. Suppose, for example, that a group changes its name. Is this merely old wine in new bottles, or is it really a different entity? If it is nothing more than relabeling, surely it is a case of double counting to treat it as a different challenging group.

There is also a problem of new wine in old bottles. Sometimes a minority faction seizes control of an organization's apparatus and its name. The organization may then radically change its direction, organization, and strategy. Surely, at some point, one would want to consider it a new challenger that happens to bear the old name.

As I write, the Ku Klux Klan is marching again in the South. Are we to treat this as the same challenging group as the Klan of the Reconstruction era, the Klan of the 1890s, and the Klan of the 1920s? The members are, after all, different people who may adopt different organizational forms and strategies, may have different interactions with agents of social control, and may have different outcomes.

The choice of a name by a group was never a criterion for inclusion or exclusion.[5] Two names were considered to represent the same challenging group if and only if the major goals, programmatic efforts, and constituency remained the same, and the average challenging group member and potential member would agree that the new-name group was essentially the old group relabeled.[6]

Strategy focused on a sustained effort or campaign as the basis for putting boundaries around the challenging group. An organization that carries a new mobilization effort by a new generation is a new challenging group, even if it bears an old name and has ideology and general values similar to those of earlier campaigns many years ago.

There are good reasons why challengers may choose to make use of existing names and organizational identities to launch new campaigns. The Ku Klux Klan is a symbol of terror and successful racial oppression in the South. Today it reappears, defanged, its members no longer able to hide their identity behind a ghoulish mask. Today's Klan still means to intimidate. Indeed, the symbolism of the Klan is chosen as an aid in that purpose. But to consider today's Klan the same challenging group as the Klan of Reconstruction is to be mesmerized by a symbol.

Goldstone considers that these methodological decisions were "errors." (I envy him his certainty that there are right and wrong answers to such questions instead of merely more and less useful ones.) Our differences stand out most clearly on the cases of the National Student League and the American Student Union. Goldstone calls it "double counting." They should, he suggests, be considered a single case. They were, he claims, "pursuing the same goals, with the same or related constituencies, and similar tactics, during the same time period."

---

[5]Goldstone says that "if a group's name changes over time, consistency [was] achieved by simply coding the longest-used name as the unique name of the group." This is false. We recorded every name that a group had and, for purposes of identification, used whatever initials or nickname was most convenient. The issue of a unique name arises only as a *sampling* problem. If one group has 20 names and another has only one, then the first one has 20 times the probability of being selected. Hence, in drawing our sample, we linked every group to a unique name. Our conventions were to use the most common or popular name if this was unambiguous and to use the name with the most letters if there were two or more competitors for the most common. This is quite separate from the question of whether, when a group changes its name, it has become an independent challenging group.

[6]This discussion of how name changes are handled appears in *Strategy*, p. 30.

Why should one consider them two independent challenging groups? Start with the fact that they had different outcomes. The National Student League grew out of the fratricidal struggles of the campus left in the early 1930s. Dissatisfied with the socialist politics of the Student League for Industrial Democracy, radical members formed this new communist-oriented challenger. From 1931 to 1935, the group pursued a number of specific campaigns— for the elimination of compulsory ROTC and compulsory chapel on campuses, equal educational opportunity for women and blacks, employment security for college graduates, and better working conditions for coal miners. The National Student League was generally met with hostility by university administrations, although the administration at Columbia University did, briefly negotiate with the group. They ended up gaining neither acceptance nor advantages.

The period of combat and separate paths among communist and socialist groups on campuses gave way to the era of the popular front. The American Student Union was a popular front challenger, combining socialist and communist efforts in a single challenging group. Some of the new efforts were continuations of those begun by the National Student League—for example, the campaign to end ROTC. But the American Student Union took up new issues such as economic aid to students and reform of college administrations. It took up foreign policy issues, promoting the Oxford Pledge "not to support any war which the government may undertake."

This challenger was much more successful than the National Student League in gaining acceptance. During its 1938 convention, for example, the delegates received a letter of greeting from President Roosevelt, as well as messages from the mayor of New York, the president of CCNY, and the women's director of the Democratic National Committee. While neither the National Student League nor the American Student Union gained new advantages, they *could* have had different outcomes on this variable, given the differences in where they placed their efforts.

But even if these two groups really had operated at the same time and had had the same outcome,[7] there would be ample reason for considering them independent. The National Student League

---

[7]By Goldstone's rules, they necessarily *do* have the same outcome, since he would credit either or both with the successes won by the student movement a generation later in the 1960s.

was involved in violent interactions with the police; the American Student Union was not. Members of the National Student League were arrested; members of the American Student Union were not. The American Student Union was 10 times the size of the National Student League. The National Student League made use of constraints as a means of influence; the American Student Union did not. The National Student League was competing with other, rival challenging groups for the same constituency, while the American Student Union had the field pretty much to itself. If we treat the two groups as a single case, what value should we assign it on these variables? Goldstone's claim of double counting here is unwarranted, and his advice to treat the two groups as one can only muddy the antecedents of success, making it more difficult to discover and interpret the relationships that may exist.[8]

THE ISSUE OF PSEUDOSUCCESS

Goldstone believes that *Strategy* employs too restrictive a definition of success. There is irony in this charge because the book is, in fact, much more vulnerable to the opposite critique. It fails to distinguish the genuine article from two possible kinds of pseudosuccess. Hence, it is insufficiently restrictive.

Consider the shadow success: a group that realizes the changes it is seeking only to have the changes turn out empty of real meaning or impact. There is no more poignant example of such a group than the American Committee for the Outlawry of War. The committee carried on a decade-long campaign in the 1920s to gain American support and participation in a treaty that would make

---

[8]While I concede nothing to Goldstone's general arguments on independence, I am prepared to second guess the coding of individual cases in *Strategy*. The American Anti-Slavery Society provided a particularly difficult set of dilemmas. Our procedures excluded satellite groups of a parent organization. A satellite group—for example, a women's auxiliary or a vigilante protection unit—has no programmatic goals separate from those of the parent group and merely provides a service or additional resources for the parent group. Perhaps the Female Anti-Slavery Society should have been excluded as merely a satellite of the American Anti-Slavery Society, and this does represent a genuine instance of double counting. The American Anti-Slavery Society also confronted us with a case of a faction seizing control of an organizational apparatus. In 1840 the original organization split, but the Garrison faction continued to mount a challenge under the original name. We chose to use this watershed as the end of the challenge. But by the logic of our procedures, we should have then considered the Garrison American Anti-Slavery Society from 1840 onward as a new, independent challenging group to be included in the sample. Hence, one might say that we failed to double count here when we should have.

war illegal under international law. Salmon O. Levinson, an energetic and well-connected lawyer, made the committee's effort his
own personal crusade, paying more than 95% of the expenses of
the campaign from his own pocket, even when it was costing more
than $15,000 a year. The committee got what it was seeking when
the U.S. Senate ratified the Pact of Paris (the Kellogg-Briand Pact)
in 1929. Within a few years, legalities notwithstanding, the Japa-
nese invaded Manchuria, the Italians attacked Ethiopia, and the
Germans dismembered Czechoslovakia. History played a cruel
joke on Levinson and his supporters.

Consider the tag-along group: a group that realizes the changes
it is seeking because of what another, more powerful and effective,
challenging group is doing. It joins successful campaigns but, in
reality, contributes little of importance to them. Hence, it appears
successful, riding on the success of others. The Federal Suffrage
Association, for example, was not the most important of the wom-
en's suffrage groups. It fell in the sample, while the National American Woman Suffrage Association did not. The Federal Suffrage
Association was inactive during the crucial years from 1916 to the
passage of the federal suffrage amendment in 1920. The measure
of success in *Strategy* does not distinguish this situation from one
in which a group is the sole organizational carrier of a challenge.

These problems of pseudosuccess are acknowledged in *Strategy*,
but they are not solved. The route to improving the quality of this
data set is through further discriminations of this sort, allowing us
to sort pseudosuccesses from genuine ones in some reliable fashion. Goldstone's efforts to redefine the measure of success used in
Strategy would have been better directed in showing us how to
disaggregate these cases rather than aggregating even more.

BUREAUCRACY AND SUCCESS

If one had not read *Strategy*, but relied only on Goldstone's
presentation of its argument, his table 2 might appear to be a major
embarrassment.[9] It shows that when one looks only at groups without displacement goals, there is no relationship between bureau-

[9]Goldstone states that *Strategy* rests "on frequently spurious zero-order correlations"
but, in fact, table 2 is the only shred of evidence he offers for this assertion. All of his
other tables rest on the recoding of individual cases, using his own definition of successful groups.

cracy and the ability to gain new advantages. One might think, from Goldstone's account, that *Strategy* argues that bureaucracy is an important determinant of gaining new advantages, but the book does not make that argument.

What does it say about bureaucracy and success? For a challenging group to operate effectively in conflict situations, two separate functional problems must be solved. On the one hand, the group must be able to maintain a series of commitments from members that can be activated when necessary—essentially a problem of *pattern maintenance*. Pattern maintenance exists when members of a group carry around their membership in latent form, even while not actively participating in collective action. When they convene, the individuals are ready to begin functioning immediately as group members again. In this sense, the group continues to exist even while individual members are scattered about and not in direct interaction with each other. On the other hand, the group must be able to solve problems of internal conflict so that power struggles within the group do not paralyze its ability to act— essentially a problem of *integration*.

Centralization of power, *Strategy* argues, helps a group with the problem of managing internal conflict. It does so in particular because it helps a group to avoid debilitating factional splits. Bureaucratic organization helps a group with the problem of pattern maintenance. By creating a structure of roles with defined expectations in the place of diffuse commitments, a challenging group can better assure that certain necessary tasks will be routinely performed.

Strategy created two organizational variables intended to capture the theoretical distinction. One, labeled "power centralization," differentiated those groups with either a dominant leader or another form of centralized power structure (e.g., a central committee) from the rest. The second, labeled "bureaucracy," might more precisely have been labeled "formalization and role differentiation." It distinguished groups that had a written constitution or charter, maintained a formal list of members, and possessed at least three distinct levels of internal divisions from those that lacked one or more of these characteristics. These two summary measures are empirically independent in this sample of groups.

What *Strategy* argues is that centralization of power is more strongly related to gaining new advantages, while bureaucratization is more strongly related to gaining acceptance. Both characteristics are helpful, but coopted groups are particularly likely to be bureaucratic, and preempted groups are particularly likely to be power centralized.

In the chapter on these organizational issues, *Strategy* works with a cluster of variables including centralization of power, bureaucracy, factional splits, external attack by antagonists or hostile third parties, inclusive versus exclusive organization, and the two measures of successful outcome. It looks at the relationships among these variables sequentially, typically analyzing three or four variables at a time, to explore different parts of a complex argument. I was remiss in not including the variable of displacement goals in this analysis.[10] Let me use this opportunity to rectify the omission.

We coded a number of specific questions about the concerns of the challenging group. Specifically, we asked whether in its influence attempts, the group was concerned with (1) altering the scope of authority of all or some of its antagonists, (2) altering the procedures used by these antagonists, (3) altering the personnel of its antagonists, and/or (4) destroying or replacing all or some of its antagonists. Some 16 groups were coded "yes" on the last of these items; these are groups with displacement goals. They have a very poor rate of either new advantages or acceptance.

How do groups with displacement goals organize themselves compared with nondisplacement groups? Figure 1 shows the relationships for bureaucracy and centralization. Displacement groups are strikingly less likely to be bureaucratic than the others but only a little less likely to be centralized. No displacement groups are both bureaucratic and centralized, and only one is bureaucratic.

In considering why displacement groups fail, there is no way to disentangle the extent to which organizational characteristics such as lack of bureaucracy may contribute in important ways. Perhaps it is their choice of an impossible goal that leads them to ultimate failure, regardless of their organization. But it is just as plausible to argue that it is the inability of such groups to solve the problem

---

[10]Goldstone misleads the reader by suggesting that the role of displacement goals is omitted in other discussions in *Strategy* where it is relevant. The chapter dealing with the unruliness of a group's tactics and the extent to which it is attacked by others includes displacement goals as a variable throughout. Similarly, this variable plays an important role in the discussion of the relationship of war and other crises to acceptance and new advantages.

FIGURE 1
Bureaucracy, Centralization, and Displacement Goals

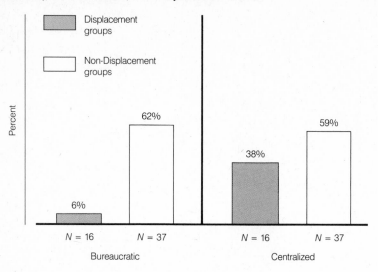

FIGURE 2
Bureaucracy and Centralization by Outcome for Nondisplacement Groups Only

of pattern maintenance through becoming bureaucratic that really produces the failure. In any event, groups with displacement goals are especially likely to lack bureaucracy, suggesting a problem of pattern maintenance.

How does the argument fare when we examine the 37 nondisplacement groups? Figure 2 presents the same analysis as figure 7.4 in *Strategy* (p. 95) but this time for nondisplacement groups only. It shows, perhaps more clearly than the earlier figure, how bureaucracy is associated with acceptance while centralization is associated with new advantages. If a group is centralized, bureaucracy does not add to its ability to gain new advantages. Indeed, the nonbureaucratic, centralized groups do as well as or better than groups that have both characteristics.

A complementary result holds for acceptance. Here, bureaucracy is the more important organizational variable, while centralization does not add to the group's ability to gain acceptance. Indeed, the bureaucratic, decentralized groups do even better than those that have both characteristics.

Many of the groups with neither bureaucracy nor centralization have displacement goals. Hence, we are reduced to only four cases in this category for this analysis. It is worth noting that the only one of these four that enjoyed both acceptance and new advantages was the Federal Suffrage Association—a group pointed to earlier as a possible pseudosuccess.

LENGTH OF TIME OF SUCCESS: A CRITIQUE OF GOLDSTONE

Goldstone goes beyond a critique of *Strategy* to offer a positive contribution to our understanding of how challenging groups gain entry into the American polity. How does this contribution stand up? Goldstone first makes a series of unwise methodological choices that result in an indiscriminate measure of success. The consequence is that virtually every group appears to succeed and, hence, there is no variance in outcome to explain. Thus, he turns to the length of the challenger's career as a variable.

In trying to use this measure, he immediately comes to grief on his inability to distinguish the challenger from the challenge. Recall that the end point of a challenge is defined by acceptance or disappearance of the organization. Goldstone accepts this definition for those cases in *Strategy* that are already defined as successes. For his recoding, however, he uses a different measure to mark the end point, based on new advantages. These two measures frequently yield different values. The challenge of the Steel Workers Organizing Committee, for example, ended in 1942 when the union won recognition from its remaining antagonists after a six-year struggle. But it was not until several years later, after World War II ended, that significant new advantages were won. Goldstone is apparently unaware that the end point of a challenge in his data set means different things: sometimes that a group gained new advantages for its beneficiary; sometimes that the challenging group was accepted by its antagonists; and sometimes, in the case of pre-emption, that the challenging group collapsed.

What kind of model might fit such a muddy set of observations? I would suggest a null model as follows: success is unrelated to whether agents of social control physically attack or arrest members of a group; it is unrelated to the techniques that a group uses to gain and sustain the commitment of its constituency; unrelated to the strategy and tactics that a group employs to influence its antagonist; unrelated to the internal organization of the challenger.

This weakness-of-everything model assumes that the process is essentially random. In any given year, every extant challenging group has an equal, constant probability of success. In some years it may be a little easier, in other years a little harder, but for everybody equally. Nothing that the group does or undergoes really affects its chances in this stochastic process.

The poorer the quality of the data set, the more likely this null model is to fit. Poor quality is what one gets when the success of a challenge and a challenging group are confused, an indefinite follow-up period is used, groups with very different organization and strategy are treated as identical, and different definitions of the end point of a challenge are used. Indeed, this is the major lesson to be learned from Goldstone's analysis.

He encounters three awkward moments in his efforts to make a positive contribution. The first occurs when he presents table 6, assessing the impact of six variables on the time distribution of success. To his credit, he presents the analysis two ways—once using the definition of success and length of challenge from *Strategy*, and once with his revised, enlarged, and supposedly improved data set.

It is of some interest to compare the strength of the relationships in the two data sets. If Goldstone has, indeed, improved the quality, the relationships should appear more clearly. It turns out that Goldstone loses six-love on this comparison. The relationships are consistently stronger on the original data set from *Strategy* than they are on the revisions, sometimes very substantially so. He deftly sidesteps this potential embarrassment by not noticing it.

His second awkward moment occurs when he attempts to explain why bureaucracy and selective incentives are associated with slower rather than more rapid success. To explain this result, he finds himself echoing arguments made in *Strategy* and acknowledges as much in his footnote 11. He does not, however, actually present the argument, so let us look at what *Strategy* has to say on this point (p. 122):

> We noted in Chapter Seven . . . that bureaucracy had a stronger relationship to one measure of success—acceptance—while centralization was more strongly related to the other—new advantages. Now we note that long-term challenges tend to be more bureaucratic than short-timers, but not more centralized and, further, that groups with a challenge in progress when a crisis arrives have a clear advantage in winning acceptance but a more equivocal one in gaining new advantages. Putting these results together suggests that third-party pressure in a crisis may be a mechanism that connects bureaucracy and acceptance. Bureaucracy helps a group to survive for a longer period in the absence of tangible results; a system-wide crisis then occurs and outside pressures push the group's antagonist to make some accommodation with it. The result is a higher rate of acceptance for bureaucratic groups.

Goldstone's final awkward moment occurs in his discussion of crises and the timing of success. Again, he finds himself making an argument that has already appeared quite explicitly in *Strategy*. He suggests that "social protest groups, even if seeking nondisplacement goals, will get serious attention only when some external shock occurs, such as a major war or economic or political crisis. Only at such times, when the need for integration and support of the established order is particularly strong, are established interests likely to feel the need to compromise and accommodate to new social protest groups."

While I prefer my version of this argument, Goldstone's is similar, as he acknowledges. But he fails to describe the analysis in

Strategy that bears on this issue. Groups during whose period of challenge a war occurs are compared with the other groups. It turns out that the wartime challengers are considerably more successful, but mainly on the acceptance criterion. The results for new advantages are considerably weaker.

Strategy also compares groups that launched a challenge prior to the Great Depression—a challenge that was still unresolved when the depression came—with those that began their challenge while the country was in the throes of that national crisis. The predepression groups were markedly more successful than their depression counterparts, especially on new advantages. When one removes groups with displacement goals, the results on wartime challengers continue to hold for nondisplacement groups, but the depression results do not. Here, the interpretation must be complicated by the fact that the depression stimulated the formation of challenging groups with goals of replacing their antagonist. Six of the 10 depression-spawned groups were of this type, while none of the predepression groups had such goals.

Goldstone offers a different analysis, and in my view it is much less helpful in evaluating the crisis argument. Crisis is a loose label, and if it is to be anything other than a sponge concept, it needs a tight definition. Not only does Goldstone neglect to offer us one; he also shows a remarkable flexibility in deciding what is or is not a crisis period. The period before the panic of 1837 is a crisis but the period after is not; the postwar years of 1946–48 are considered a crisis but the prewar years, 1939–41, are not; the Vietnam years, 1970–72, are considered a crisis but the Korean War years of 1950–53 are not. I do not disagree with the underlying argument, but it is hard to see how one can evaluate it when so much flexibility and arbitrariness are allowed in deciding what constitutes a crisis period.

To summarize my criticisms of Goldstone, he has diluted the quality of the data set in *Strategy* in four ways: (*a*) he fails to distinguish between social movements and their organizational carriers; (*b*) he employs a definition of success so loose that it fails to distinguish among very different challenging group careers; (*c*) he treats quite different cases as if they were identical; and (*d*) he fails to use a consistent definition in determining the length of a challenge. Furthermore, his attempt at a positive contribution employs the concept of crisis in such a sloppy fashion that it is deprived of any possible explanatory power.

CONCLUSION

Strategy explores a number of arguments from the literature on protest groups, bringing evidence to bear on them whenever possible. Some of these arguments bear on the general issue of the permeability of the American polity but many of them have little direct bearing. An attempt is made to draw out empirical implications from these arguments whenever possible and to examine how well the set of 53 groups fits these implications. Typically, clusters of variables are presented that deal with particular arguments. To make the analysis easier to follow, relationships are presented sequentially, using very simple graphs, but this mode of presentation does not make it any less a multivariate analysis.

There are some advantages to this mode of analysis and presentation. It makes it quite easy to identify deviant cases, forcing one to question why they do not fit the main pattern. It helps one to remain close to the reality underlying the labels and numbers, to remember the concrete experiences they supposedly reflect. By going back and forth between argument and data at many different points, one can develop a theoretical argument that is grounded in a large number of different concrete relationships.

Although I may be a critic of pluralist theory as an interpretation of American politics, I am a dyed-in-the-wool pluralist on methodological approaches in sociology. I readily concede that there are other ways of handling these data that might yield additional insights. *Strategy* includes the summary codes for the 53 groups in an appendix as an invitation to other scholars to pursue such analyses, and Goldstone's is the fourth such analysis that I know of.[11]

---

[11]The others are Steedly and Foley (1979), Weisburd (1979), and Mirowsky and Ross (1979). Steedly and Foley took 30 of the summary measures and used nonmetric multidimensional scaling to reduce them to a smaller number of clusters. Five clusters were derived, using a similarities matrix. These empirically derived clusters turn out to be quite similar to the theoretically derived clusters considered in *Strategy* and, in fact, the authors use the chapter headings of *Strategy* to label most of them. Steedly and Foley then explored this data set with both multiple regression and discriminant function analyses, using, in turn, the five composite variables which they identified and the underlying set of 30 discrete variables. Most of their analysis supports the general thrust of *Strategy* and, indeed, they conclude that "through multivariate analysis we confirmed the propositions of Ash, Turner and Killian, Garner, Gamson, and others" (p. 12). Their analysis provides some additional insight. In particular, the number of alliances that a group has (a variable that is not given much emphasis in *Strategy*) emerges as an important predictor of success. This theme of third-party help is an important one in a number of studies of more recent protest movements including the work of Jenkins and Perrow (1977) on farm worker movements and Lipsky (1970) on the tenant rights movement in New York City. Weisburd (1979) uses the data to explore a number of issues concerned with the integrative and disintegrative effects of conflict. While many have argued that

Just as there are matters of taste or style in data analysis and presentation, there are issues of taste in the type of theoretical argument with which one chooses to work. In a world where phenomena are overdetermined, one can pick different levels of analysis. To focus on systemwide crises, for example, is to pick a nonmanipulable variable—unless one considers the possibility that challenging groups through their actions can create such crises.

My personal preference is to pursue arguments that rely on manipulable variables. *Strategy* emphasizes strategies of mobilization, strategies of influence, and internal organization because these are things that challenging groups can control. Hence, the argument has immediate relevance for practice. The impact of nonmanipulable events, such as wars and depressions, must be considered in the argument. Even crises, though, take on more implications for practice when they are viewed as opportunities or threats with implications for the mobilization and influence strategies of challenging groups.

Clearly, Goldstone has a different perspective on these issues. I respect the time he has spent with the historical materials analyzed in *Strategy*, and his willingness to take on the question how individual groups should be coded on the variables of interest. Unfortunately, he offers us poor methodological advice that shows insensitivity to important issues of data quality. Nor do I think he really understands what *Strategy* is saying theoretically about the careers of challenging groups. In the end, the book emerges from

---

external conflict causes internal unity, Weisburd attempts to show that causality runs in the reverse direction as well. He codes a number of additional variables concerned with group unity and external conflict for most of the groups in the sample. (For nine of them, he was unable to find all of the relevant information for his additional codes.) His analysis explores the relationships by estimating a linear regression model with reciprocal effects between social conflict and group unity. Finally, Mirowsky and Ross (1979) analyze the data using both measures of success in *Strategy*. The antecedent variables are divided into five categories on a priori grounds: movement context, beliefs and goals, organization, action and interaction, and length of challenge. The middle three categories involve clusters of from eight to 12 variables which were factor analyzed. Three orthogonal factors were extracted in each cluster. Since the dependent variables were dichotomous, multidimensional scaling with embedded hierarchical clustering was also used. The resulting indexes correlated between .85 and 1.0 with the corresponding factor analytically derived indexes. A path analytic model was estimated for both dependent variables with the causal flow following the order listed above. Again, the general thrust of the results is consistent with *Strategy* but there are refinements and different emphases. Mirowsky and Ross conclude, for example, that bureaucracy has a "decisive effect" on acceptance but, in contrast to Steedly and Foley's analysis, "protest group success does not generally depend on the intercession of third parties."

his critical examination unscathed. But I am a partisan, and this is a matter for others to judge.[12]

APPENDIX

A few clarifications and corrections not bearing on any important issues between Goldstone and myself need brief comment.

Interviewing.—Goldstone states that *Strategy* relied on interviews, where possible, for some of its data on the 53 groups. This is not so. It relied on historical documents and secondary sources only. Goldstone's memory was probably playing a trick on him here, since my description in the book used the metaphor of an interview. "Instead of employing our questionnaire to interview individuals as one would on a survey, we employed it to interview books and documents" (p. 24).

First International.—Goldstone thinks that the International Workingmen's Association should have been coded as a displacement group. Although the IWA had a long-range objective of gaining political power and establishing a socialist society, its immediate program focused on the economic emancipation of the working class. The IWA in America spent most of its energy in fratricidal combat, paralleling the split between Marx and Bakunin in Europe. But there were some programmatic efforts to achieve nondisplacement goals. During the financial panic and depression of 1873–74, the IWA presented demands for relief of the unemployed to the city governments of New York and Chicago—demands which would not have required the replacement of city officials.

International Association of Machinists.—Weisburd (1979) calls attention to an error in the violence code for this group. It was coded as not being involved in violent interactions, but it was so involved during the period from 1901 to 1911. The evidence appeared in one of our major sources on this group (Perlman 1961), but our compiler simply missed it. Since *Strategy* argues that unruliness is positively related to success, this correction tends to strengthen the argument at this point.

---

[12]A further comment, by Foley and Steedly, and Goldstone's reply to both comments are scheduled to appear in the next issue of the *AJS.*—ED.

REFERENCES

Jenkins, Craig, and Charles Perrow. 1977. "Insurgency of the Powerless: Farm Worker Movements, 1946–1972." *American Sociological Review* 42 (April): 249–68.

Lipsky, Michael. 1970. *Protest in City Politics*. Chicago: Rand-McNally.

McCarthy, John D., and Mayer N. Zald. 1977. "Resource Mobilization and Social Movements: A Partial Theory." *American Journal of Sociology* 82 (May): 1212–41.

Mirowsky, John, II, and Catherine E. Ross. 1979. "Protest Group Success: The Impact of Group Characteristics, Social Control, and the Situation." Unpublished manuscript. Department of Sociology, Yale University, New Haven, Conn.

Oberschall, Anthony. 1973. *Social Conflict and Social Movements*. Englewood Cliffs, N.J.: Prentice-Hall.

Perlman, Mark. 1961. *The Machinists: A New Study of American Trade Unionism*. Cambridge, Mass.: Harvard University Press.

Steedly, Homer R., Jr., and John W. Foley. 1979. "The Success of Protest Groups: Multivariate Analyses." *Social Science Research* 8:1–15.

Tilly, Charles. 1978. *From Mobilization to Revolution*. Reading, Mass.: Addison-Wesley.

Weisburd, David. 1979. "Unity, Conflict and the Necessity of Reciprocal Causation in Conflict Theory." Unpublished manuscript. Department of Sociology, Yale University, New Haven, Conn.

Zald, Mayer N., and Roberta Ash. 1966. "Social Movement Organizations: Growth, Decay and Change." *Social Forces* 44 (March): 327–41.

The Strategy of Social Protest:
A Comment on a Growth Industry

JOHN W. FOLEY

Center for the Study of Middle-Size Cities, Sangamon State University

HOMER R. STEEDLY, JR.

University of South Carolina

William A. Gamson in *The Strategy of Social Protest* (1975) examined the organizational determinants of protest-group success using a sample of 53 U.S. protest groups. In an appendix, he thoughtfully provided the raw data that were the basis for the variables used in the analysis. This invitation to reanalyze his data has led to the beginning of a burgeoning growth industry in sociology.[1] The Gamson data have generated at least four manuscripts reporting further research (Weisburd 1979; Steedly and Foley 1979; Mirowsky and Ross 1979; and now Goldstone).[2]

Jack A. Goldstone's "The Weakness of Organization: A New Look at Gamson's *The Strategy of Social Protest*" (*AJS* 85 [March 1980]: 1017–42) is the most recent of these articles. While Goldstone's work is an innovative contribution to the collective behavior literature, we were surprised by his findings that protest-group structure, organization, and other attributes were, if anything, negatively related to the success of the group.

We were surprised because earlier work by ourselves and others using a wide variety of multivariate techniques including path analysis, discriminant function analysis, and nonmetric multidimensional scaling had confirmed and extended Gamson's initial data analysis. Upon carefully reading Goldstone's article, we found several serious problems.

The problem area that first came to mind is table 5, where Goldstone constructs a stochastic model (without an error term?) to predict group success or failure from a time distribution of the probability of success. Not only is the relationship basically

---

[1] The term "social movement industry" would seem most appropriate had not McCarthy and Zald (1977) already used it in a different scholarly context.

[2] These data have also generated papers presented at national meetings such as the 1977 American Sociological Association meetings.

Reprinted, with permission, from the *American Journal of Sociology*.

a tautology, correlating parts with wholes (see Bartko and Pettigrew 1968 and Fuguitt and Lieberson 1974); it is also statistically
problematic. The use of regression analysis to explain a categorical
dependent variable is inappropriate. Discriminant function analysis is clearly a more legitimate technique. (See Aldrich and Cnudde
[1975] for a comparison of these techniques and Steedly and Foley
[1979] for use of this technique with these data.)

But the most debilitating problem in Goldstone's reanalysis of
the Gamson data set is a simple data-coding problem. Goldstone
finds, for example, that bureaucratic groups and groups that employ selective incentives are slower than others to achieve success
(table 6). Without dwelling on the direction of the relationship, he
finds a *negative* relationship between the time-distribution measure and group success (table 5). How can this be possible? The
answer lies in Gamson's original coding. For example, the variable
measuring the extent of overall new advantages ranges from 1 (no
new advantages) to 4 (partial advantages), while the variable measuring selective incentive ranges in the opposite direction from 1
(yes, selective incentives) to 2 (no, no selective incentives).

Similarly, the variables measuring outcome and target displacement are coded to vary inversely if they are positively related.
Goldstone apparently missed this. If anything, then, his negative
findings should be interpreted as a reaffirmation of the findings
that protest-group organization, tactics (including alliances), and
resource management strongly predict protest-group outcome. Indeed, it has been shown that knowledge of a group's value on
certain key variables measuring these concepts enables us to predict group success or failure with a great deal of confidence.

REFERENCES

Aldrich, John, and Charles F. Cnudde. 1975. "Probing the Bounds of
   Conventional Wisdom: A Comparison of Regression, Probit, and Dis-
   criminant Analysis." *American Journal of Political Science* 29:571–608.
Bartko, J. J., and K. D. Pettigrew. 1968. "A Note on the Correlation of
   Parts with Wholes." *American Statistician* 22:41.
Fuguitt, Glenn U., and Stanley Lieberson. 1974. "Correlation of Ratios
   and Difference Scores Having Common Terms." *Sociological Method-
   ology, 1973–74*, edited by H. L. Costner. San Francisco: Jossey-Bass.
Gamson, William A. 1975. *The Strategy of Social Protest*. Homewood,
   Ill.: Dorsey.

McCarthy, John D., and Mayer N. Zald. 1977. "Resource Mobilization and Social Movements: A Partial Theory." *American Journal of Sociology* 82 (6): 1212–41.

Mirowsky, John, II, and Catherine E. Ross. 1979. "Protest Group Success: The Impact of Group Characteristics, Social Control, and the Situation." Mimeographed. New Haven, Conn.: Yale University, Department of Sociology.

Steedly, Homer R., Jr., and John W. Foley. 1979. "The Success of Protest Groups: Multivariate Analyses." *Social Science Research* 8:1–15.

Weisburd, David. 1979. "Unity, Conflict, and the Necessity of Reciprocal Causation in Conflict Theory." Mimeographed. New Haven, Conn.: Yale University, Department of Sociology.

Mobilization and Organization: Reply to Foley and Steedly and to Gamson

JACK A. GOLDSTONE

Harvard University

As Foley and Steedly's criticisms are few, and Gamson's comment (*AJS* 85 [March 1980]: 1043–60) is largely a defense of his original position, I am for the most part content to let my paper speak for itself. On a few points, however, I think clarification of my arguments will be useful.

Foley and Steedly seem to misunderstand the analysis in table 5. The correlation between the stochastic model and the data presented in table 5 is so far from being tautologous that an alternative stochastic model—the Poisson distribution—is decisively rejected in a comparison of the model and the data (see my n. 10). Moreover, since the variables in table 5 are measured in interval-level data, the comment that regression analysis is inappropriate for categorical data is simply irrelevant.[1]

---

[1] The variables are: x = years, the data ranging from 1 to 88; and y = the fraction of challenges succeeding in x years or less, the data ranging from 0.052 to 1.00.

Reprinted, with permission, from the *American Journal of Sociology*.

They also mistakenly assert that I have misused Gamson's 1–4 success scale, reversing the scale's order. In fact, table 6 does not use Gamson's success scale at all. Gamson's measure denotes the *degree* of success: full, partial, or none; table 6 deals with the *timing* of success. The negative *D*'s for bureaucracy and selective incentives show that groups with those characteristics simply take longer to attain success than groups lacking them. My negative findings on the impact of these characteristics, therefore, should be interpreted as just that—negative findings. Incidentally, I dwell at some length on the direction of these relationships on pages 1034–35.

I do not know why Foley and Steedly are so surprised at my negative findings regarding bureaucracy, centralization, and the use of selective incentives. In their analysis of Gamson's data (Steedly and Foley 1979), they present in tables 5 and 6 all "variables . . . changing the coefficient of determination [of the multiple regression equation for success] more than .015" (p. 7). That is, in plain English, they present all the variables they found to have a significant effect on outcomes. In these tables, displacement goals are the dominant factor; bureaucracy (levels of hierarchy), centralization, and the use of selective incentives are conspicuously absent. Thus, though their interpretation of their overall results is that they have "confirmed the propositions of . . . Gamson" (p. 13), their data analysis, at least in these tables, is in full accord with my arguments on the lack of effect of organization on success.

Gamson attempts to clarify his position on the effects of bureaucracy and centralization in his figure 2 (1980). In *Strategy* (Gamson 1975), he was careful to test the significance of all his results, using the χ^2 test. Yet he has neglected to do so here. He should have paused in his attempt to bolster his argument, however, for as table 1 in this reply shows, the differences in success rates among the four classes of groups in his figure 2 are not statistically significant. This is true whether one looks at new advantages or acceptance. Thus, Gamson's figure only serves to prove my point: when displacement groups are excluded, his data fail to demonstrate significant effects of organization on group success.[2]

---

[2] The same result holds when we look behind statistical significance and examine the strength of the associations Gamson presents. When displacement groups are included, as in fig. 7-4 in *Strategy* (p. 95), lambda for new advantages and for acceptance are .31 and .40, respectively. When displacement groups are excluded, as shown in table 1, even these modest strengths of association plummet: lambda for new advantages and for

TABLE 1
Significance Test of Data in Gamson's (1980) Figure 2

	Group Characteristics				
	Bureaucracy and Centralization	Centralization Only	Bureau-cratization Only	Neither	Totals
New advantages	9 (8.11)	8 (6.76)	6 (7.43)	2 (2.70)	25
No new advantages	3 (3.89)	2 (3.24)	5 (3.57)	2 (1.30)	12
	$\lambda_{rc} = .0$, df $= 3$, $\chi^2 = 2.42$, N.S.				
Acceptance	8 (7.46)	5 (6.22)	9 (6.84)	1 (2.49)	23
No acceptance	4 (4.54)	5 (3.78)	2 (4.16)	3 (1.51)	14
	$\lambda_{rc} = .14$, df $= 3$, $\chi^2 = 4.88$, N.S.				

NOTE.—For df $= 3$, the critical value of χ^2 for rejection of the null hypothesis is 7.81 (.05 confidence level). Null hypothesis expected frequencies in parentheses.

In discussing my analysis, Gamson attributes the success of the stochastic model of the timing of success to my muddying of his data. This is simply untrue; as my figure 2 and table 5 show, the stochastic model fits Gamson's original success data and fits it well. Moreover, let us consider the charge that the modifications I suggest "muddy" the data. Examine the confidence limits on the parameters in my table 5. In every case, the modified data set yields parameter estimates with narrower confidence intervals; that is, there is less random variation in the modified data set. Examine my table 6. Gamson mistakenly notes that since the "relationships" are "stronger" for the unmodified data, his data are more precise. Yet he misunderstands the table. A D value does not measure strength of relationship; the D measures the divergence in the timing of success between groups having and lacking a specified characteristic. Such divergence reflects, in part, the impact of the characteristics; in part, it reflects random differences due to sampling. Since smaller samples have larger sampling fluctuations, one expects larger D's in small samples. Thus, the larger D's in the upper half of my table 6 do not imply stronger relationships.

---

acceptance become .0 and .14. Thus, it is not merely the small sample size that affects the significance of Gamson's results; by any measure, the association of bureaucracy and centralization with success in his data is very weak when displacement groups are removed.

They simply reflect, as one would expect from a smaller sample size, larger random-sampling fluctuations. In both tables 5 and 6, the data analyses for both Gamson's original data and the modified data yield similar results, with the modified data set exhibiting less random variation throughout. This is exactly what one would expect if the modifications simply added cases of success similar to those Gamson had included.

Gamson should also understand that the stochastic model I propose, though a null model, is not a "nihil" model. That is, it is not from lack of content that the model, though representing a random process, fits the data. To see this, consider two alternative null models.

These are pictured in figure 1. Let us say that, as group characteristics make no difference, the time to attain success will vary normally around some mean time to attain success, X_o. Some groups will succeed more rapidly, some more slowly; but most will succeed after some time near the mean. This is graph *a*. As another alternative, let us suppose that sheer longevity is the main factor in group success: then, the longer a challenge, the more likely it is to achieve success; there will be few quick victories. This is graph *b*. Now consider the model in my paper, the geometric distribution with low *p*. Under this model, groups do not face a similar mean time of success, but a similar annual probability of success, *p*. This is graph *c*. It is also, as figure 2 in my paper shows, the shape of Gamson's data. Thus, the model is not a nihil model; it describes a very specific pattern of success—a pattern that Gamson's data fit.

Finally, Gamson criticizes me for not offering a tighter definition of crises. The crises cited are a diverse lot—they include major

FIGURE 1
Alternative Models of the Timing of Success, *x* = Years; *y* = Fraction of Challenges Expected to Succeed in *x* Years or Less.

wars, depressions, population movements, and institutional over-hauls. To my mind, the first question to ask about these crises is not how to circumscribe them with a general definition, but how did they contribute to protest-group success. Did they stir up potential constituents, making recruitment and mobilization easier? Did they weaken antagonists' ability to resist? Both? Sometimes one, sometimes the other? These topics still await study.[3] Before I venture a general definition of the nature of these crises, I would like more information than Gamson's aggregate success data provide. Nonetheless, the evidence for the association of protest-group success with the specific crises cited is quite strong. This seems an inescapable datum for theories of protest-group success.

In deference to Gamson, let me add to Foley and Steedly's clever comment that the analysis of his data is a "growth industry." This is because Gamson, in *Strategy*, presents the best data extant on the attributes of social movement organizations and their success. It is both a proof of Gamson's courage and a model for all social scientists that he has presented his data in full for both friends and critics to explore. Let me add, in case it was not clear enough in my paper, that I do not oppose all of *Strategy*'s findings; indeed, I have taken certain points, as I explicitly noted (p. 1037 and n. 11), from Gamson's analysis.

As Gamson notes, the issues raised by my paper go far beyond the merits of *Strategy*. Resource-mobilization theorists have long believed that organization greatly contributed to the effective mobilization of support and eventual success. I hope to have called this straightforward link into question. Instead of the conventional model

$$\text{organization} \longrightarrow \text{mobilization} \longrightarrow \text{success}$$

I suggest an alternative model

---

[3] One illuminating, albeit controversial, study of these issues is Piven and Cloward (1977). Their argument, presented through a series of case studies, is that crises—"large scale changes [that] undermine political stability" (p. 28)—contribute both to the mobilization of constituents and to the weakening of established adversaries. Their case studies lack an explicit theoretical analysis, and there is no attempt to measure precisely the beginnings or outcomes of challenges; yet they offer persuasive case evidence of the diverse roles of crises in facilitating protest-group success.

as a starting point for research on the success of social protest groups.[4]

This does not mean that organization per se is unimportant. A host of rich questions remains. Does superior organization contribute to an unsuccessful group's survival while it struggles for success? Among competing social movement organizations within the same social movement, do superior organization or tactics affect the outcome of struggles within the movement? Moreover, if organization is of so little benefit in the chances or timing of success, why do groups organize? Might it be primarily to increase their leaders' control over them? Or, in part, simply to meet the needs of group members for structure and social order? Even after the oft-presumed connection between organization and success is challenged, a host of provocative questions remains.

REFERENCES

Gamson, William A. 1975. *The Strategy of Social Protest*. Homewood, Ill.: Dorsey.

Goldstone, Jack A. 1980. "Theories of Revolution: The Third Generation." *World Politics* 32 (March): 425–53.

Piven, Frances Fox, and Richard A. Cloward. 1977. *Poor People's Movements*. New York: Pantheon.

Skocpol, Theda. 1979. *States and Social Revolutions*. Cambridge: Cambridge University Press.

Steedly, Homer R., Jr., and John W. Foley. 1979. "The Success of Protest Groups: Multivariate Analyses." *Social Science Research* 8:1–15.

---

[4] It is interesting to note that recent theories of revolutions have held that the organization of revolutionary movements contributes less to successful revolutions than do large structural aspects of societies, including political and social crises (see Skocpol 1979; Goldstone 1980). I venture the same may apply to social protest movements in general.

appendix b

The 53 Challenging Groups: A Brief Description

The members of the sample of challenging groups are very briefly identified and described below. The dates following the name represent the beginning and end of the period of challenge. The beginning is usually marked by the year in which the group was formed or, in some cases, began a new burst of organizing activity after an inactive period. The end is more complicated and to some degree arbitrary (see pp. 30–31). It is sometimes marked by the disappearance of the group and sometimes by the resolution of active conflict with its target. The outcome of the group's challenge is also listed.

1. American Association of University Professors (1914–22)

   A group that attempted to mobilize university professors for the achievement of academic freedom and, more specifically, over the right of trustees to fire teachers and for the establishment of definite rules of tenure. *Co-optation.*

2. *American Free Trade League (1869–72)*

A group that attempted to mobilize wage-earners along the eastern seaboard and western farmers for the repeal of high tariffs. *Preemption.*

3. *American Committee for the Outlawry of War (1921–29)*

A group that attempted to mobilize a middle-class reform constituency for American support for a treaty that would make war illegal under international law. The period of challenge ended with the ratification of the Pact of Paris (the Kellogg-Briand Pact) by the United States Senate. *Full response.*

4. *National Brotherhood of Baseball Players (1885–91)*

A group that attempted to mobilize professional baseball players for the achievement of greater benefits for this group. *Collapse.*

5. *Brotherhood of the Kingdom (1892–1915)*

A group that was part of the social gospel or social Christianity movement of the late 19th and early 20th century. They attempted to mobilize Christians for a redirection of the energies of the church toward the improvement of social conditions in this world. *Collapse.*

6. *Social Revolutionary Clubs (Anarcho-Communists) (1880– 87)*

A group that based its program on European socialist thought, in particular, the Bakunin wing. It attempted to mobilize primarily German immigrant workers for the abolition of the wage system and the system of private property more generally and to replace them with its particular vision of socialist organization. After initial hesitation, the group chose to support the eight-hour day movement and participated with many others in the meeting in the Haymarket in Chicago on May 4, 1886, in which a bomb was thrown killing a policeman. The leaders of the group were blamed for the incident, tried as accessories to murder, and four were executed. *Collapse.*

7. *National Urban League (1910–30)*

A group that attempted to mobilize a black and white middle-class reform constituency for efforts to improve the living conditions of urban blacks, particularly migrants from the rural South to the industrial centers of the North. *Full response.*

8. *United Brotherhood of Carpenters and Joiners of America (1881–1912)*

A group that attempted to mobilize carpenters and other wood workers for the achievement of greater benefits for this group. *Full response.*

9. *International Seamen's Union of America (1892–1921)*

A group that attempted to mobilize seamen for the achievement of greater benefits for this group. *Co-optation.*

10. *National Union for Social Justice (1934–36)*

A group, led by the "radio priest" Father Coughlin, that attempted to mobilize working-class Catholics, small farmers, and the masses of unemployed for the achievement of inflationary monetary policies through a variety of means. *Collapse.*

11. *Amalgamated Association of Street and Electrical Railway Workers (1892–1921)*

A group that attempted to mobilize streetcar and trolley workers for the achievement of greater benefits for this group. *Full response.*

12. *American Birth Control League (1921–37)*

A group, led originally by Margaret Sanger, that attempted to mobilize a middle-class reform constituency of women for the greater acceptance of birth control and more specifically to influence legislation affecting this goal. *Collapse.*

13. *American Labor Union (1902–5)*

A group that attempted to mobilize industrial workers for industrial unionism and socialist political goals. The group was an important forerunner of the I.W.W. *Preemption.*

14. *American Federation of Labor (1881–1935)*

A group that attempted to mobilize workers in a variety of trades and industries for the achievement of legislative and political support for the labor movement. *Full response.*

15. *Revolutionary Workers League (Revolt) (1938–43)*

A splinter group of left-wing Trotskyists that attempted to mobilize industrial workers, especially those in the automobile, steel, and maritime industries, for the replacement of the existing economic and political system with a socialist system. *Collapse.*

16. *American Republican Party (Native American Party) (1843–47)*

A nativist group that attempted to mobilize urban native-born Protestants against the rising economic and political power of Catholic immigrants. *Collapse.*

17. *League of Deliverance (1882)*

A nativist group that attempted to mobilize West Coast workers to prevent the employment of Chinese labor. *Full response.*

18. *National Student League (1931–35)*

A group, formed by former members of the Student League for Industrial Democracy, that attempted to mobilize university students for the achievement of an antiwar, antiracist, and antifascist political program. It also concerned itself with campus issues such as the achievement of a free student press and the elimination of compulsory R.O.T.C. *Collapse.*

19. *German-American Bund (1936–43)*

A group that attempted to mobilize the German-American population for the achievement of an American political system along National Socialist lines. *Collapse.*

20. *Brotherhood of the Cooperative Commonwealth (1896–1914)*

A group that attempted to mobilize socialist workers and other sympathizers to gain political control of the state of Washington through establishing cooperative settlements there that would eventually become an electoral majority. *Collapse.*

21. *National Female Anti-Slavery Society (1832–40)*

A group that attempted to mobilize a reform constituency of

middle-class, northern white women to achieve the abolition of slavery. *Collapse.*

22. *American Student Union (1935–41)*

A group, formed by former members of the National Student League and the Student League for Industrial Democracy, that attempted to mobilize university students behind a broad and somewhat changing set of leftist political goals. *Co-optation.*

23. *Young People's Socialist League #1 (YPSL I) (1915–19)*

This group mounted two separate challenges, separated by a period of inactivity, which are treated here as independent challenges (cf. #44). The group was formed by members of the Socialist Party and attempted to mobilize young workers and students toward the achievement of socialist political and economic goals. *Collapse.*

24. *Grand Eight Hour Leagues (1865–72)*

A group that attempted to mobilize primarily skilled workers for the support of eight-hour day legislation. *Preemption.*

25. *Order of Railway Conductors (1885–1934)*

A group that attempted to mobilize railway conductors for the achievement of greater benefits for this group. *Full response.*

26. *American Proportional Representation League (1893– 1932)*

A group that attempted to mobilize a middle-class reform constituency for the adoption of proportional representation as a means of breaking the power of urban political machines. *Preemption.*

27. *International Longshoreman's Association (West) (1934– 48)*

Two separate challenges are included under the name of the ILA (cf. #49). Although a West Coast branch of the ILA existed before 1934, under Harry Bridges it became essentially an independent union with open defiance of the national president of the union. This challenge deals with the attempt of the group to mobilize West Coast longshoremen for the achievement of greater benefits for this group. *Full response.*

28.   International Association of Machinists (1888–1935)

A group that attempted to mobilize machinists for the achievement of greater benefits for this group. *Full response.*

29.   League of American Wheelmen (1880–1905)

A group that attempted to mobilize bicycle owners and riders to remove restrictions on the use of the bicycle. Later it became a major participant in the good roads movement. *Full response.*

30.   American Federation of Teachers (1916–37)

A group that attempted to mobilize elementary and secondary school teachers for the achievement of greater benefits for this group. *Full response.*

31.   Church Peace Union (1914–45)

A group that attempted to mobilize the religious community in support of American participation in the League of Nations and later the United Nations. *Full response.*

32.   Bull Moose Party (Progressive Party) (1912–16)

A group that attempted to mobilize progressives of both parties for the election of Theodore Roosevelt to the Presidency. *Co-optation.*

33.   Packinghouse Workers Organizing Committee (1937–43)

A group that attempted to mobilize meatpackers for the achievement of greater benefits for this group. *Full response.*

34.   United Hebrew Trades (1888–1910)

A group that attempted to mobilize Jewish immigrant workers in different industries for the achievement of greater benefits for this group. *Full response.*

35.   Tobacco Night Riders (1906–11)

A group that attempted to mobilize tobacco farmers of the black patch area to achieve control of the marketing of tobacco and to break the power of the tobacco trust. *Preemption.*

36.   United Sons of Vulcan (1858–73)

A group that attempted to mobilize boilers, puddlers, and other iron workers for the achievement of greater benefits for this group. *Full response.*

37. Steel Workers Organizing Committee (1936–42)

A group that attempted to mobilize steelworkers for the achievement of greater benefits for this group. *Full response.*

38. March on Washington Committee (1942)

A group that attempted to mobilize urban blacks for the elimination of racial discrimination in employment. The period of this particular challenge was essentially over after President Roosevelt issued an executive order establishing a Fair Employment Practices Committee (FEPC). *Full response.*

39. Prison Discipline Society (1825–30)

A group that attempted to mobilize a middle-class reform constituency ᶠor the adoption of the "Auburn-system" of prison organization. *Full response.*

40. Christian Front against Communism (1938–42)

A group, led by Father Coughlin, that attempted to mobilize a broad-based, predominantly working-class Catholic constituency behind a program of isolationism and neutrality in the developing European conflict, anti-Communism, and anti-Semitism. *Collapse.*

41. American Party (1886–88)

A nativist group that attempted to mobilize a constituency of predominantly young workers and white-collar employees to achieve greater restrictions on immigration and naturalization. *Collapse.*

42. Communist Labor Party (1919–20)

A group, formed by delegates from the left-wing caucus of the Socialist Party (the so-called Gitlow-Reed faction), that attempted to mobilize industrial workers for the establishment of a communist state in America. *Collapse.*

43. Dairymen's League (1907–20)

A group that attempted to mobilize dairy farmers for the achievement of benefits for this group. *Co-optation.*

44. Young Peoples Socialist League, #2 (YPSL II) (1929–54)

This group began a renewed challenge with the onset of the stock market crash and the depression (cf. #23). It attempted to mobilize young workers and students toward the achievement of socialist political and economic goals. *Collapse.*

45. Independence League (1905–10)

A group, formed by William Randolph Hearst, to mobilize a middle-class reform and working-class constituency behind a variety of reform goals to be achieved through Hearst's acquisition of political power. *Collapse.*

46. Progressive Labor Party (1887)

A group that attempted to mobilize workers for the election of socialist political candidates. *Collapse.*

47. Federal Suffrage Association (1892–1920)

A group that attempted to mobilize middle-class women in support of a constitutional amendment giving women the right to vote. The period of challenge ended with the ratification of the federal suffrage amendment. *Full response.*

48. Society for the Promotion of Manual Labor in Literary Institutions (1831–33)

A group that attempted to mobilize a middle-class reform constituency to improve the physical fitness of students in colleges, theological seminaries, and other institutions by introducing programs of physical labor into the curriculum. *Preemption.*

49. International Longshoreman's Association (East) (1892–1933)

A group that attempted to mobilize dockworkers for the achievement of benefits to this group. This challenge (cf. #27) focuses on efforts on the East Coast, Great Lakes, and Gulf district. *Full response.*

50. Union Trade Society of Journeymen Tailors (1833–36)

A group that attempted to mobilize journeymen tailors for the achievement of benefits to this group. *Collapse.*

51. International Workingmen's Association (First International) (1869–76)

This group, the first real Marxist effort in America, attempted to mobilize a constituency of immigrant workers and American intellectuals to achieve the organization of the working class into trade unions and cooperative societies looking ultimately toward the building of a socialist state. *Collapse.*

52. American Anti-Slavery Society (1833–40)

A group that attempted to mobilize a middle-class male reform constituency for the abolition of slavery. *Collapse.*

53. North Carolina Manumission Society (1816–34)

A group that attempted to mobilize religious white southerners, especially Quakers, to achieve the elimination of slavery through a program of voluntary granting of freedom by slave-holders. *Collapse.*

appendix c

Compiling the Sampling Frame

The sampling frame consisted of a gross list of some 4,500 cards, compiled from the indexes of a series of general and specialized histories. A coder went through each index and listed on a separate card every formal organization — for example, General Motors or the United Automobile Workers — and every collective behavior episode — for example, "Raid on Harper's Ferry" or "Bonus Marchers." High reliabilities were achieved between independent coders using this procedure.

We began with a list of types of social movements or protest groups plus some general bibliographic sources, especially *The Harvard Guide to American History* and *A Guide to the History of the United States*. The categories were agricultural, labor, ethnic (including immigrant), women, religious, prohibition (temperance), nativist, reform, professional, business and commerce, conservation, black, utopian, socialist and communist, peace, veterans, rightist, radicals, cranks and crackpots, sports and recreation, and education. Our concern was that every challenging group be covered by at least one of these categories, and it mattered not at all if it fit into several. Through this method, we developed a bibliography of some 75 books.

We started the list or file with some general sources: six volumes and a supplement of the *Dictionary of American History, The Oxford Companion to American History,* Richard Morris' *An Encyclopedia of American History* and Louis Filler's *A Dictionary of Social Reform.* From here, we proceeded to the more specialized histories within each category.

A list of the entries from each new source was checked against the growing file to avoid making duplicate entries. If some group was already in the file, the additional source was recorded on its card. As each source was used, a tally was made of the percentage of new entries it provided to the file. The final dozen sources, from several different categories, yielded an average of 10 percent new entries, and all were below 20 percent. In examining these new entries, we gained the strong impression that very few, if any, would actually meet the criteria for a challenging group. To check this impression, we did further investigation on the final 20 new entries. Seven were local chapters of larger groups that had already been included. One was not a formal organization or collective behavior episode. Two were federally funded institutions or projects. One was a pseudonym for the Ku Klux Klan, which, of course, was already included, and five were local organizations dealing strictly with local issues. The remaining four were international organizations or organizations in other countries whose activities were not directed primarily at American antagonists. Thus, none of the last 20 new entries actually added any challenging groups to the gross list.

The entries in the gross list consisted of valid entries—that is, challenging groups—and blanks, where a blank was defined as any card entry which, upon investigation, did not meet the criteria for a valid entry.

Our sampling procedure consisted of drawing a random sample, actually an interval sample, of 11 percent of the cards, 467 in all. Once we filtered the challenging groups from these cards and dealt with problems of duplication and multiple listings, our valid entries represented a random sample of all valid entries in the gross file. Of course, having filtered only those cards that were selected in our sample, we could not produce a total list of valid entries, but it was quite unnecessary to do so.

The process of culling valid entries from blanks was quite time-consuming. Many could be eliminated quickly by simple inspection—for example, "socialism," "industrial-unionism," "Paris Commune," "class struggle doctrine," "U.S. Department of Agriculture." Others required further investigation. Frequently, it was sufficient to turn to the source that yielded the index listing, but some cases required many hours of library work before we learned that they failed to meet one of the criteria described in the text (see pp. 16–18).

It was important to give each challenging group only one card. Many groups were known by a variety of names, and, to insure that such a group had only one chance of entering the sample, it was necessary to adopt conventions that would link it with a unique name. If there was a most common or popular name for the group, we used this. If there were two or more equally common names, we treated the longest name as the unique name. A sample card was considered a valid entry only if it contained the unique name of the challenging group. The file was also checked for exact duplicates, something which could occur through error. If another card appeared for the same group, the chosen card was given a .5 probability of remaining in the sample to correct for the double probability that it had inadvertently been given earlier.

In the case of cards with collective behavior episodes, we attempted to associate these with some sponsoring organization whenever this was appropriate—for example, the Butte Miner's Strike was associated with the Western Miner's Union. The card with the name of the organization was designated as the unique way for the challenging group to enter in such cases. In theory, a collective behavior listing might have yielded a challenging group, in the absence of any appropriate organization listing, but this, in fact, never occurred. Thus, all of our final sample listings are organizations.

Although the file was considered complete when we drew the sample, it was perfectly possible to add new entries that we might uncover in the course of the research. All we required is that every additional entry be given the same .11 probability of entering the sample as earlier entries. For example, we drew the card, "Good Roads Movement." On investigating this entry, we discovered seven different organizations that had some involvement, not necessarily all challenging groups. Some were in the file already, and some were not. Those that were not in the file were given cards and a .11 probability of coming in, and one of these, the League of American Wheelmen, was selected and qualified as a challenging group.

Sometimes a challenging group goes into a period of dormancy and then mounts a new mobilization effort after a quiet period of five years or more. These are new challenging groups with independent careers, and we do not wish to eliminate them merely because they use the same banner as an earlier challenge. The Ku Klux Klan is a good example. The revived Klan in the 1920s took the name of the earlier organization, but it might have chosen another. The choice of a name by a group should not be a criterion for its inclusion or exclusion. To handle this, we included all challenges under the same name as independent challenging groups, treating a new burst of activity after a dormant period of five years or longer as an additional sample entry. The KKK did not fall into the sample, but two cases of this type did. The International Longshoreman's Association was involved in two rather separate challenges, one begun in the 1890s, concentrating mainly in the East and the Great Lakes region, and another in the 1930s under Harry Bridges' leadership on the West Coast. The Young People's Socialist League also had two separate efforts, one during the period of World War I and one during the depression. Each of these single entries, then, yielded two separate challenging groups, since only in this manner would the separate efforts have an equal probability of inclusion.

When the culling and duplicate eliminating process was completed, we were left with 64 apparently valid entries. We were able to get sufficient information on 83 percent of them, but 11 eluded our efforts. We know a little about these nonrespondents, and they apparently are valid entries, although it is quite possible that if we knew more some of them could be discarded. Of course, if we knew more, we could presumably have completed·protocols on some of them and added them to our analysis. The 11 are briefly described below:

1. The Order of Secularists

A secret society of the 1860s intent on creating a proper climate for social reform in the United States by propagating atheism. It was composed primarily of German immigrants and included among its members Fredrich Sorge, the dominant figure in the First International and the so-called Father of Marxism in America. It was successfully secret, and there is inadequate information on its nature and activities.

2. *Lower Taxes, Less Legislation League*

A reform group of the progressive era.

3. *Union of Russian Workers*

A major target of the Palmer Raids following World War I. Many of its members were among the 249 aliens deported in January 1920.

4. *Lithuanian Socialist Federation*

A group of Lithuanian immigrants, perhaps no more than a branch or satellite of the Socialist Party without independent status, but we do not know.

5. *Corn Belt Committee*

A group of midwestern farmers who wanted Congress to institute a plan to pay farmers their cost of production plus profit, regardless of market prices.

6. *The American Negro Labor Congress*

A group that attempted to organize blacks into unions during the 1920s.

7. *National Christian Citizenship League*

One of several Christian Socialist organizations during the 1880s and 1890s.

8. *National Direct Legislation League*

A group formed in the 1890s to gain various governmental reforms.

9. *Seamen and Harbor Workers Union*

An alleged communist-front organization of the 1930s.

10. *Philadelphia Journeymen House Painters Association*

A group of the 1860s that was involved in efforts to form a city-wide trades assembly. It may have been localized, but journeymen house painters were not; therefore, it can not be ruled invalid out of hand.

11.　National Labor Defense Council

A group of civil libertarians formed in 1917 to support the Industrial Workers of the World (IWW) and other labor groups that were harassed by the government.

It is conceivable that enough information could be found on some of these groups but not within the resources available to this project. They do not appear to be concentrated in any particular time period although none are pre-Civil War. Nor are they of any particular type. They are well distributed over occupational, reform, and socialist categories although right-wing groups are apparently not represented among these nonrespondents.

We conclude this appendix with the list of sources used to compile the gross sampling list or card file.

Agriculture

Benedict, M. R., *Farm Policies of the United States, 1790–1950*
Shannon, Fred A., *American Farmer's Movements*
Taylor, Carl C., *The Farmer's Movements, 1620–1920*
Hicks, J. D., and Saloutos, T., *Agricultural Discontent in the Middle West*
Buck, S. J., *Agrarian Crusade*
Taylor, Carl C., *Rural Life in the United States*
Gates, Paul E., *The Farmers Age*

Labor

Saposs, *Left-Wing Unionism*
Commons, J. R., et al., *History of Labor in the United States,* vols. 2, 3, 4
Fine, Nathan, *Labor and Farmer Parties in the United States – 1828–1928*
Dulles, R. F., *Labor in America*
Yellen, Samuel, *American Labor Struggles*

Ethnic Groups (Immigrants)

Higham, John, *Strangers in the Land*
Brown, F. J., and Roucek, J. S., *One America*
Commons, J. R., *Races and Immigrants in America*
Hansen, M. L., *The Immigrant in American History*
Kohler, M. J., *Immigration and Aliens in the United States*
Wittke, Carl, *We Who Built America*

Women

Stanton, Elizabeth, et al., *History of Woman Suffrage,* 6 vols. Many other listings are included in books on social reform with sections on women's movements.

Religious Groups

Stokes, Anson P., *Church and State in the United States*
Sweet, W. W., *Religion in America*

Prohibition Groups (Temperance)

Colvin, D. L., *Prohibition in the United States*
Asbury, Herbert, *The Great Illusion*

Nativist

Higham, John, *Strangers in the Land*
Billington, R. A., *The American Protestant Crusade 1800–1860*

Reform Groups

Filler, Louis, *A Dictionary of Social Reform*
Aaron, Daniel, *Men of Good Hope—A Story of American Progressives*
Nye, R. B., *Midwestern Progressive Politics*
Warbasse, J. P., *Co-operative Democracy through Voluntary Association*
Filler, Louis, *Crusaders for American Liberalism*
"The Arbitrator," William Floyd, ed., *Social Progress*
Daniels, John, *Co-operation—An American Way*

Professions

Warren, Charles, *A History of the American Bar*
Packhard, F. R., *History of Medicine in the U.S.,* Vol. II

Business and Commerce

Shultz, W. J. and Caine, *Financial Development of the United States*
Studenski, Paul and Kross, *Financial History of the U.S.*

Conservation

Van Hise, C. R., *Conservation of Our Natural Resources*

Black (and Other Racial, Religious, and Ethnic Minorities)

Frazier, E. F., *The Negro in the United States*
McWilliams, Carey, *A Mask for Privilege — Anti-Semitism in America*
Rose, Arnold and Caroline, *America Divided*
Franklin, J. H., *From Slavery to Freedom*
Bennett, Lerone, Jr., *Before the Mayflower: A History of the Negro in America*

Utopias

Bestor, A. E., *Backwoods Utopias*
Tyler, A. F., *Freedom's Ferment — Phases of American Socialism to 1860*

Socialism and Communism

Hillquit, Morris, *History of Socialism in the United States*
Gitlow, J. B., *The Whole of Their Lives*
Egbert, et al., *Socialism and American Life*
Kipnis, Ira, *The American Socialist Movement 1897–1912*
Cannon, J. P., *History of American Trotskyism*
Herreshoff, David, *American Disciples of Marx*
Quint, H., *The Forging of American Socialism*
Bimba, Anthony, *History of the American Working Class*

Peace

Curti, M. E., *Peace or War — The American Struggle 1636–1936*

War, Veterans, and Rightist Groups

Evan, Wallace, *Patriotism on Parade*
Harrison, Gordon, *Road to the Right*
Rossiter, Clinton, *Conservatism in America*
Wector, Dixon, *When Johnny Comes Marching Home*

Radicals, Cranks and Crackpots

Preston, William, *Aliens and Dissenters*
Chafee, Z., Jr., *Free Speech in the United States*
Adamic, Louis, *Dynamite — the Story of Class Violence in America*

Greer, Thomas H., *American Social Reform Movements, Their Pattern Since 1865*

Destler, Chester M., *American Radicalism*

Jaker, F. C., *Doubters and Dissenters — Cataclysmic Thought in America 1885–1918*

David, Henry, *The History of the Haymarket Affair*

Allen, Frederick Lewis, *Only Yesterday*

Sports

Dulles, R. F., *America Learns to Play*

Education

Knight, Edgar W., *Education in the United States*

Butts, R. F. and Cremin, *A History of Education in American Culture appendix d*

The Questionnaire

1. Background Information

1.1   Name of compiler.

1.2   Sample listing from card file (e.g., "anarcho-communists").

1.3   Constituency of the CG.[1]

1.4   Check list of criteria for inclusion as a CG. Compiler must note whether the sample entry passes all validity tests, including checks for duplication.

1.5   Aliases. Other names by which the CG was known.

1.6   Time reference points. Significant events in the CG's history which can be used to establish time boundaries for its activities and relationships (e.g., strike begins at X company: June 12, 1937 = T3).

1.7   Sources used in compiling the protocol. Note any general biases or overall point of view.

1.8   Background briefing. A short (one page) general description to orient the coder.

1.9   Context of the times. A brief description of the historical context in which the CG arose.

1.10   Primary antagonists of the CG.

---

[1] We will employ the abbreviation CG for challenging group.

2. Law Enforcement System

This section of the questionnaire deals with the relationship between the CG and the *law enforcement system*. This latter term is intended to include police, special investigatory agencies (e.g., FBI, Narcotics Agents, etc.), and the judicial system. The police may be the local police department or sheriff's office, state police, or federal law enforcement officials. The investigatory agencies referred to above are those connected with law enforcement and do not include legislative investigating committees or regulatory commissions which are covered elsewhere. The judicial system includes everything from local magistrates through the Supreme Court.

The questionnaire sometimes makes use of the term police as a shorthand for this entire system. If relevant information is discovered about parts of the law enforcement system other than the police, this should be included also—for example, the military, national guard, and militia.

2.1   Salience of law enforcement system.[2]

How much emotional salience, positive or negative, did the *local* law enforcement system have for the CG? How much emotional salience did the *supralocal* system have? To what extent was either an object of intense feeling or of little or no concern?

2.2   Legal police activity short of arrest.

How much legal police activity short of arrest was directed toward the CG? To what extent were CG members investigated, subjected to surveillance, and interrogated?

2.3   Arrests.

To what extent were CG members subject to arrest?

2.4   Illegitimate police activity.

How much illegal police activity or activity beyond the spirit of the law was directed at the CG?

2.5   Police protection of CG.

How adequate was police protection of CG members and rendering of normal police services? How adequately did police respond to requests for aid? How adequately were CG members protected from hostile third parties?

---

[2] Under each question the compiler was given a set of additional instructions concerning the information sought. These additional instructions are not included here but are available on request.

2.6   Collusion against.

How much collusion was there between the law enforcement system and hostile third parties? To what extend did police and judges hold membership in hostile third-party groups? To what extent was there informal collusion or sympathy with hostile third parties?

2.7   Collusion with.

How much joint membership was there between police or judges and CG? To what extent was there informal collusion or sympathy with CG?

2.8   CG trust in police.

What was the CG attitude toward the police?

2.9   CG trust in courts.

What was the CG attitude toward the courts?

2.10   Hostile CG activity against police.

How much hostile activity did the CG direct against members of the law enforcement system? To what extent did they verbally or physically attack the police and attempt to harass them?

2.11   Use of courts as resource.

How much use did the CG make of the judicial system as a resource in bringing about social change?

3.   Public Agencies

This section deals with the relationship between the CG and public agencies other than law enforcement agencies. Examples of such agencies are HEW, HUD, the Department of Agriculture, the State Education Commission, and the Interstate Commerce Commission. The President, any governor, and other office holders in the executive branch are included here.

3.1   Salience of public agencies.

Were public agencies relevant to the aims or tactics of the CG? If so, in what ways?

3.2   Influence attempts on public agencies by CG and allies.

What influence attempts on public agencies were made by CG or, on behalf of CG, by some ally?

3.3   Influence attempts on public agencies by hostile third parties.

Was influence applied to public agencies by hostile third parties aimed at regulating the behavior of the CG?

3.4   Favorable actions by public agencies.

What actions by public agencies occurred which were favorable to the CG?

3.5   Unfavorable actions by public agencies.

What actions by public agencies occurred which were unfavorable to the CG?

4.   (This section was integrated into section 3 above).

5.   Communication System

This section deals primarily with the relationship of the CG to the mass media. However, where relevant, it also includes information on communication in face-to-face interaction.

The mass media include (at different periods) TV, radio, newspapers, newsmagazines, newsreels, and books, among others. We *exclude* here publications of the CG — that is, internal house organs — aimed at their constituency although press releases and statements designed to reach a general audience would be included.

In face-to-face communication, we also focus on messages intended to reach an audience *outside* of the constituency. Examples here would include communication through sermons in churches, through political meetings, through talks at private clubs, employee gatherings, and other organizational functions. Typically, this includes a leader of the CG talking to some audience outside of the constituency in which he or she is justifying the demands or explaining the grievances of the CG. (An example would be that of black militants lecturing to predominantly white audiences.)

5.1   Salience of the CG for the mass media.

To what extent were the mass media aware of the CG and its activities? How much attention did they give it? How much attention did they give to the problems raised by the CG?

5.2   Salience of communications system for CG.

To what extent did the CG show sensitivity or concern about the communications system? To what extent did it see communications with an outside audience as relevant and important?

5.3   Public relations attempts by CG.

To what extent did the CG carry out activities aimed at influencing the content and extent of publicity about them?

5.4   Public relations attempts directed against CG by antagonists.

To what extent did antagonists carry out activities aimed at influencing the content and extent of publicity about the CG and its activities?

5.5   Favorableness of mass media coverage.

How favorable or unfavorable was the content of the media coverage?

5.6   Favorableness of public opinion toward CG.

To what extent was the CG a focus of conversation and concern for large segments or all of the general public? What was the dominant attitude(s) toward the CG, its leaders, goals, activities, etc.? Was there consensus or polarization among those concerned in their attitudes toward the CG?

6. Electoral System

This section deals with the CG experience with the electoral process. This experience can be mediated through one of the established major parties, through an existing third party, or through the creation of a new third party. We also include here experiences which are a precondition to participation in electoral politics — namely CG activities aimed at enfranchisement (or antagonist activities aimed at disenfranchisement.)

6.1   Salience of electoral politics.

To what degree were electoral politics seen as a relevant arena of political action by CG?

6.2   Primary relationship to political party system.

What type of political party experience did the CG regard as most relevant for its participation in electoral politics — working through a major established political party, through an existing third party, through an emerging third party, or through preparty activity?

6.3   Influence attempts by CG on major political parties.

In what ways did the CG attempt to gain influence through the medium of a major political party?

6.4   Influence attempts by CG with respect to third parties.

In what ways did the CG attempt to gain influence through the medium of a third party?

6.5   Influence attempts by CG aimed at enfranchisement.

To what extent did the CG attempt to remove barriers to constituency participation in the electoral process and to encourage such participation?

6.6   Influence attempts by antagonists aimed at limiting degree of success of CG participation in electoral politics.

To what extent did antagonists attempt to influence CG participation in electoral politics or to limit its success?

6.7   Degree of inclusion of CG and constituency in major political parties.

To what extent was the CG successful in electing candidates to offices on major party tickets? To what extent were they successful in winning party offices and positions? To what extent did major parties adopt the CG program as part of its platform? To what extent did a major party become an agent of CG interests?

6.8   Degree of third party success.

To what extent did CG-backed third parties win electoral success? To what extent did major party platforms attempt to preempt issues and solutions promoted by CG-backed third parties?

7.   Legislative Bodies

This section deals with the relationship between the CG and legislative bodies at any level of the governmental system. Legislators sometimes function in other roles—for example, as political party leaders or as partisans for interest groups on one or another issue. We focus on them here in their role as lawmaker. The level may range from city council through Congress.

7.1   Salience of legislative bodies to CG.

To what degree was legislative action seen as relevant for CG aims and tactics? To what extent were actions initiated by legislative bodies relevant?

7.2   Influence attempts on legislative bodies by CG and allies.

To what extent and in what way did the CG attempt to influence legislation?

7.3   Influence attempts on legislative bodies by hostile third parties.

To what extent and in what way did hostile parties attempt to promote legislation against CG interests?

7.4   Favorable actions by legislative bodies.

To what extent did favorable legislative actions occur affecting either the CG or its constituency?

7.5   Unfavorable actions by legislative bodies.

To what extent did unfavorable legislative actions occur affecting either the CG or its constituency?

8.   Private Interest Groups and Other Challenging Groups

This section covers interest groups in two separate roles — as the targets of CG influence (i.e., as antagonists) and as allies or enemies in influencing some other target (i.e., as partisans). We also distinguish between private groups with well-established support from some constituency and those that are themselves challenging groups in a state of attempted mobilization. In summary, we consider three different relationships of the CG in this section of the questionnaire:

A.   Private established interest groups as antagonists or targets of influence.

B.   Established private interest groups as allies or enemies in the CG's efforts.

C.   Other challenging groups as allies or enemies in the CG's efforts.

A.   Private Interest Groups as Antagonists

8.1   Salience of specific private groups as antagonists.

To what extent was some private group the major target of CG activity — for example, as a private company or an industry is for many labor groups?

8.2   Influence attempts on private targets by CG and its allies.

To what extent and in what way did the CG attempt to influence a private target?

8.3   Influence attempts on private targets by hostile third parties.

To what extent and in what way did hostile third parties attempt to influence the private target to act against CG interests or wishes?

8.4   Favorable actions by a private group as antagonist.

To what extent did the private target take action affecting favorably either the CG or its constituency?

8.5   Unfavorable actions by a private group as antagonist.

To what extent did the private target take action affecting unfavorably either the CG or its constituency?

B.   Established Interest Groups as Allies or Enemies

8.6   Alliance ideology.

What beliefs did the CG hold about the importance and desirability of alliances with other groups?

8.7   Scope enlargement attempts short of formal alliance.

To what extent did the CG attempt to draw other interest groups into the conflict as honest broker or sympathizer?

8.8   Alliance attempts by CG toward established interest groups.

To what extent did the CG approach established interest groups in efforts to gain their support for the changes sought by the CG?

8.9   Alliance attempts by established interest groups toward CG.

To what extent was the CG offered support by established interest groups?

8.10   Actual alliance formed between CG and established interest groups.

What working relationships were developed and maintained between the CG and established interest groups?

8.11   Hostile activity directed by CG against established interest groups.

To what extent did the CG attempt to injure, discredit, or undermine established interest groups that it regarded as enemies?

8.12   Attempts by CG to appeal "over the head" of established interest groups to win support of their constituency.

To what extent did the CG attempt to woo away the membership of established interest groups against the desires of the leaders of such groups?

8.13   Hostile activity directed by established interest groups against CG.

To what extent did established interest groups attempt to injure, discredit, or undermine the CG?

8.14   Coordination of hostile activity by established interest groups.

To what extent were the hostile activities described in 8.13 (if any) coordinated and organized among different hostile third parties.

C.   Other CGs as Allies or Enemies

8.15   Alliance attempts by CG toward other CGs.

To what extent did the CG attempt to work with other CGs in a more general social movement?

8.16   Alliance attempts by other CGs toward focal CG.

To what extent did other CGs attempt to include the focal CG in its activities?

8.17   Actual alliances formed between CG and other CGs.

To what extent did the CG actively participate with other CGs as part of a larger social movement?

8.18   Hostile activity directed *by* CG at other CGs.

To what extent did the CG attempt to undermine or retard the mobilization efforts of other CGs?

8.19   Hostile activity directed *at* CG by other CGs.

To what extent did other CGs attempt to undermine or retard the mobilization efforts of the focal CG?

9.   Attributes of CG

The focus on the questionnaire shifts at this point from the relationship between the CG and other groups to its internal characteristics – its leadership, organizational structure, tactics, and ideology, among others.

9.0   Growth.

What was the peak membership of the CG and its size at different points in time?

9.1   Formal goals.

What was the generalized belief or end-state on the basis of which the CG attempted to mobilize its constituency?

9.2   Beliefs about tactics and strategy.

What are the means by which the CG hoped to achieve its goals?

9.3   Actual means of influence used.

What was the predominant means of influence employed by the CG?

9.4   Beliefs about resources needed and their availability.

What did the CG view as its primary resources, and how did it hope to obtain these in sufficient amount?

9.5   Actual availability of resources.

What resources were available to the CG and in what quantities?

9.6   Leadership structure and change.

To what extent was the CG led by a single dominant leader with a strong personal following or by a more collective leadership without a single dominant figure?

9.7   Quality and skill of leadership.

To what extent were leaders experienced and skilled in performing different leadership functions?

9.8   Bureaucratization.

To what extent were rules of membership and operation of the CG formalized in a constitution or similar document?

9.9   Secrecy.

To what extent were activities of the CG carried on secretly?

9.10   Diffusion of internal authority.

How large a group within the CG was involved in internal decision-making?

9.11   Factional strife.

How frequent and severe were internal divisions in the CG?

10.   Attributes of Constituency

While the previous section focused on the active or organizational component, the challenging group, this section focuses on the underlying constituency of the CG.

10.1   Type of solidarity.

What social characteristics distinguished the constituency of the CG?

10.2   Geograpical concentration.

To what extent was the constituency geographically dispersed or concentrated?

10.3   Socio-economic status.

To what extent was the constituency predominantly middle class or lower class in background?

10.4   Rural-urban location.

To what extent was the constituency predominantly rural or urban?

10.5   Physical distinctiveness.

To what extent did the constituency have physical characteristics or mannerisms, such as foreign accents, that set them apart from the surrounding population?

10.6   Degree of nonmovement interaction.

To what extent did the constituency members interact with each other outside of the context of CG activities?

10.7   Subcultural distinctiveness.

To what extent did the constituency form a distinctive subculture with a common life style, norms, and values?

11. Boundary Relations between CG and Its Constituency

11.1   Degree of commitment required by members.

To what extent did CG participation call for total involvement by members rather than partial and spare-time involvement?

11.2   Social distance between CG leaders and average member of constituency.

To what extent did CG leaders come from essentially the same social background and life experiences as the average member of their constituency?

11.3   Ease of constituency members becoming involved in CG activites.

How permeable were the boundaries of the CG for a would-be activist?

11.4   Degree of competition faced by CG.

To what extent did the CG have a monopoly on efforts to mobilize its constituency, and to what extent did it face competition from CGs with similar aims?

12. Outcome Variables

Outcome is viewed from two angles, the degree of acceptance that the CG gains as an organization and the degree of new advantages that the beneficiary obtains. The new advantages that are diffused to the beneficiary are examined twice, once at the time point at the end of the challenging period of the CG and again over the fifteen-year time span that follows the end of the period of challenge. The end of the period of challenge is called TN, and TN + 15 years is called TU. For a discussion of how TN is determined, see Chapter Three (pp. 30–31).

A.   Acceptance of CG

12.0   Organizational fate of the challenge.

What was the state of the CG as an organization at TN?

12.01   Inclusion of CG leaders and members in the organization of its antagonist.

To what extent were CG leader(s) and/or members offered positions of power, prestige, and/or influence within the formal structure of the antagonist?

12.1   Formal recognition.

To what extent was the CG extended formal recognition by its antagonist as a spokesman for the CG's beneficiary?

306 The Strategy of Social Protest

12.2   Acceptance through negotiation.

To what extent was acceptance of the CG implied by the willingness of its antagonist to engage in negotiations with it over matters affecting its beneficiary?

12.3   Acceptance through consultation.

To what extent did the antagonist contact the CG to consult with it on matters affecting the beneficiary?

12.4   Antiacceptance and discrediting efforts.

To what extent did the antagonist attempt to deny that the CG was an agent for or representative of the beneficiary?

B.   *New Advantages to Beneficiary by TN*

12.5   Formal concessions or agreements.

To what extent was the CG able to win specific advantages for its beneficiary through formal agreement or contract?

12.6   Policy changes dealing with stated CG goals — undisputed.

To what extent did policy changes occur which were acknowledged by both the CG and its target to meet explicit grievances?

12.7   Policy changes aiding beneficiary but unconnected with explicit CG grievances — undisputed.

To what extent did policy changes occur which were acknowledged by both the CG and its target to aid the beneficiary.

12.8   Disputed policy changes.

To what extent were there claims that new benefits had been extended which were disputed by one or another protagonist?

12.9   Policy changes decreasing benefits.

To what extent were new policies introduced that decreased benefits to the beneficiary during the period of challenge?

C.   *New Advantages to Beneficiary: TN to TU*

12.10   Formal concessions or agreements.

To what extent was the CG or its successors able to win specific advantages for its beneficiary through formal agreement or contract from TN to TU?

12.11   Policy changes dealing with stated CG goals — undisputed.

To what extent did policy changes occur which were acknowledged by both the CG, or its successors, and the target to meet explicit grievances during TN to TU?

12.12 Policy changes aiding the beneficiary but unconnected with explicit CG grievances – undisputed.

To what extent did policy changes occur which were acknowledged by both the CG, or its successor, and its target to aid the beneficiary from TN to TU?

12.13 Disputed policy changes.

To what extent were there claims that new benefits had been extended which were disputed by one or another protagonist during TN to TU?

12.14 Policy changes decreasing benefits.

To what extent were new policies introduced that decreased benefits to the beneficiary during the period between TN and TU?

appendix e

Basic Codes and Data

Some readers may wish to analyze the data described in this book to address additional issues not discussed here or to check other interpretations of the results. To facilitate this, the basic codes are presented here along with the data on these codes for the 53 groups in the sample. Missing code columns cover identifying information or variables of questionable reliability that have been omitted.

Col. 14: Type of group.
    1. Occupational groups including unions, farmers.   20 (38%)
    2. Reform groups including peace groups, civil rights groups, social gospel groups, abolitionists.   17 (32%)
    3. Socialist groups including leftist student groups.   10 (19%)
    4. Right wing groups including nativist groups.   6 (11%)

Col. 18: Minimal acceptance relationship.
    1. Yes.   21 (40%)
    2. Consultation only.   4 (8%)
    3. No.   28 (53%)

Col. 20: Overall new advantages.
    1. No new advantages.   20 (38%)
    2. Equivocal advantages.   3 (6%)

308

3.	New advantages.		26	(49%)
4.	Partial and peripheral advantages.		4	(7%)

Col. 21: Combined outcome measure: Unequivocal advantages and minimal acceptance relationship.

		Col. 18	Col. 20		
1.	Full response.	1, 2	3	20	(38%)
2.	Preemption.	3	3	6	(11%)
3.	Co-optation.	1, 2	1, 2, 4	5	(9%)
4.	Collapse.	3	1, 2, 4	22	(42%)

Col. 24: Is violence present in the interaction between the CG and others?

1.	No.	36	(68%)
2.	Yes, undisputed and unequivocal.	15	(28%)
3.	Yes, but disputed or equivocal—for example, only an isolated incident in which a small scuffle broke out with no arrests or serious injuries.	2	(4%)

Col. 25: Did the group use violence either in self-defense or in pursuit of its goals?

1.	No.	44	(83%)
2.	Yes, undisputed and unequivocal.	8	(15%)
3.	Yes, but disputed and equivocal.	1	(2%)

Col. 26: Was the group subjected to violence by others including the police? (Do not include arrests per se unless accompanied by beating or other physical abuse.)

1.	No.	40	(75%)
2.	Yes, by hostile third parties.	4	(8%)
4.	Yes, by police or militia.	7	(13%)
6.	Yes, by both hostile third parties and by police or militia.	2	(4%)

Col. 27: Were group members subject to arrests or other nonviolent constraints by the police?

1.	No.	32	(60%)
2.	Yes, undisputed and unequivocal.	18	(34%)
3.	Yes, but disputed and equivocal.	2	(4%)
4.	Yes, but only in test cases deliberately initiated by the group.	1	(2%)

310   *The Strategy of Social Protest*

Col. 28:   Group ideology on violence.
   1.   Rejection, implicit or explicit. Either vio-
        lence was not an issue and no mention is
        made of it (it is irrelevant for the CG), or it
        is mentioned and explicitly rejected, *and*
        the group does not arm itself, give its
        members paramilitary training, or in any
        other way make preparations to defend it-
        self or carry out actions using arms.   46   (87%)
   2.   Acceptance. Either violence is explicitly
        claimed to be legitimate or necessary
        under *some* circumstances and/or the
        group arms itself, gives paramilitary train-
        ing to its members or in other ways pre-
        pares to defend itself or carry out actions
        using arms.   7   (13%)
Col. 30:   Violence status summary.
   1.   No violence or arrest in history (1 in Col.
        24–27).   30   (57%)
   2.   Violence user (2 in Col. 25).   8   (15%)
   3.   Violence recipient (1 in Col. 25 and 2, 4, or
        6 in Col. 26).   7   (13%)
   4.   Arrest only (1 in Cols. 25 and 26 and 2 in
        Col. 27).   8   (15%)
Col. 32:   Target displacement. Was the CG trying to
        either destroy or replace the target(s) as a
        way of realizing its goals/demands?
1. or 2.   Yes.   16   (30%)
   5.   No.   37   (70%)
Col. 34:   Public good/private good.
   1.   CG constituents get it especially, not
        pooled.   27   (51%)
   2.   CG constituents get it especially, but
        pooled. (Do not code here if #1 is possible.) 16   (30%)
   3.   Everyone gets it and it's pooled. (Do not
        code if #1 or #2 is possible.)   6   (11%)
   4.   Those who are not part of CG constitu-
        ency get it especially.   4   (8%)
Col. 35:   More than benefits.
   1.   More than simply boundaries or benefits is
        at issue.   35   (66%)

2. Only boundaries or benefits.   18 (34%)

Col. 37: Systemic versus local.

1. Target of change is system qua system, not merely one element, not one industry or specific institution (e.g., fighting communism or capitalism, achieving world peace or national socialism).   11 (21%)

2. Local: a particular and specific institution, organization, or industry (e.g., university administrations, slavery, prisons, etc.).   42 (79%)

Col. 39: Dominant leader.

1. There was a single dominant leader with whom the group was identified. The group could be considered in some sense a vehicle for a single leader.   20 (38%)

3. Several prominent leaders; or a single leader but one who is clearly subordinate to group or organization; or a succession of leaders. Group is in no sense a vehicle for a single dominant leader.   33 (62%)

Col. 40: Secrecy.

1. Group practiced secrecy in the form of secret rituals, covert activity, etc. Secrecy is institutionalized and represents more than merely a private planning meeting on occasion.   9 (17%)

2. Group did not practice institutionalized secrecy. Include here groups whose only secrecy was maintaining private membership lists. The fact that a group does not publicize every fact about itself is not sufficient for inclusion here.   44 (83%)

Col. 41: Factionalism.

1. No major factional splits in history of the group nor was group born out of a factional split. Internal disputes in group did not result in members leaving, through expulsion or resignation, to set up a new group.   30 (57%)

2. Group was born out of factional dispute, but it did not experience any splits during its challenge.   7 (13%)

3. Group was born out of factional dispute and experienced factional splits after birth.   1   (2%)
4. Group not born out of factionalism but experienced it after birth.   15   (28%)

Col. 42:   Timing of factionalism — relationship to external attack.
1. No factionalism (1 on Col. 41).   30   (57%)
2. Factionalism prior to attack. Internally generated but external attack follows within two years of factional split or factional birth.   3   (6%)
3. Factionalism but no attack within two years after split or factional birth. Internally generated.   17   (32%)
4. Factionalism after external attack. Factional split or factional birth follows within two years of external attack.   3   (6%)
    (Note: external attack is defined as the application of violence, arrest, or other constraints applied to group members by outsiders.)

Col. 44:   Written constitution or charter.
1. Written document existed stating both purposes of organization and provisions for operation.   33   (62%)
2. Written document existed stating purposes only but without provisions for operation (e.g., a manifesto).   13   (25%)
3. No written document is known to have existed.   7   (13%)

Col. 45:   Formal membership list.
1. Organization maintained a list of members.   38   (72%)
2. No formal list was maintained.   15   (28%)

Col. 46:   Full-time employees.
1. CG had more than one full-time paid employee.   29   (55%)
2. CG had one full-time paid employee.   4   (8%)
3. CG had no paid, full-time employees, only volunteers or part-time help.   20   (37%)

Col. 48:   Levels of hierarchy.
1. Three or more levels — officers; division,

	committee, or chapter heads; rank and file.	31	(58%)
2.	Two levels – officers and council; rank and file.	3	(6%)
3.	Two levels – officers or leaders and rank and file.	19	(36%)

Col. 50: Size of group at peak.

1.	Under 1,000.	11	(21%)
2.	1,000–9,999.	16	(30%)
3.	10,000–99,999.	12	(23%)
4.	100,000 plus.	14	(26%)

Col. 51: Bureaucracy summary code.

| 1. | Full formal bureaucracy (1 on Cols. 44, 45, *and* 48). | 24 | (45%) |
| 2. | Not full formal bureaucracy (not #1 above). | 29 | (55%) |

Col. 56: Electoral system salience. (Code in terms of practice, not simply belief.)

1.	Electoral challenge. CG formed third party and/or attempted to elect its members to office and/or to use referenda as a means of reform.	8	(15%)
2.	Electoral challenge through existing parties only. Group supported candidates it deemed sympathetic and worked for them or against unsympathetic candidates. (Code here only if #1 is not an appropriate code.)	13	(25%)
3.	Nonelectoral challenge. CG took no interest in the electoral system.	32	(60%)

Col. 58: Means of influence.

1. Group accepted in principle *and* made use of constraints as a means of influence in one of the following forms:
   a. Doing injury to persons or property,
   b. Strikes or boycotts,   20   (38%)
   c. Efforts to discredit and humiliate individual enemies by personal vituperation; discrediting efforts are individualized and not simply directed against "the system" or other more abstract targets; ad hominem attacks.

2. Group made use of but never tried to justify constraints in principle, even as a necessary evil.   1   (2%)
3. Group justified, advocated, or accepted as necessary the use of constraints under appropriate circumstances but never got around to actually using them.   10   (19%)
4. Group rejected constraints implicitly or explicitly in both action and belief.   22   (41%)

Col. 59:   Alliances excluding physical attacks and arrest.

Some definitions: *Help* = more than verbal support; some pooling of resources to help the CG. *Hindrance* = more than verbal condemnation; more tangible harassment that hinders the group in its efforts to mobilize and influence. Exclude physical violence and arrests here since they are coded elsewhere. Include, for example, censorship. (Note: Focus here is on help or hindrance in influence. Do not include actions which could be regarded as an outcome measure—for example, legislation which the group is seeking as part of its goals or which deals unfavorably with the issues and causes that the group is pursuing. Include only if it is action which helps or hinders the group in its capacity for influence or mobilization. For example, legislation prohibiting or permitting "yellow dog" contracts would be included; legislation guaranteeing a minimum wage would not.) *Outsider* = not a target of influence and not another CG. Outsider refers to an established interest group or political party or government agency that is not itself the target of change but can, by its actions, help or hinder the efforts of the group.

1. Group received only help from outsiders.   13   (25%)
2. Group received both help and hindrance from outsiders.   5   (9%)

3. Group received neither help nor hindrance from outsiders.   29   (55%)
4. Group received only hindrance from outsiders.   6   (11%)

Col. 60: Help and hindrance summary. (The same as Col. 59 only arrests and violence are added to hindrance.)

1. Help only (1 in Col. 59, 1 in Col. 26 *and* 1 or 4 in Col. 27).   11   (21%)
2. Help and hindrance (2 in Col. 59; *or* 1 in Col. 59 *and* 2, 4, 6 in Col. 26 or 2, 3 in Col. 27).   7   (13%)
3. Neither help nor hindrance (3 in Col. 59 and 1 in Col. 26 and 1 or 4 in Col. 27).   18   (34%)
4. Hindrance only (4 in Col. 59 *or* 3 in Col. 59 *and* 2, 4, 6 in Col. 26 *or* 2, 3 in Col. 27).   17   (32%)
(Note: Col. 26 = subjected to violence; Col. 27 = subjected to arrest.)

Col. 62: Class origins of constituency.

1. Middle class and professional, including wives of same.   13   (24%)
2. Blue-collar workers, manual workers, craftsmen.   21   (40%)
3. Farmers.   3   (6%)
4. Mixture of working class and middle class or workers and farmers.   10   (19%)
5. Students.   2   (4%)
6. Ethnic groups, including blacks.   4   (8%)

Col. 63: Initial resources – sponsorship.

1. No patron.   39   (74%)
2. Yes. Group had wealthy backers who were willing to finance it.   3   (6%)
3. Yes. Group had the patronage of figures of considerable prestige among outsiders, high status patrons. (Refers to more than upper-middle-class status: to people who have reputations as individuals outside of challenge.)   4   (8%)
4. Yes. Group had the patronage of those who occupied important decision-making positions in institutional hierarchies.   5   (9%)

5. Yes. More than one of the above. 2 (4%)
(Note: Don't include as a patron anyone whose status grew out of the challenge itself. Refer only to status prior to the challenge.)

Col. 65: Competition—other CGs in the field.
1. Yes. Other groups existed at the same time attempting to appeal to roughly the same constituency about similar issues, but not necessarily using the same tactics or program. 30 (57%)
2. No. No real competition from another group existed. Include here even if many members of the constituency belonged to other groups as long as these other groups were not offering an *alternative* vehicle. 23 (43%)

Col. 66: Class composition of constituency: summary code.
1. Middle class and students (1 or 5 in Col. 62). 15 (28%)
2. Blue collar and ethnic (2 or 6 in Col. 62). 25 (47%)
3. Farmers (3 in Col. 62). 3 (6%)
4. Mixed (4 in Col. 62). 10 (19%)

Col. 67: Sponsorship: summary code.
1. No sponsor (1 in Col. 63). 39 (74%)
2. Yes. Sponsorship (2–5 in Col. 63). 14 (26%)

Col. 69: Number of antagonists and concerns.
1. Single type of antagonist and single area of concern. 10 (19%)
2. More than one type of antagonist but a single area of concern. 34 (64%)
3. Single type of antagonist but more than one area of concern. 0 (0%)
4. More than one type of antagonist, more than one area of concern. 9 (17%)
(Note: The "government" as an antagonist is considered to be more than one type—i.e., code #2 or #4 above.)

The "emancipation of the working class," the "establishment of a socialist state," are considered single areas of concern unless specific subgoals are formulated by the group (e.g., elimination of ROTC on campus; staying out of war; establishing an FEPC; etc.).

Col. 70: Selective incentives.
   1. Yes. Group provides some form of tangible selective incentive, nonsymbolic, to members before TN. (Code #2 if provided only after TN.)   9   (17%)
   2. No. No evidence of any selective incentives beyond such things as emotional satisfaction and social interaction valued for itself.   44   (83%)

Col. 71: Inclusiveness versus exclusiveness.
   1. Inclusive organization. Any eligible member who wants to can join. No period of probation or formal induction.   48   (91%)
   2. Exclusive. Members are required to go through probationary period or investigation after which they are formally inducted into the group.   5   (9%)

Col. 72: Diffusion versus centralization of internal authority.
   1. Centralized. A single center of internal power. This may be a single leader or a group, with or without official authority. Where there are branches or chapters, their freedom of action is clearly limited.   28   (53%)
   2. Decentralized. More than one center of power in the organization. May be diffused through membership at large or in chapters and divisions with a considerable amount of freedom of action. Coalition-like.   19   (36%)
   3. Probably decentralized. No positive evidence of centralization exists; no dominant leader or other indication of centralization.   6   (11%)

Col. 73: Date of beginning of challenge.
   1. Before 1860.   8   (15%)
   2. 1860–1879.   3   (6%)
   3. 1880–1899.   18   (34%)
   4. 1890–1913.   6   (11%)

	5.	1914–1928.	7	(13%)
	6.	1929–1945.	11	(21%)

Col. 74: Relationship of CG to competitor CGs.

1. CG is less moderate than principal competitor. Advocates or uses more militant means, i.e., constraints, or goals implying higher degree of conflict with antagonist.   10   (19%)

2. CG is more moderate than principal competitor.   7   (13%)

3. No difference between CG and competitor or inconsistent differences. Put jurisdictional disputes here. Put here if CG's only claim is that it is more effective than rival without any connotation of greater or lesser militancy.   13   (25%)

4. No competitor (2 on Col. 65).   23   (43%)

Column

Group	14	18	20	21	24	25	26	27	28	30	32	34	35	37	39	40	41	42	44	45	46	48	50	51	56	58	59	60	62	63	65	66	67	69	70	71	72	73	74
1. American Association of University Professors	1	2	2	3	1	1	1	1	1	1	5	1	1	2	3	2	1	1	1	1	1	1	2	1	3	4	3	3	1	3	2	1	2	1	2	1	3	5	4
2. American Free Trade League	2	3	3	2	1	1	1	1	1	1	5	2	1	2	3	2	1	1	3	2	1	3	2	2	1	4	1	1	4	3	2	4	2	1	2	3	2	2	4
3. American Committee for the Outlawry of War	2	2	3	1	1	1	1	1	1	1	5	3	1	2	2	2	1	1	3	2	3	3	1	2	2	4	1	3	1	5	1	1	2	2	1	1	5	3	3
4. National Brotherhood of Baseball Players	1	3	1	4	1	1	1	1	1	1	5	1	1	2	3	2	1	1	2	1	3	3	1	2	3	3	3	3	2	1	2	2	1	2	1	1	3	4	4
5. Brotherhood of the Kingdom	2	3	2	4	1	1	1	1	1	1	5	3	2	2	3	2	1	1	2	2	3	3	2	2	3	4	3	3	1	1	1	1	1	1	2	2	3	4	4
6. Anarcho-Communists	3	3	1	4	2	4	4	2	2	3	1	2	1	1	3	2	1	1	1	2	3	3	1	2	3	3	3	4	2	1	1	2	2	2	1	2	3	1	1
7. National Urban League	2	1	3	3	1	1	1	1	1	1	5	1	2	2	3	2	1	1	1	2	3	1	3	2	3	4	1	1	6	4	2	2	2	2	1	2	4	4	4
8. United Brotherhood of Carpenters and Joiners	1	1	3	1	1	1	1	2	1	4	5	1	2	2	1	2	1	3	1	1	1	1	4	1	3	1	3	4	2	1	1	2	1	1	1	1	3	3	3
9. International Seamen's Union of America	1	1	4	3	1	1	1	1	1	1	5	1	2	2	1	2	4	1	1	1	1	1	3	1	3	1	3	3	2	1	2	2	1	2	1	1	3	2	2
10. National Union for Social Justice	4	3	4	4	1	1	1	1	1	1	2	1	2	2	1	2	1	1	2	1	1	2	4	2	1	4	3	3	4	1	2	4	1	4	1	1	6	4	4
11. Amalgamated Assn. of Street & Elec'l Railway Workers	1	1	3	1	2	2	6	2	1	2	5	1	2	2	1	1	1	1	1	1	1	1	4	1	2	1	3	4	2	1	1	2	2	2	1	1	3	3	3
12. American Birth Control League	2	3	3	4	1	1	1	2	1	4	5	1	2	2	1	2	4	3	1	1	1	2	3	2	3	4	4	4	2	1	1	1	1	2	1	1	5	3	3
13. American Labor Union	1	3	3	2	1	1	1	1	1	1	5	1	2	1	3	2	1	1	1	1	1	1	3	1	2	1	3	3	2	1	1	2	2	2	1	1	4	1	1
14. American Federation of Labor	1	1	3	1	1	1	1	1	1	1	5	1	1	2	1	2	4	3	1	1	1	4	4	2	2	1	1	1	2	1	2	2	2	2	1	1	3	2	2
15. Revolutionary Workers League (Revolt)	3	3	1	4	3	1	1	3	2	4	2	2	1	2	3	2	2	2	2	2	3	3	1	2	3	3	2	2	2	1	1	2	2	2	2	3	6	6	3
16. Native American Party	4	3	4	4	2	2	4	3	1	2	2	2	1	2	3	2	2	3	1	2	3	1	3	2	1	2	2	2	4	1	2	4	4	4	1	1	1	4	4
17. League of Deliverance	4	1	3	1	1	1	1	2	2	4	2	2	1	2	1	2	2	1	1	1	2	3	1	2	3	1	3	4	4	1	2	4	2	2	1	1	3	3	4

Group	14	18	20	21	24	25	26	27	28	30	32	34	35	37	39	40	41	42	44	45	46	48	50	51	56	58	59	60	62	63	65	66	67	69	70	71	72	73	74
18. National Student League	3	3	1	4	2	1	4	2	1	3	1	1	1	2	3	2	2	3	1	1	3	1	2	1	3	1	4	4	5	1	1	1	1	4	2	1	2	6	1
19. German-American Bund	4	3	1	4	3	1	1	2	2	4	2	3	1	1	1	1	4	3	2	1	1	1	3	2	2	3	4	4	6	4	2	2	2	2	2	2	1	6	1
20. Brotherhood of the Cooperative Commonwealth	3	3	1	4	1	1	1	1	1	1	2	2	1	2	3	2	4	3	2	1	2	3	2	2	3	4	3	3	2	1	1	2	1	1	2	1	3	3	3
21. National Female Anti-Slavery Society	2	3	1	4	2	1	2	1	1	3	5	4	1	2	3	2	4	4	1	1	3	1	2	1	3	4	4	4	1	1	2	1	1	2	2	1	2	1	4
22. American Student Union	3	1	1	3	1	1	1	1	1	1	5	1	1	2	3	2	3	3	1	1	1	1	3	1	3	3	3	3	5	1	2	1	1	4	2	1	2	6	4
23. YPSL	3	3	1	4	1	1	1	1	1	4	2	2	1	2	3	1	4	4	1	1	3	3	2	2	2	3	3	4	5	1	2	4	1	2	2	1	2	5	2
24. Grand Eight Hour Leagues	1	3	3	2	1	1	1	1	1	1	5	1	2	2	1	2	1	1	1	2	3	3	1	2	2	4	3	3	4	1	4	4	1	2	2	1	2	2	3
25. Order of Railway Conductors	1	1	3	1	1	1	1	1	1	1	5	1	1	2	3	2	1	1	1	1	1	1	3	1	3	3	3	3	2	1	2	1	1	1	1	2	2	3	2
26. American Proportional Representation League	2	3	3	2	1	1	1	1	1	1	5	2	1	2	3	2	1	1	1	1	1	1	1	1	1	4	1	1	1	1	2	1	1	2	2	1	3	3	4
27. International Longshoreman's Assn. (West)	1	3	1	1	2	2	6	2	1	2	5	1	1	2	1	2	1	1	3	1	1	1	3	2	3	1	2	2	2	1	2	2	2	2	2	1	1	6	4
28. International Assn. of Machinists	1	3	1	1	1	1	1	1	1	1	5	1	1	2	3	1	1	1	1	1	1	1	4	1	2	1	1	2	2	1	2	2	1	2	1	1	2	3	3
29. League of American Wheelmen	2	2	3	1	1	1	1	4	1	1	5	2	2	2	3	2	4	3	1	1	1	1	4	1	2	4	3	3	2	1	2	1	1	2	2	1	2	3	4
30. American Federation of Teachers	1	1	3	1	1	1	1	1	1	1	5	1	1	2	3	2	4	3	1	1	1	1	3	1	3	4	2	2	1	1	1	1	1	2	2	1	2	5	1
31. Church Peace Union	2	2	3	1	1	1	1	1	1	1	5	3	2	1	3	2	1	1	1	2	1	2	2	2	3	4	3	3	1	2	2	2	2	4	2	1	1	5	4
32. Bull Moose Party	2	1	1	3	1	1	1	1	1	1	2	2	1	2	1	2	2	3	1	1	1	1	4	2	1	1	1	1	4	3	1	2	2	2	2	1	1	4	3
33. Packinghouse Workers Organizing Committee	1	1	3	1	2	2	1	2	1	2	5	1	1	2	3	2	4	3	1	1	1	1	3	3	3	1	1	2	4	4	2	2	1	2	2	1	1	6	1
34. United Hebrew Trades	1	1	3	1	2	2	4	1	1	2	5	1	1	2	3	1	1	1	1	1	1	1	4	1	3	1	3	4	6	1	1	1	1	1	2	1	1	3	2
35. Tobacco Night Riders	1	3	2	2	2	2	2	2	2	2	5	2	2	2	1	2	1	1	2	2	3	1	2	2	1	3	4	3	1	2	2	3	1	1	2	2	1	4	4

Group	14	18	20	21	24	25	26	27	28	30	32	34	35	37	39	40	41	42	44	45	46	48	50	51	56	58	59	60	62	63	65	66	67	69	70	71	72	73	74
36. United Sons of Vulcan	1	1	3	1			1			1	5	2	2	2	3	1	1	1	1	1		1	2	3	3	1	3	3	2	1	2	2	2	2	2	1	2	1	4
37. Steel Workers Organizing Committee			3		2	2	4	2	2	2	5	1	1	2	3	2	1	1	1		1		4	1	2		2	2	2	4	1	2	2	2	2	2	1	6	1
38. March on Washington Committee	2	1	3		1	1	1	1	1	1	5	1	2	2	1	2	1	1	3	2	3	3	2	2	3	1	2	1	6	4	2	2	2	1	2	1	1	6	4
39. Prison Discipline Society	2	1	3	1	1	1	1	1	1	1	5	4	2	2	1	2	1	1	1	2	2	3	2	2	3	4	3	3	1	4	1	1	1	1	1	1	1	1	3
40. Christian Front against Communism	4	3	1	4	2	2	1	2	1	2	2	3	1	1	1	2	1	1	1	2	3	3	4	2	2	4	4	4	2	3	2	2	4	4	2	1	1	6	4
41. American Party	4	3	1	4	1	1	1	1	1	1	2	2	1	2	3	2	4	3	2	2	3	1	2	2	1	4	3	4	4	1	2	2	2	2	2	1	2	3	4
42. Communist Labor Party	3	3	1	4	1	1	1	2	2	4	2	2	1	1	3	1	2	2	2	2	1	3	3	2	3	3	2	2	2	1	2	3	1	1	1	2	2	5	1
43. Dairymen's League	1	1	4	3	2	1	2	1	1	3	5	1	1	2	3	1	1	3	1	1	1	1	4	1	3	3	3	4	3	1	2	3	1	1	1	1	2	4	4
44. YPSL II	3	3	1	4	1	1	2	2	1	4	2	2	1	1	3	2	4	3	1	2	3	3	2	2	2	3	3	4	4	1	1	4	2	4	2	1	2	6	3
45. Independence League	2	3	1	4	1	1	1	1	1	1	2	1	1	2	1	2	1	1	2	2	3	3	4	2	1	1	1	1	4	5	1	2	2	4	2	1	1	4	3
46. Progressive Labor Party	3	3	1	4	1	1	1	1	1	1	2	2	1	2	3	2	2	3	2	2	3	3	2	2	1	4	3	3	2	1	2	1	2	2	2	2	3	3	3
47. Federal Suffrage Association	2	2	3	1	1	1	1	1	1	1	5	1	1	2	3	2	1	1	1	2	3	3	1	2	2	4	1	1	1	1	1	1	2	2	1	1	2	3	3
48. Soc. for the Promotion of Manual Labor in Literary Inst.	2	3	3	2	1	1	1	1	1	1	5	3	1	2	3	2	1	1	3	2	2	2	1	2	3	4	1	1	1	2	2	1	1	1	2	1	1	1	4
49. International Longshoreman's Assn. (East)	1	1	3	1	1	1	1	1	1	1	5	1	2	2	1	2	4	3	1	1	1	1	4	1	3	3	3	3	2	1	1	1	1	1	1	1	1	3	2
50. Union Trade Society of Journeymen Tailors	1	3	1	4	2	3	4	2	1	3	5	1	2	2	3	2	2	3	3	1	3	3	1	2	3	1	3	4	2	1	2	2	2	2	2	1	3	1	4
51. First International	3	3	1	4	2	1	4	2	1	3	5	1	2	1	1	2	4	2	1	1	1	1	2	1	3	3	3	4	2	2	2	2	2	2	2	1	1	2	2
52. American Anti-Slavery Society	2	3	1	4	2	1	2	1	1	3	5	4	1	2	3	2	4	4	1	1	1	1	4	3	3	4	4	4	1	1	1	2	2	2	2	1	1	1	1
53. North Carolina Manumission Soc.	2	3	2	4	1	1	1	1	1	1	5	4	2	2	3	2	4	3	1	1	3			3	3	4	3	3	1	1	2	3	2	2	2	1	2	1	4

Some Negative Results

I have tried in the body of this book to give coherence to a set of results. Readers, of course, may make their own interpretations, and, in some cases, their interpretations may rest on variables that were not discussed. There are basically two reasons why theoretically interesting variables are omitted. By far the most important reason was our frequent inability to extract what we considered meaningful and reliable measures of them. We have tried not to force our data beyond its natural limits.

There was a second reason for exclusion. A few variables that we were able to measure reasonably well yielded equivocal or uninteresting results. Of course, interest and equivocality are not intrinsic characteristics of results but a function of the interpretation one makes. Some readers, making different interpretations, may see more meaning in these results than we have, and they are presented here to allow this possibility.

NATURE OF ANTAGONIST

Some groups such as labor unions directed their challenge primarily in the private sector; others had a set of governmental authorities as a target. This distinction is less than clear-cut. It is quite common for groups to have both public and private antagonists. Some student groups in the 1960s, for example, made the government in Washington the target of action on one occasion, university administration the target on another, and a private corporation such as Dow Chemical the target on a third. Such a mixture is not untypical among our 53 challengers.

Nevertheless, we were able to classify challengers by whether their most frequent or predominant antagonists were in the public or private sector. A little more than half (55 percent) of the groups had predominantly governmental targets. At first glance, challengers with public targets seem to enjoy less success than the others. Only 34 percent won acceptance and 41 percent new advantages, against 62 percent and 58 percent respectively for groups with private targets.

However, these differences can be largely accounted for by the presence of all but two of the 16 groups with target displacement goals among the challengers with public targets (see pp. 41–44). When these groups are removed from the analysis, the results disappear or even reverse themselves. Of the nondisplacing groups with public targets, 60 percent win acceptance, compared to 64 percent of the nondisplacing groups with private targets. The figures for new advantages are 80 percent and 59 percent respectively.

ELECTORAL VERSUS NONELECTORAL CHALLENGERS

Some 21 of the challenging groups attempted to utilize the electoral system at some point during their period of challenge. In some cases this involved forming or supporting a third party, in others supporting or working through existing major parties. The remaining 32 challengers took no particular interest in the electoral system.

There is remarkably little difference in the outcomes between these two groups of challengers: 52 percent of the electoral challengers gained new advantages compared to 47 percent of the others. The advantage lay the other way with respect to acceptance: 38 percent of the electoral challengers gained acceptance compared to 53 percent of the remainder. Note, however, that this difference is partly an artifact of how acceptance was defined. A purely electoral challenger, one whose only target of influence was a set of political offices, was considered accepted only if it enjoyed some electoral success. Thus, there is a degree of noncomparability in the measure of acceptance for some of the electoral challengers that can easily account for the slight difference found.

COMPETITION WITH OTHER CHALLENGING GROUPS

Only 23 groups had the field to themselves; no other challenger was attempting to mobilize a significant part of their constituency at the same time they offered their mobilization efforts. The other 30 groups did not enjoy such a monopoly; for them, other challenging groups existed at the same time attempting to appeal to roughly the same constituency on similar issues. Of course, these rival challengers did not necessarily use the same tactics or program in their appeals.

Again there is a striking lack of difference in success on what seems like a potentially important variable. Exactly half of the groups with competition and 48 percent of the others were successful in gaining new advantages. For acceptance, the figures were 50 percent and 44 percent, respectively.

SECRECY

We suspected that secrecy might be positively related to success since it might enhance the ability of a group to wage political combat. Only nine of the challengers practiced secrecy in the form of secret rituals, covert activity, or the like. To be classified as a practicer of secrecy, the practices had to be institutionalized and to represent more than merely a private planning meeting on occasion.

It turns out that secrecy has no apparent relationship to outcome for this sample. Four of the nine secret groups gained new advantages and acceptance; the percentage for the remaining 44 groups is virtually identical.

SOCIAL CLASS ORIGINS

One of the most interesting variables on which to compare groups is the social class origin of their constituency. Is the system more open for challenging groups with a middle-class as opposed to a working-class constituency?

Unfortunately, we found it difficult to get a fully reliable measure of the class composition of many challengers; a good many attempted to appeal across class lines, and our information on their success in doing so is spotty and incomplete. We were able to identify with reasonable reliability 15 groups that directed their appeal primarily to middle-class people and/or to college students.

There is almost no difference in the success rate of these groups when compared to the remainder. Fifty-three percent gained acceptance and a like percentage gained new advantages; for the others, 45 percent and 47 percent gained acceptance and new advantages, respectively. Even these negligible differences wash out or are reversed when one controls for target-displacement goals. Only one of the middle-class-based groups, a student group, attempted to displace its antagonist. Thus, the nonmiddle-class groups achieve their virtually equal success rate in spite of a sizable number of target displacers in their ranks.

When these groups are removed from the analysis, the nonmiddle-class groups actually do better than their middle-class counterparts. Seventy-four percent gain new advantages compared to 57 percent of the middle-class challengers. Their greater militancy and combativeness can account for much of the advantage (see pp. 72–88).

Finally, it is worth noting that middle-class status does not exempt a group from attack. More than a quarter (27 percent) of the middle-class groups were either the passive recipients of violence or were subject to arrests, only slightly lower than the 29 percent of the nonmiddle class groups receiving similar treatment.

Bibliography

Adamic, Louis.
    1944   *A Nation of Nations.* New York: Harper & Bros.
Adams, Alice Dana.
    1964   *The Neglected Period of Anti-Slavery in America, 1808–1831.* Gloucester, Mass.: P. Smith.
Adorno, Theodore W.; Frenkel-Brunswik, Else; Levinson, Daniel J.; and Sanford, R. Nevitt.
    1950   *The Authoritarian Personality.* New York: Harper & Row.
Agger, Robert; Goldrich, Daniel; and Swanson, Bert E.
    1964   *The Rulers and the Ruled.* New York: Wiley.
Albrecht, Arthur Emil.
    1923   *International Seamen's Union of America: A Study of Its History and Problems.* Washington, D.C.: U.S. Printing Office.
Allen, Lee.
    1950   *100 Years of Baseball.* New York: Bartholomew House.
    1961   *The National League Story: The Official History.* New York: Hill & Wang.
American Federation of Teachers, Commission on Educational Reconstruction.
    1955   *Organizing the Teaching Profession: The Story of the American Federation of Teachers.* Glencoe, Ill.: Free Press.
Aminzade, Ronald.
    1973   "Revolution and Collective Political Violence: The Case of the Working Class of Marseille, France 1830–1871." Working

Paper #86, Center for Research on Social Organization. Ann Arbor: University of Michigan, October.

Anderson, L. F.
1913   "The Manual Labor School Movement." *Educational Review*, 46.

Anson, Adrian.
1900   *A Baseball Player's Career*. Chicago: Era Publishing.

Ash, Roberta.
1972   *Social Movements in America*. Chicago: Markham.

Bancroft, Hubert Howe.
1890   *The Works of Hubert Howe Bancroft, Vol. 24, History of California 1860–90*. San Francisco: History Co.

Barkan, Steven E.
1979   "Strategic, Tactical, and Organizational Dilemmas of the Protest Movement against Nuclear Power." *Social Problems*, 27:19–37.

Barnes, Gilbert H.
1957   *The Anti-Slavery Impulse, 1830–1844*. Gloucester, Mass.: P. Smith.

Barnes, Gilbert H., and Dumond, Dwight L.
1934   *Letters of Theodore Dwight Weld, Angela Grimké Weld, and Sarah Grimké, 1822–1844*. New York: D. Appleton-Century.

Barnes, Harry Elmer.
1918   *A History of the Penal, Reformatory and Correctional Institutions of the State of New Jersey, Analytical and Documentary*. Trenton, N.J.: MacCrellish & Quigley.
1926   *The Repression of Crime: Studies in Historical Penology*. New York: George H. Doran.

Bartlett, Roland Willey.
1931   *Cooperation in Marketing Dairy Products*. Springfield, Ill.: C. C. Thomas.

Bassett, John Spencer.
1898   *Anti-Slavery Leaders of North Carolina*. Baltimore: Johns Hopkins Press.
1899   *Slavery in the State of North Carolina*. Johns Hopkins University Studies in Historical and Political Science, ser. 17, no. 7–8. Baltimore: Johns Hopkins Press.

Bean, Walton.
1968   *California: An Interpretive History*. New York: McGraw-Hill.

de Beaumont, Gustave, and de Tocqueville, Alexis.
1833   *On the Penitentiary System in the United States, and Its Application in France*. Tr. by Francis Lieber. Philadelphia: Carey, Lea & Blanchard.

Bennett, David H.
1969   *Demagogues in the Depression: American Radicals and the Union Party, 1932–1936.* New Brunswick, N.J.: Rutgers University Press.
Bernheimer, Charles S., ed.
1905   *The Russian Jew in the United States.* Philadelphia: J. C. Winston.
Bernstein, Irving.
1970   *Turbulent Years: A History of the American Worker, 1933–1941.* Boston: Houghton Mifflin.
Billington, Ray Allen.
1963   *The Protestant Crusade, 1800–1860: A Study of the Origins of American Nativism.* Gloucester, Mass.: P. Smith.
Blackstock, Nelson.
1976   *COINTELPRO: The FBI's Secret War on Political Freedom.* New York: Vintage Books.
Bloom, Bernard H.
n.d.   "Yiddish Speaking Socialists in America: 1892–1905." *American Jewish History.* Vol. 3.
Bodein, Vernon Parker.
1944   *The Social Gospel of Walter Rauschenbusch and Its Relation to Religious Education.* New Haven, Conn.: Yale University Press.
Bolton, Charles D.
1972   "Alienation and Action: A Study of Peace Group Members." *American Journal of Sociology,* 78:537–61.
Bose, Atindranath.
1967   *A History of Anarchism.* Calcutta: World Press.
Boulware, Marcus H.
1969   *The Oratory of Negro Leaders, 1900–1968.* Westport, Conn.: Negro Universities Press.
Breines, Wini.
1982   *Community and Organization in the New Left.* New York: Praeger.
Brissenden, Paul F.
1957   *The I.W.W.: A Study of American Syndicalism.* New York: Columbia University Press.
Broderick, Francis L., and Meier, August, eds.
1966   *Negro Protest Thought in the Twentieth Century.* Indianapolis, Ind.: Bobbs-Merrill.
Brody, David.
1964   *The Butcher Workmen: A Study of Unionization.* Cambridge, Mass.: Harvard University Press.

Brown, Olympia, ed.
>   1917   *Democratic Ideals: A Memorial Sketch of Clara B. Colby.*
>   Federal Suffrage Association.

Butts, R. Freeman, and Cremin, Lawrence A.
>   1953   *A History of Education in American Culture.* New York: Holt.

Caplan, Nathan S., and Paige, Jeffery M.
>   1968   "A Study of Ghetto Rioters." *Scientific American,* August,
>   219:15–21.

Carlson, John R.
>   1943   *Under Cover.* Philadelphia: Blakiston.

Carlson, Oliver, and Bates, Ernest S.
>   1936   *Hearst, Lord of San Simeon.* New York: Viking Press.

Chapman, Maria W.
>   1839   *Right and Wrong in Massachusetts.* Boston: Dow and Jack-
>   son's Anti-Slavery Press.

Chilton, Paul.
>   1988   "Critical Discourse Moments and Critical Discourse Analy-
>   sis." Working Paper #7, Institute on Global Conflict and Co-
>   operation. San Diego: University of California.

Christie, Robert A.
>   1956   *Empire in Wood: A History of the Carpenters' Union.* Ithaca,
>   N.Y.: Cornell University.

Cochran, Thomas.
>   1968   *The Great Depression and World War II: 1929–1945.* Glenview,
>   Ill.: Scott, Foresman.

Coleman, James S.
>   1973   "Loss of Power." *American Sociological Review,* February,
>   38:1–17.

Commons, John R.; Phillips, Ulrich B.; Gilmore, Eugene A.; Sumner,
Helen L.; and Andrews, John B.
>   1958   *Documentary History of American Industrial Society.* Vols.
>   3–6, 9. New York: Russell & Russell.

Commons, John R., et al.
>   1966   *History of Labor in the United States.* New York: A. M.
>   Kelley.

Crenson, Matthew A.
>   1971   *The Unpolitics of Air Pollution.* Baltimore: Johns Hopkins
>   Press.

Cross, Ira B.
>   1935   *A History of the Labor Movement in California.* Berkeley:
>   University of California Press.

Cruse, Harold.
>   1967   *The Crisis of the Negro Intellectual.* New York: Morrow.

Curti, Merle Eugene.
    1959   *Peace or War: The American Struggle, 1636–1936.* Boston:
            J. S. Cunner.
Dahl, Robert.
    1961   *Who Governs?* New Haven, Conn.: Yale University Press.
    1967   *Pluralist Democracy in the United States: Conflict and Con-
            sent.* Chicago: Rand-McNally.
David, Henry.
    1958   *The History of the Haymarket Affair: A Study in the Ameri-
            can Social-revolutionary and Labor Movements.* 2d ed. New
            York: Russell & Russell.
Davis, Winfield J.
    1893   *History of Political Conventions in California, 1849–1892.* No.
            1. Sacramento: California State Library.
Dawes, Robyn M., and Thaler, Richard H.
    1988   "Anomalies: Cooperation." *Journal of Economic Perspec-
            tives*, 2:187–97.
Dearing, Charles Lee.
    1941   *American Highway Policy.* Washington, D.C.: Brookings
            Institution.
Desmond, Humphrey J.
    1905   *The Know-Nothing Party.* Washington, D.C.: New Century
            Press.
Destler, Chester McArthur.
    1946   *American Radicalism, 1865–1901.* New London: Connecticut
            College Press.
Dillon, John J.
    1941   *Seven Decades of Milk: A History of New York's Dairy Indus-
            try.* New York: Orange Judd.
Dombrowski, James.
    1936   *The Early Days of Christian Socialism in America.* New York:
            Columbia University Press.
Donner, Frank J.
    1980   *The Age of Surveillance.* New York: Knopf.
Draper, Hal.
    1967   "The Student Movement of the Thirties." In Rita Simon, ed.
            As We Saw the Thirties. Urbana: University of Illinois Press.
Draper, Theodore.
    1957   *The Roots of American Communism.* New York: Viking
            Press.
Dubofsky, Melvyn.
    1969   *We Shall Be All: A History of the Industrial Workers of the
            World.* Chicago: Quadrangle Books.

Dulles, Foster Rhea.
    1940   *America Learns to Play: A History of Popular Recreation, 1607–1940.* New York: D. Appleton-Century.
    1949   *Labor in America.* New York: Thomas Y. Crowell.
Dumond, Dwight L.
    1939   *Anti-slavery Origins of the Civil War in the United States.* Ann Arbor: University of Michigan Press.
    1961   *Anti-slavery: The Crusade for Freedom in America.* Ann Arbor: University of Michigan Press.
Earle, Thomas, comp.
    1969   *Life, Travels and Opinions of Benjamin Lundy.* New York: Arno Press.
Egbert, Donald Drew, and Persons, Stow, eds.
    1952   *Socialism and American Life.* Vol. 1. Princeton, N.J.: Princeton University Press.
Eisinger, Peter K.
    1973   "The Conditions of Protest Behavior in American Cities." *American Political Science Review*, March, 67:11–28.
Epstein, Melech.
    1950   *Jewish Labor in the U.S.A.: An Industrial History of the Jewish Labor Movement, 1882–1914.* New York: Trade Union Sponsoring Committee.
Erdman, Henry E.
    1921   *The Marketing of Whole Milk.* New York: Macmillan.
Ferrell, Robert H.
    1968   *Peace in Their Time: The Origins of the Kellogg-Briand Pact.* Hamden, Conn.: Archon Books.
Feuer, Lewis.
    1969   *The Conflict of Generations.* New York: Basic Books.
Filler, Louis.
    1960   *The Crusade against Slavery, 1830–1860.* New York: Harper Bros.
Fine, Nathan.
    1961   *Labor and Farmer Parties in the United States, 1828–1928.* New York: Russell & Russell.
Finnie, Gordon E.
    1969   "The Anti-Slavery Movement in the Upper South before 1840." *Journal of Southern History*, August, 35.
Fireman, Bruce, and Gamson, William A.
    1979   "Utilitarian Logic in the Resource Mobilization Perspective." In Mayer N. Zald and John D. McCarthy, eds. *The Dynamics of Social Movements.* Cambridge, Mass.: Winthrop.

Fisher, Clyde Olin.
   1922   *Use of Federal Power in Settlement of Railway Labor Disputes*. Washington, D.C.: U.S. Printing Office.
Flacks, Richard W.
   1967   "The Liberated Generation: An Exploration of the Roots of Student Protest." *Journal of Social Issues*, July, 23:52–75.
   1988   *Making History*. New York: Columbia University Press.
Floyd, William, ed.
   1925   *Social Progress; A Handbook of the Liberal Movement*. New York: Arbitrator.
Foner, Phillip.
   1965   *History of the Labor Movement in the U.S. Vol. 3: The Policies and Practices of the AFL, 1900–1909*. New York: International Publishers.
Franklin, John Hope.
   1943   *The Free Negro in North Carolina, 1790–1860*. Chapel Hill: University of North Carolina Press.
Franklin, John Hope, and Starr, I.
   1967   *The Negro in Twentieth Century America*. New York: Vintage Books.
Fromm, Erich.
   1941   *Escape from Freedom*. New York: Rinehart.
Galenson, Walter.
   1960   *The CIO Challenge to the AFL*. Cambridge, Mass.: Harvard University Press.
Gamson, William A.
   1968a *Power and Discontent*. Homewood, Ill.: Dorsey.
   1968b "Stable Unrepresentation in American Society." *American Behavioral Scientist*, November/December, 12:15–21.
   1988   "Political Discourse and Collective Action." In Bert Klandermans, Hanspeter Kriesi, and Sidney Tarrow, eds. *From Structure to Action*. Greenwich, Conn.: JAI Press.
Gamson, William A., and Modigliani, Andre.
   1989   "Media Discourse and Public Opinion on Nuclear Power: A Constructionist Approach." *American Journal of Sociology* 95: July, 1–37.
Gamson, Zelda F.; Goodman, Jeffery; and Gurin, Gerald.
   1967   "Radicals, Moderates, and Bystanders during a University Protest." Paper presented at American Sociological Association meetings. San Francisco, August.
Garfinkel, Herbert.
   1969   *When Negroes March*. New York: Atheneum.

Gerlach, Luther P., and Hine, Virginia H.
    1970   *People, Power, and Change.* Indianapolis, Ind.: Bobbs-Merrill.

Gitlin, Todd.
    1980   *The Whole World Is Watching.* Berkeley: University of California Press.
    1987   *The Sixties.* New York: Bantam.

Gitlow, Benjamin.
    1940   *I Confess: The Truth about American Communism.* New York: E. P. Dutton.

Glasgow University Media Group.
    1976   *Bad News.* London: Routledge and Kegan Paul.

Goldberg, Joseph P.
    1958   *The Maritime Story: A Study in Labor-Management Relations.* Cambridge, Mass.: Harvard University Press.

Gorter, Wytze, and Hildebrand, George H.
    1952   *The Pacific Coast Maritime Shipping Industry, 1930–1948.* Berkeley: University of California Press.

Granovetter, Mark.
    1973   "The Strength of Weak Ties." *American Journal of Sociology,* 78:1360–80.

Gregory, Paul M.
    1956   *The Baseball Player: An Economic Study.* Washington, D.C.: Public Affairs Press.

Hagel, Otto, and Goldblatt, Louis.
    1963   *Men and Machines.* San Francisco: International Longshoreman's and Warehousemen's Union.

Harris, Joseph P.
    1930   *The Practical Workings of Proportional Representation in the United States and Canada.* New York: National Municipal League.

Hawgood, John A.
    1940   *The Tragedy of German-America.* New York: G. P. Putnam's Sons.

Hawkins, Hugh, ed.
    1964   *The Abolitionists: Immediatism and the Question of Means.* Boston: Heath.

Hicks, John Donald.
    1961   *The Populist Revolt: A History of the Farmers' Alliance and The People's Party.* Lincoln: University of Nebraska Press.

Higham, John.
    1950   "The American Party: 1886–1891." *Pacific Historical Review,* 19.

1963   *Strangers in the Land: Patterns of American Nativism, 1860–1925.* New York: Atheneum.
Hillquit, Morris.
1965   *History of Socialism in the United States.* 5th rev. and enl. ed. New York: Russell & Russell.
Hirschman, Albert O.
1970   *Exit, Voice and Loyalty.* Cambridge, Mass.: Harvard University Press.
Hoag, Clarence G., and Hallett, George H., Jr.
1926   *Proportional Representation.* New York: Macmillan.
Hoffer, Eric.
1951   *The True Believer.* New York: Harper & Row.
Hoke, Henry.
1946   *It's a Secret.* New York: Reynal & Hitchcock.
Hopkins, Charles Howard.
1942   *The Rise of the Social Gospel in American Protestantism, 1865–1915.* New Haven, Conn.: Yale University Press.
Horowitz, Morris Aaron.
1962   *The Structure and Government of the Carpenters' Union.* New York: Wiley.
Howland, Harold.
1921   *Theodore Roosevelt and His Times.* New Haven, Conn.: Yale University Press.
Hughes, Langston.
1962   *Fight for Freedom: The Story of the NAACP.* New York: Norton.
Johnson, Claudius O.
1967   *Borah of Idaho.* Seattle: University of Washington Press.
Joyner, Fred Bunyan.
1939   *David Ames Wells: Champion of Free Trade.* Cedar Rapids, Ia.: Torch Press.
Kaplowitz, Stan A.
1977   "The Influence of Moral Considerations on the Perceived Consequences of an Action." *Journal of Conflict Resolution*, September, 21:475–500.
1979   "The Just World and the Tendency to Infer Outcomes from the Morality of an Action: A Second Confirmation." *Journal of Social Psychology*, 108:125–6.
Kaufman, Jacob A.
1954   *Collective Bargaining in the Railroad Industry.* New York: King's Crown Press.
Kellogg, Charles Flint.
1967   *NAACP, A History of the National Association for the Ad-*

vancement of Colored People, Vol. 1: 1909–1920. Baltimore: Johns Hopkins Press.

Keniston, Kenneth.
  1968 *Young Radicals.* New York: Harcourt, Brace, & World.
Kennedy, David M.
  1970 *Birth Control in America.* New Haven, Conn.: Yale University Press.
Kerner Commission.
  1968 *National Advisory Commission on Civil Disorders: Final Report.* New York: Bantam.
Kipnis, Ira.
  1968 *The American Socialist Movement, 1887–1912.* New York: Greenwood Press.
Klandermans, Bert.
  1984 "Social Psychological Expansions of Resource Mobilization Theory." *American Sociological Review.* October, 49:583–600.
  1986 "New Social Movements and Resource Mobilization: The European and the American Approach." *Journal of Mass Emergencies and Disasters: Special Issue on Collective Behavior and Social Movements in Comparative Perspective.*
Klandermans, Bert; Kriesi, Hanspeter; and Tarrow, Sidney, eds.
  1988 *From Structure to Action: Comparing Social Movement Research Across Cultures.* Greenwich, Conn.: JAI Press.
Klandermans, Bert, and Oegema, Dirk.
  1987 "Potentials, Networks, Motivations and Barriers: Steps towards Participation in Social Movements." *American Sociological Review.* August, 52:519–31.
Kornhauser, William.
  1959 *The Politics of Mass Society.* New York: Free Press.
Kraditor, Aileen S.
  1969 *Means and Ends in American Abolitionism.* New York: Pantheon Books.
Lavine, Harold.
  1939 *Fifth Column in America.* New York: Doubleday, Doran.
LeBon, Gustave.
  1896 *The Crowd.* London: Ernest Benn.
Leiserson, William M.
  1924 *Adjusting Immigrant and Industry.* New York: Harper Bros.
Lenin, V. I.
  1929 *What Is To Be Done?* New York: International Publishers.
Lewis, Orlando F.
  1922 *The Development of American Prisons and Prison Customs, 1776–1845.* Albany: Prison Association of New York.

Lewis, Walter David.
  1965   *From Newgate to Dannemora: The Rise of the Penitentiary in New York, 1796–1848*. Ithaca, N.Y.: Cornell University Press.
Lingley, Charles Ramsdell.
  1920   *Since the Civil War*. New York: Century.
Lipsky, Michael.
  1968   "Protest as a Political Resource." *American Political Science Review*, December, 62:1144–58.
  1970   *Protest in City Politics*. Chicago: Rand-McNally.
Livernash, E. Robert.
  1961   *Collective Bargaining in the Basic Steel Industry*. Washington, D.C.: U.S. Department of Labor.
Lloyd, C.
  1912   *Henry Demarest Lloyd, 1847–1903*. New York: G. P. Putnam's Sons.
Lorwin, Lewis.
  1933   *The American Federation of Labor*. Washington, D.C.: Brookings Institution.
Lowi, Theodore J.
  1971   *The Politics of Disorder*. New York: Basic Books.
Lutz, Alma.
  1968   *Crusade for Freedom—Women of the Antislavery Movement*. Boston: Beacon Press.
Lyons, Eugene.
  1941   *The Red Decade: The Stalinist Penetration of America*. Indianapolis, Ind.: Bobbs-Merrill.
MacFarland, Charles S.
  1946   *Pioneers for Peace through Religion*. New York: Fleming H. Revell.
Maddox, Robert J.
  1970   *William E. Borah and American Foreign Policy*. Baton Rouge: Louisiana State University Press.
Martin, James Joseph.
  1953   *Men against the State: The Expositors of Individualist Anarchism in America, 1827–1908*. DeKalb, Ill.: Adrian Allen Associates.
Marwell, Gerald, and Ames, Ruth.
  1981   "Economists Ride Free, Does Anyone Else?" *Journal of Public Economics*, 15:295–310.
Marx, Gary T.
  1974   "Thoughts on a Neglected Category of Social Movement Participant: The Agent Provocateur and the Informant." *American Journal of Sociology*, 80:402–42.

1988   *Undercover: Police Surveillance in America*. Berkeley: University of California Press.

Mason, P. P.
n.d.   "The League of American Wheelman and the Good Roads Movement." Ph.D. dissertation.

May, H. F.
1949   *Protestant Churches and Industrial America*. New York: Harper Bros.

McAdam, Doug.
1982   *Political Process and the Development of Black Insurgency*. Chicago: University of Chicago Press.
1986   "Recruitment to High-Risk Activism: The Case of Freedom Summer." *American Journal of Sociology*, July, 92:64–90.

McCarthy, John D., and Zald, Mayer N.
1977   "Resource Mobilization and Social Movements." *American Journal of Sociology*, May, 82:1212–41.

McDonald, David J.
1969   *Union Man*. New York: E. P. Dutton.

McEvoy, James III.
1971   *Radicals or Conservatives: The Contemporary American Right*. Chicago: Rand-McNally.

McKelvey, Blake.
1936   *American Prisons: A Study in American Social History Prior to 1915*. Chicago: University of Chicago Press.

McKenna, Marian C.
1961   *Borah*. Ann Arbor: University of Michigan Press.

McLaughlin, Martin Michael.
1948   *Political Processes in American National Student Organizations*. South Bend, Ind.: University of Notre Dame Press.

McNeill, George E., ed.
1892   *The Labor Movement: The Problem of Today*. New York: M. W. Hazen.

McPherson, James M.
1964   *The Struggle for Equality: Abolitionists and the Negro in the Civil War and Reconstruction*. Princeton, N.J.: Princeton University Press.

Melucci, Alberto.
1980   "The New Social Movements: A Theoretical Approach." *Social Science Information*, 19:199–226.
1985   "The Symbolic Challenge of Contemporary Movements." *Social Research*, 52:789–816.

Metzger, Walter P.
1961   *Academic Freedom in the Age of the University*. New York: Columbia University Press.

Michels, Robert.
    1949   *Political Parties.* Glencoe, Ill.: Free Press.
Middleton, Phillip Harvey.
    1941   *Railways and Organized Labor.* Chicago: Railway Business Association.
Miller, James.
    1987   *"Democracy Is in the Streets": From Port Huron to the Siege of Chicago.* New York: Simon and Schuster.
Mills, C. Wright.
    1956   *The Power Elite.* New York: Oxford University Press.
Molotch, Harvey.
    1979   "Media and Movements." In Mayer N. Zald and John D. McCarthy, eds. *The Dynamics of Social Movements.* Cambridge, Mass.: Winthrop.
Morris, Aldon D.
    1984   *The Origins of the Civil Rights Movement.* New York: The Free Press.
Morris, Richard B.
    1970   *Encyclopedia of American History.* New York: Harper & Row.
Morrison, Charles Clayton.
    1927   *The Outlawry of War, A Constructive Policy for World Peace.* Chicago: Willett, Clark & Colby.
Muse, Benjamin.
    1968   *The American Negro Revolution: From Nonviolence to Black Power, 1963–1967.* Bloomington: Indiana University Press.
Mushkat, Jerome.
    1971   *Tammany: The Evolution of a Political Machine, 1789–1865.* Syracuse, N.Y.: Syracuse University Press.
Myrdal, Gunnar.
    1944   *An American Dilemma: The Negro Problem and Modern Democracy.* New York: Harper Bros.
Nall, J. O.
    1939   *Tobacco Night Riders of Kentucky and Tennessee, 1905–1909.* Louisville, Ky.: Standard Press.
Nevins, Allan.
    1935   *Abram S. Hewitt: With Some Account of Peter Cooper.* New York: Harper Bros.
Nye, Russel B.
    1955   *William Lloyd Garrison and the Humanitarian Reformers.* Boston: Little, Brown.
    1964   *Fettered Freedom: Civil Liberties and the Slavery Controversy, 1830–1860.* East Lansing: Michigan State University Press.

Oberholtzer, Ellis Paxson.
  1936 *A History of the United States since the Civil War.* New York: Macmillan.
Oberschall, Anthony.
  1973 *Social Conflict and Social Movements.* Englewood Cliffs, N.J.: Prentice-Hall.
O'Connor, Richard.
  1968 *The German-Americans.* Boston: Little, Brown.
Oliver, Pamela.
  1984 "If You Don't Do It, Nobody Else Will: Active and Token Contributions to Local Collective Action." *American Sociological Review*, 49:601–10.
Olson, Mancur, Jr.
  1965 *The Logic of Collective Action.* Cambridge, Mass.: Harvard University Press.
Orum, Anthony M.
  1974 "On Participation in Political Protest Movements." *Journal of Applied Behavioral Science*, 10:181–207.
Paige, Jeffery M.
  1971 "Political Orientation and Riot Participation." *American Sociological Review*, October, 36:810–20.
Parsons, Lucy Eldine.
  1889 *Life of Albert R. Parsons, With Brief History of the Labor Movement in America.* Chicago: L. E. Parsons.
Parsons, Talcott.
  1960 "The Distribution of Power in American Society." In T. Parsons, ed. *Structure and Process in Modern Societies.* New York: The Free Press.
Payne, George Henry.
  1912 *The Birth of the New Party.* Atlanta: J. L. Nichols.
Perlman, Mark.
  1961 *The Machinists: A New Study of American Trade Unionism.* Cambridge, Mass.: Harvard University Press.
  1962 *Democracy in the International Association of Machinists.* New York: Wiley.
Peterson, Lorin W.
  1961 *The Day of the Mugwump.* New York: Random House.
Pilisuk, Marc, and Hayden, Thomas.
  1965 "Is There a Military Industrial Complex which Prevents Peace?" *Journal of Social Issues*, July, 21:67–117.
Pinchot, Amos.
  1958 *History of the Progressive Party, 1912–1916.* New York: New York University Press.

Polsby, Nelson W.
   1960   "Toward an Explanation of McCarthyism." *Political Studies*, October, 8:250–71.
Porter, Kirk H., and Johnston, Donald Bruce, comps.
   1970   *National Party Platforms, 1840–1968*. Urbana: University of Illinois Press.
Porter, Luther H.
   1892   *Wheels and Wheeling*. Boston: Wheelman.
Poulshock, S. Walter.
   1965   *The Two Parties and the Tariff in the 1880s*. Syracuse, N.Y.: Syracuse University Press.
Purcell, Theodore V.
   1953   *The Worker Speaks His Mind on Company and Union*. Cambridge, Mass.: Harvard University Press.
   1960   *Blue Collar Man: Patterns of Dual Allegiance in Industry*. Cambridge, Mass.: Harvard University Press.
Quin, Mike.
   1949   *The Big Strike*. Olema, Calif.: Olema Publishing.
Quint, Howard H.
   1964   *The Forging of American Socialism: Origins of the Modern Movement*. Indianapolis, Ind.: Bobbs-Merrill.
Rayback, Joseph G.
   1966   *A History of American Labor*. New York: The Free Press.
Renshaw, Patrick.
   1967   *The Wobblies: The Story of Syndicalism in the U.S.* New York: Doubleday.
Richards, Leonard L.
   1970   *Gentlemen of Property and Standing: Anti-abolition Mobs in Jacksonian America*. New York: Oxford University Press.
Ring, Elizabeth.
   1933   *The Progressive Movement of 1912 and the Third Party Movement of 1924 in Maine*. Orono: University of Maine Press.
Robbins, Edwin Clyde.
   1914   *Railway Conductors: A Study in Organized Labor*. New York: Columbia University Press.
Robinson, Jesse S.
   1917   "The Amalgamated Association of Iron, Steel, and Tin Workers." Ph.D. dissertation.
Rochester, Anna.
   1943   *The Populist Movement in the United States*. New York: International Publishers.
Rogge, O. John.
   1961   *The Official German Report*. New York: Thomas Yoseloff.

Rogin, Michael Paul.
 1967   *The Intellectuals and McCarthy: The Radical Specter.* Cambridge, Mass.: M.I.T. Press.
Rogoff, Abraham M.
 1945   "Formative Years of the Jewish Labour Movement in the U.S. (1890–1900)." Ph.D. dissertation. Columbia University.
Rollins, Richard.
 1941   *I Find Treason.* New York: William Morrow.
Roney, Frank.
 1941   *Irish Rebel and California Labor Leader: An Autobiography.* Berkeley: University of California Press.
Rothman, David J.
 1971   *The Discovery of the Asylum: Social Order in the New Republic.* Boston: Little, Brown.
Rowan, Richard W.
 1939   *Secret Agents against America.* New York: Doubleday, Doran.
Russell, Maud.
 1966   *Men along the Shore.* New York: Brussel and Brussel.
Ryan, Charlotte.
 1990   *Media Strategies for Organizers.* Boston: The South End Press.
Sale, Kirkpatrick.
 1973   *SDS.* New York: Random House.
Saxton, Alexander Plaisted.
 1971   *The Indispensable Enemy: Labor and the Anti-Chinese Movement in California.* Berkeley: University of California Press.
Schattschneider, E. E.
 1960   *The Semi-Sovereign People.* New York: Holt, Rinehart & Winston.
Schmeidler, Emilie.
 1980   "Shaping Ideas and Actions: CORE, SCLC, and SNCC in the Struggle for Equality, 1960–66." Ph.D. dissertation. Ann Arbor, Mich.: University Microfilms International.
Schmidt, Emerson Peter.
 1937   *Industrial Relations in Urban Transportation.* Minneapolis: University of Minnesota Press.
Scisco, Louis Dow.
 1901   *Political Nativism in New York State.* New York: Columbia University Press.
Selznick, Philip.
 1960   *The Organizational Weapon.* Glencoe, Ill.: Free Press.

Seymour, Harold.
    1960   *Baseball, Vol. 1: The Early Years*. New York: Oxford University Press.
Smelser, Neil J.
    1963   *Theory of Collective Behavior*. New York: The Free Press.
Smith, Robert Miller.
    1961   *Baseball in America*. New York: Holt, Rinehart & Winston.
Snow, David A., and Benford, Robert D.
    1988   "Ideology, Frame Resonance, and Participant Mobilization." In Bert Klandermans, Hanspeter Kriesi, and Sidney Tarrow, eds. *From Structure to Action*. Greenwich, Conn.: JAI Press.
Snow David A.; Rochford, E. Burke, Jr.; Worden, Steven K.; and Benford, Robert D.
    1986   "Frame Alignment and Mobilization." *American Sociological Review*, 51: 464–81.
Snow, David A.; Zurcher, Louis A., Jr.; and Eckland-Olson, Sheldon.
    1980   "Social Networks and Social Movements: A Microstructural Approach to Differential Recruitment." *American Sociological Review*, 45:787–801.
Sorin, Gerald.
    1972   *Abolitionism: A New Perspective*. New York: Praeger.
Sowles, Patrick.
    1965   "The North Carolina Manumission Society, 1816–1834." *North Carolina Historical Review*, January, 42.
Spalding, Albert Goodwill.
    1911   *America's National Game*. New York: American Sports Publishing.
Stampp, Kenneth.
    1943   "The Fate of the Southern Anti-slavery Movement." *Journal of Negro History*, January, 28.
Stanton, Elizabeth Cady; Anthony, Susan B.; and Gage, Matilda Joslyn.
    1887   *History of Woman Suffrage, Vol. 1: 1848–1861*. Rochester, N.Y.: Elizabeth Cady Stanton, Susan B. Anthony, and Matilda Joslyn Gage.
Stanwood, Edward.
    1903   *American Tariff Controversies in the Nineteenth Century, Vol. II*. Boston: Houghton Mifflin.
Steeger, Henry.
    1969   *You Can Remake America*. Garden City, N.Y.: Doubleday.
Stegner, Wallace.
    1949   "The Radio Priest and His Flock." In Isabell Leighton, ed. *The Aspirin Age, 1919–1941*. New York: Simon & Schuster.

Stein, Leon, and Taft, Philip, eds.
1969 *Religion, Reform, and Revolution: Labor Panaceas in the Nineteenth Century.* New York: Arno.
Stewart, Ethelbert.
1913 "Two Forgotten Decades in the History of Labor Organizations: 1820–1840." *American Federationist*, 20.
Stewart, Frank M.
1950 *A Half-century of Municipal Reform: The History of the National Municipal League.* Berkeley: University of California Press.
Stokes, Arson Phelps.
1950 *Church and State in the United States, Vol. 1.* New York: Harper Bros.
Stone, Roy.
1894 *New Roads and Road Laws in the United States.* New York: D. Van Nostrand.
Stoner, John E.
1942 *S. O. Levinson and the Pact of Paris.* Chicago: University of Chicago Press.
Stowell, Charles Jacob.
1918 "The Journeymen Tailors' Union of America." Ph.D. dissertation. University of Illinois.
Swanberg, W. A.
1963 *Citizen Hearst: A Biography of William Randolph Hearst.* New York: Bantam.
Sweeney, Vincent D.
1956 *The United Steelworkers of America: Twenty Years Later, 1936–1956.* Pittsburgh: The United Steelworkers of America.
Taft, Philip.
1964 *Organized Labor in American History.* New York: Harper & Row.
Taussig, F. W.
1888 *The Tariff History of the United States.* New York: G. P. Putnam's Sons.
Tcherikower, Elias, ed.
1961 *The Early Jewish Labor Movement in the United States.* Tr. and rev. by Aaron Antonovsky. New York: Yivo Institute for Jewish Research.
Thomas, Benjamin P.
1950 *Theodore Weld: Crusader for Freedom.* New Brunswick, N.J.: Rutgers University Press.
Tilly, Charles.
1970 "From Mobilization to Political Conflict." Center for Re-

search on Social Organization. Ann Arbor: University of Michigan.

1973a "Collective Action and Conflict in Large-Scale Social Change: Research Plans, 1974–78." Center for Research on Social Organization. Ann Arbor: University of Michigan, October.

1973b "The Chaos of the Living City." In Herbert Hirsch and David C. Perry, eds. *Violence as Politics*. New York: Harper & Row, 1973.

1974 "Revolutions and Collective Violence." In Fred I. Greenstein and Nelson W. Polsby, eds. *Handbook of Political Science*. Vol. 3. Reading, Mass.: Addison-Wesley, 1974.

1978 *From Mobilization to Revolution*. Reading, Mass.: Addison-Wesley.

Tuchman, Gaye.

1974 *The TV Establishment*. Englewood Cliffs, N.J.: Prentice-Hall.

Tull, Charles J.

1965 *Father Coughlin and the New Deal*. Syracuse, N.Y.: Syracuse University Press.

Uhl, Alexander.

1954 *Trains and the Men Who Run Them*. Washington, D.C.: Public Affairs Institute.

Vinson, John Chalmers.

1957 *William E. Borah and the Outlawry of War*. Athens, Ga.: University of Georgia Press.

Voigt, David Quentin.

1966 *American Baseball*. Norman: University of Oklahoma Press.

Vreeland, Francis McLennon.

1929 "The Process of Reform with Especial Reference to Reform Groups in the Field of Population." Ph.D. dissertation. University of Michigan.

Wagstaff, H. M., ed.

1934 *Minutes of the N. C. Manumission Society, 1816–1834*. Chapel Hill: University of North Carolina Press.

Waite, Frederick Clayton.

1943 *Western Reserve University: The Hudson Era*. Cleveland: Western Reserve University Press.

Warren, Roland L., ed.

1969 *Politics and Ghettos*. New York: Atherton Press.

Wechsler, James A.

1935 *Revolt on the Campus*. New York: Covici, Friede.

Weeks, Stephen B.

1896 *Southern Quakers and Slavery: A Study in Institutional History*. Baltimore: Johns Hopkins Press.

Wehberg, Hans.
    1931   *The Outlawry of War*. Tr. by Edwin H. Zeydel. Washington,
            D.C.: Carnegie Endowment for International Peace.
Wilson, K., and Orum, Anthony M.
    1976   "Mobilizing People for Collective Political Action." *Journal
            of Political and Military Sociology*, 4:187–202.
Winkler, Fred A.
    1948   *Railroad Conductor*. Spokane, Wash.: Pacific Books.
Wohlforth, Tim.
    1960   *Revolt on the Campus: The Student Movement in the 1930s*.
            New York: Young Socialist Forum.
Wooden, Evans.
    1892   "Labor Troubles between 1834 and 1837." *Yale Review*, May.
Yellen, Samuel.
    1936   *American Labor Struggles*. New York: Harcourt, Brace.
Yergin, Daniel.
    1977   *Shattered Peace: The Origins of the Cold War and the Na-
            tional Security State*. Boston: Houghton Mifflin.
Zald, Mayer N., and Ash, Roberta.
    1966   "Social Movement Organizations: Growth, Decay and
            Change." *Social Forces*, March, 44:327–41.

Index